11/18

CRAVE

CRAVE

a Memoir
of Food and
Longing

Christine S. O'Brien

St. Martin's Press ≈ New York

CRAVE. Copyright © 2018 by Christine S. O'Brien. All rights reserved. Printed in the United States of America. For information, address St. Martin's Press, 175 Fifth Avenue, New York, N.Y. 10010.

www.stmartins.com

Designed by Anna Gorovoy

Library of Congress Cataloging-in-Publication Data

Names: O'Brien, Christine Scherick, author.
Title: Crave : a memoir of food and longing / Christine S. O'Brien.
Other titles: Memoir of food and longing
Description: First edition. | St. Martin's Press : New York, [2018]
Identifiers: LCCN 2018022097 | ISBN 9781250128836 (hardcover) |
    ISBN 9781250128850 (ebook)
Subjects: LCSH: Mothers and daughters—United States—Biography. |
    Romann, Carol Ruth. | Natural foods—United States. | O'Brien,
    Christine Scherick—Family. | Scherick, Edgar J.—Family. | Adult children
    of divorced parents—United States—Biography. | Television producers
    and directors—United States—Biography. | New York Metropolitan
    Area—Social life and customs—20th century. | Dakota, The (New York, N.Y.) |
    California—Social life and customs.
Classification: LCC CT275.O227 A3 2018 | DDC 306.874/3—dc23
LC record available at https://lccn.loc.gov/2018022097

Our books may be purchased in bulk for promotional, educational, or business use. Please contact your local bookseller or the Macmillan Corporate and Premium Sales Department at 1-800-221-7945, extension 5442, or by email at MacmillanSpecialMarkets@macmillan.com.

First Edition: November 2018

10 9 8 7 6 5 4 3 2 1

To Tim
For his unwavering belief

Acknowledgments

I'd like to thank my writing professors from the Saint Mary's College of California MFA in Creative Writing program: Marilyn Abildskov, for her passion and dedication to her students, and for seeing me as a writer, so for the first time I saw myself as a writer, too; and the late Wesley Gibson, who also saw in my writing ability what I was not yet ready to recognize.

I also want to acknowledge my Book Writing World mentor and teacher, Elizabeth Stark, for her razor-sharp insight and for driving home the practical nuts and bolts of story craft. I'd like to thank my fellow BWW writers, mainly Susan Sasson, Robert Ward, Vijaya Nagarajan, Jody Brettkelly, Mollie McNeil, and Maureen Fan, for setting the writing bar so high; for their support, positive feedback, and companionship in the trenches. I want to acknowledge editors Sydny Miner and Brooke Warner, who helped with the shaping of my original proposal.

Thank you to my children, Emily and Luke, for your confidence in me and willingness to listen and let me bounce ideas off of you, even when you had better things to do.

I want to acknowledge my brothers, who, despite being characters in *Crave,* have never offered me anything but encouragement and love.

Thank you to my agent, Carole Bidnick, for her "hunch" when she read my initial query letter and for her relentless business sense. Thank you to Michael Flamini, my editor at St. Martin's Press, for his guidance and his story instinct and for helping to bring *Crave* to its fullest potential. I'd like to acknowledge Gwen Hawkes, for her willingness and generosity of spirit and patience during the editing process, and all the editors whose eyes have been on this book for their attention to detail. Thank you, as well, to Dori Weintraub, Clare Maurer, Jordan Hanley, and Brant Janeway. I so appreciate St. Martin's Press for its professionalism and for taking on *Crave*.

I'd like to also thank Susan Pollock, my father's literary arm while I was growing up, who served as a role model and a source of loving validation.

Thank you to my friends for encouraging me every step of the way. I appreciate all the championing that has come from so many.

With great love.

CRAVE

Prologue

My mother's bedroom is hot and stuffy and exactly as it was when she died in it a month ago. Every inch of space has been piled high with stuff. I feel my once-familiar claustrophobia as my brother Jay and his wife, Macie, and Tim and I step around folders, piles of linens, stacks of papers and jazz and classical music CDs, and boxes filled with various health devices. In one corner alone there are three boxes of Himalayan salt lamps, another three filled with portable air ionizers, as we vie for somewhere to stand. Though she managed to distill an entire lifetime and eight moves from her farm-girl childhood in Illinois to a glamorous life in New York City, to Beverly Hills, and back to the East Coast, to all that remains here in one bedroom and one hall closet in this two-bedroom apartment in West LA, it's impossible to ignore the heaviness of purpose that descended when my mother set her mind to something. Heaviness evidenced by the press surrounding us now.

"How do we even start?" I say.

The cedar chest from my father's bachelor apartment on Fifth Avenue, where she lived when they were first married, sits against one wall alongside the queen-size headboard. The bed itself fills the small room. The upright piano my brother Greg bought her last year takes up another wall. A tall, many-drawered dresser and a floor-to-ceiling bookshelf each fill a wall; her rolltop desk and exercise machine—a treadmill type of thing but really, with all its handles and protrusions and knobs, unexplainable, maybe it vibrated, she had something she used to lie on that vibrated at the house in Queens—have been pushed up against the fourth. Around these larger structures and piled on them, covering every available surface, items have been laid one on top of the next, like strata, each representing a different period of her life. The musty crocheted throws from my father's study in the Dakota sit folded on top of the braided rug my Midwestern grandmother sewed from my grandfather's socks and ties. Boxes of newspaper articles about Illinois Jacquet, jazz great and my mother's late partner of twenty-three years, are stacked in corners. Boxes and crates filled with who knows what have been jammed under the bed so tightly, there isn't even a sliver of light. There are layers of smells, too, clinging to their objects: another, invisible kind of strata. The minty stink coming from the jars of all-natural oint-ments and salves sitting on her bedside table and crowding the small sink by the hallway closet, decades-old incense from the ashram tucked out of sight and sweetly cloying with the edge of something sharp—sandalwood?—the smell reminding me once again of my mother's ramrod allegiance to these adopted spiri-tual practices, the ever-present sweet spice of ginger and tur-meric and cumin and the oregano aroma of Ayurvedic herbs that clung to everything of hers, even in life.

Macie lifts the top off the cedar chest to reveal the silk and wool comforters I remember from our visits to my grandparents' farm—the silk worn through, the wool stuffing coming apart now—and the sheet music that sat propped on my mother's Stein-way grand during our childhood. Also inside, my grandfather's WWI uniform, each piece of clothing wrapped carefully in gauze: green wool trousers, shirt, jacket, hat, dog tags that bear his name. This isn't a bedroom; it's a museum, the reason she could endure this suffocating squeeze. Each day, even, she was living the important purpose of preserving and teaching what she had come to know to all who entered the space and looked upon these items.

Jay has turned to the bookshelf and is fingering a stack of ashram photographs, which will later be burned per instructions from the ashram when none of us claim them. The wall-size bookshelf is filled with book after book on various spiritual philosophies; recently she had been most interested in the Vedantic teachings and the peoples of the Indus River in the Indian subcontinent, which she said was the cradle of civilization. Most of these books she had mentioned to me; many she had sent me duplicates of.

"Look at this." Jay stoops to pull a thin folder from between two books, how-tos about improving eyesight and the danger of wearing glasses because they weaken eye muscles, and hands it to me. The folder, made of thin cardboard reprinted with photos of Princess Leia, Han Solo, and Luke Skywalker, is one of ours from high school. Inside I find pages filled with the unmistakable ink, dotted with bright stars of Wite-Out and covered in the darker typewriter letters that had pressed into the wet, from the typewriter on which my brothers and I used to write our precomputer high school papers. But I have never seen these particular pages, the date 1981 typed in the top corner, the year her marriage to my father was ending. There are some longer paragraphs, but mostly these are notes, a start to something, about her love of wandering her family's farm as a child, of the majesty of the Mississippi, of her companionship with Topsy, her beloved Saint Bernard: subjects she often liked to share with us, but here are recorded in snippets of notes that in places are poetic and detailed.

First treat of the day—walk to fruit orchard w father to sample freshly ripened fruit favorite—yellow sweet cherry, birds' favorite too, often beat me to it . . . sister's and my job to pick fruit as it ripened for eating or canning . . . peach fuzz itched.

Pool of water left after flood on concrete walkway from swollen slough, watched family of tadpoles grow.

During war years when wheat prices were at their highest, Mosenthein Island farm flooded 5 yrs. out of 6 . . . If flooded early enough, sufficient time to plant soybeans and recoup some of loss.

"Mom *wrote?*" I feel stunned by this compilation, maybe a touch betrayed. I have been writing my whole life, since I begged her to buy me my first journal at the drugstore on Seventy-second Street, a block from the Dakota, and rushed home to make my first journal entry. *I'm nine. I have three brothers, two Siamese cats, and a golden retriever named Sandy.* And while she had recently said to me, "It will be you who will tell our story," I hadn't understood the implications because she had never shared with me her own attempts to do so.

"You should have the folder, Chris," Jay says. Jay writes screenplays, but I am the prose writer, so our mother's prose is by default, apparently, my domain. When I get home, I look the folder over more carefully. Tucked in the pages behind her childhood reminiscing I find more notes documenting the physical symptoms that plagued her all her life and the supplements she experimented with, supplements that were seen as *crackpot*—my father's favorite word—remedies by most of the population at the time. The list and accompanying descriptions of her ailments seem to be written for a health practitioner; there is such attention to detail, to the minutiae of each symptom, details I know no one else was listening to, I realize she is writing to someone she expects is going to finally hear her.

1968–69—Adversely affected by air pollutants—up nights with pains in chest and arms from incinerators. Also sick from too much automobile exhaust on streets. (We lived in New York City.)

1971, January—severe allergic attact (sic) after 2 Bufferin— swelling & redness over face, hands, & chest.

After this, every attempt to eat, no matter what, gave me immediate diarrhea, very rapid pulse beat, flushed feeling, and engorged and painful blood vessels in hands and feet.

Lost 20 lbs.

Allergist merely shook his head as to what to do, except to pre-scribe tranquilizers and antihistamines, both of which I refused.

In these pages, I also sense the same intent I felt in her crowded bedroom and in our daily lives growing up under the dietary re-strictions she enforced: to pass down what she felt was impor-tant, to teach, to impose. But the stories of her childhood she told and that I find reiterated in these notes, also felt like the start to something, the setup to some important payoff yet to come. I know she didn't expect to die as she had, in an instant, after ly-ing back on her bed, legs crossed, arm across her forehead, tak-ing a moment to rest. She didn't expect to die at all; isn't that what she had been fighting all along? *I think dark thoughts*, I find, listed with her symptoms; *I have fears of death*, confirmation of the gloom I sensed, growing up, but couldn't place. But she *had* died and we didn't expect it either.

"Do you mind that I'm going to be writing a book about the fact that I was hungry?" I asked her once, after reading to her a section I had written about our first week on the Program.

"Just tell a good story," my mother said.

Chapter 1

I am ten and standing in the doorway of my parents' bedroom. My mother is lying in her evening clothes, a cream pantsuit and heels, her towering five-foot-eight frame prone like a felled tree on the hardwood floor of the hallway. It's almost midnight. My father is crouched beside her, one hand on his bent thigh. Murtle, our latest live-in, is crouching, then standing, then crouching again. She is in her uniform, though it is half zipped, revealing the upper part of her bare back, and she is barefoot and not wearing stockings.

"Go back to bed, Christine," my father says, barely glancing at me.

Murtle takes my arm and gently guides me away from my parents' room, where I had been asleep in their bed, waiting for their return from a dinner party. She leads me through the door of my brothers' rooms and into the playroom.

"The ambulance weel be coming," Murtle says. Her voice is lilting and soft, though the pressure of her squeeze on my arm is firm. "Your mother weel be fine."

From the playroom I peer through the crack in the door and into the dim hallway. Murtle and my father stand as men in jumpsuits lift my mother onto a gurney, then follow the men as they push it, its wheels rolling loudly on the bare wood, away down the hall.

It's springtime and my mother, nine, walks through her father's orchards with Topsy, her family's Saint Bernard. Topsy touches the back of my mother's leg with her cold nose. When her father brought the puppy home, she was tiny with oversize paws. Now, at three, she is big enough for my mother to ride. Though the farm is filled with dogs, her mother always keeps a small dog—there have been multiple Tippys, Jippys, Trixies, Skippys, Spottys, Fidos, and two Lassies, but Topsy is my mother's favorite. The dog never leaves my mother's side, even standing guard across her body as she plays in the sandbox.

My mother reaches out to pet Topsy with her left arm, crooked at the elbow, the result of a fall from a stepladder when she was fourteen months old. The doctor, who had been retrieved from a Sunday night church meeting, didn't set the bone correctly. He also administered too much ether, which resulted in ether pneumonia. By the time her parents took her to a specialist in St. Louis, it was too late to correct the set.

Girl and dog pass through the rows of fruit trees. It is the job of my mother and her older sister, Audrey, to pick the fruit for eating or canning, but it is early in the season and the trees are still heavy with blossoms. Spring is the time to catch bullfrogs and bring them home to eat, their legs still jumping in the pot while they cook. It's a time of waiting, for the lilacs to bloom at the Nessings' up the street, for the yellow roses to open along her mother's trellises, and of course for the fruit blossoms: apricot, apple, peach, plum, pear. Spring brings freshness and life, the dark of the freshly plowed pasture, the feel of the smooth, slick, black soil of her father's first furrow between my mother's bare toes—the first plow line determining all the others, its degree of straightness being the mark of a good farmer. Spring brings the winds of March, the thundershowers of April, the tiny streams rushing down the tracks of the field road, the peachy oranges and pinks of the sunsets after a late-afternoon rain, the green-and-yellow tornadoes. It also brings the funnel cloud when the sky becomes as dark as the newly plowed earth and my mother's family rushes to the cellar, freshly picked raspberries spilling onto the porch, a flying sheet of tin roof slicing through the air past Uncle Russell's head, her mother holding the screen door closed while the apricot tree uproots ten feet away.

My mother leaves the fruit trees and heads toward the riverbank. When my grandmother married, her own mother believed her daughter was moving to Siberia. My grandmother had spent her childhood in St. Louis; her mother had been a schoolteacher, her family city folk. In her new home as a young bride, my grandmother had to carry any water she needed from the pump in the chicken yard past the coal shed and the smokehouse, where the sausages were hung, into the house. The well was set up with ropes and pulleys to draw up the milk and butter that was kept suspended just above the water in buckets to keep it cold. There was no heating, no plumbing. In the winter, when my grandmother mopped the kitchen floor, it froze. Coal was used to light the stove in the kitchen, the oil stove in the dining room. The cistern box on the roof collected just enough rainwater for washing hair or making soap, which required an interminable amount of stirring. My grandmother used the lye and all the fats and oils she had saved for several months just for this purpose. The cistern box was also a handy place for my mother and her sister to churn ice cream using the cream their mother had saved. They sat on the freezer loaded with rock salt and covered with a gunny sack and talked while they cranked the core for homemade root beer, shaking it to see who could get the most foam. After church in the summertime, my mother's mother always cooked the same Sunday dinner: fried chicken dipped first in flour mixed with salt and pepper, mashed potatoes and milk gravy made by using grease the chicken had been fried in, adding flour to brown it slightly, and pouring the milk in until it was smooth and creamy. Vegetables were simple and incidental, always corn on the cob or something green from the garden. My mother loved these dinners, as she loved resting all Sunday afternoon, reading the funnies, playing games with the dogs. Late afternoons her family, as did most everyone else's, went for a Sunday ride, usually to the island farm to observe the progress of the crops or to the farms of customers—my mother's father sold tractors in addition to his farming—to compare progress. My mother's house had been a stagecoach stop. Her grandmother told her about storing cabbages, apples, and carrots in the ground during winter; digging the burrow and laying the vegetables with hay and dirt on top so the freeze didn't reach the food. As a little girl, this grandmother had, from my mother's upstairs bedroom window, watched Native Americans, faces bright with war paint, canoe down Choteau Slough, which ran beside their home and served as a cutoff before a dangerous stretch of the Mississippi, where the river passes over a series of rocky ledges called Chain of Rocks Reach. The house, built by these grandparents, had been a labor of love, constructed entirely with wood and pegs. Even the spiral staircase leading to the bedroom had been assembled without nails.

At the bank of the levee, my mother checks, as she does each day, to see if the pussy willows are out. It seems like magic that from a plant stalk comes curled fur as soft as the newborn kittens in the barn. Not yet—they are green buds. At the crest of the levee embankment, dog and girl meander alongside the river. The Mississippi brought my mother's family to Illinois. Her great-grandfather, a cabinetmaker from Switzerland, had come up from New Orleans on a riverboat. The money he'd earned for the trip was counterfeit, a fact he'd discovered only while attempting to settle his passage—at which point the riverboat captain steamed to shore and deposited him on a steep bank just south of St. Louis.

On this morning the river is brown and muscled, moving fast, riding high on its banks. My grandmother sits at the kitchen table in the mornings now, the radio on, listening to the river forecast. The past few days have been warm and the snows are melting in the north. The farm sits in a basin that centuries ago was part of the river itself. Now that it's spring, my mother's father and uncles police the levee daily for fox or mole holes, anything that might allow for a break. Boys from town, all the farmers within miles, and the Army Corps of Engineers help fill and carry sandbags to build the levee higher if a crest is predicted. If the levee breaks right at the house, the river will take everything in one giant roar. One morning last spring, after a levee break half a mile away, my mother woke to cold black water lapping then climbing the stairs of their basement. It filled the kitchen, the living room, and the dining room ankle-deep. Later she rode with her father in his boat across the island fields, looking down at the tops of the yellow flowers as they passed over the sunflower patch. One March, Uncle Eck, downriver, had the river change course and most of his farm washed away. But a flood is both a blessing and a curse; deafening from miles away, it carries the silt and topsoil that fertilizes the land.

My mother stops now for a moment to admire the Chain of Rocks Bridge, which spans the Chain of Rocks Reach. Here the river makes a wide curve known as Sawyer Bend, named for Tom Sawyer's legendary adventures. For all the hours she spends with Topsy, wandering along the sandy banks of the Mississippi, my mother is most excited whenever the opportunity arises to ride in the car with her father across this one-lane bridge, which, because of its forty-five-degree turn in the middle, is, in itself, a dangerous journey. At the turn, a car has to slow, but this is what my mother waits for. Suspended over the mighty bend, she drinks in the view, both upriver and down, of the Mississippi rushing on its long journey to the Gulf. My mother often imagines Huck and Tom hanging out in the sloughs she knows so well around the islands her father farms, Gabaret Island and its neighbor, Mosenthein. But she can't fathom the bravery, even in story, that allowed them to dare travel the long stretch of formidable river in between, and she is grateful to be crossing it on a bridge and not in a homemade raft.

My mother and Topsy head down from the levee, back through

the pastures, to the house and the barn. Before Topsy, my mother had loved Puzzums, named by her mother after a dog in the *Barney Google* cartoon strip. My grandfather hacked off all their small dogs' tails at the second joint, but Puzzums was born a natural bobtail. My mother dressed the little dog in doll clothes, gave her rides in her doll buggy, and set up the play table where Puzzums sat at her own place mat with her own cup of tea. One afternoon a carful of teenagers, driving on the roadway in front of my mother's house, swerved their convertible at the dog, who liked to chase passing cars. Laughing, they doubled back and ran her over as my mother and Audrey watched in horror. My grandmother consoled my mother with a doll she had stored away for Christmas. Puzzums was buried in the doll's box, beside the sandbox, the spot outlined with stones. Later a river flood caved in the dog's grave.

My mother now reaches her grandfather's potato field, which sits on a portion of her father's land. On summer nights she sits inside the screened-in porch, watching the fireflies hover over the long rows of dark green plants. Her grandfather grows potatoes, as his father did before him. When she visits his farm, my mother walks out to the tomato field, holding a tin can with a wire handle to collect the green tomato worms off the plants. On the hottest days, her grandfather drives his hay wagon filled with watermelons to the workers in the fields who are hired from the neighboring town of Venice. These workers aren't allowed on the streets in white towns after dark, but she has noticed how much they love her grandfather. As they stroll along the field road, my great-grandfather sings their spirituals to her:

I'm a comin', I'm a comin',
for my head is bending low;
I hear the angel voices calling
"Old Black Joe."

My mother and Topsy reach the barn. Just in front of the hay entrance, Jack, the hired hand's German shepherd, is gnawing a bone. Topsy trots over and Jack reluctantly gives up the bone to the bigger dog. My mother squats to put her arm over Jack's shoulders to console him. Rather than allowing himself to be soothed, the dog lunges, grabbing her face in his jaws. She sees his tongue and throat as he shakes her like a doll.

"Jack!" Uncle Russell roars. He had been setting up a combine nearby. The German shepherd drops my mother, and Russell picks her up and runs with her, her face bloodied, into the house.

In town, the doctor cauterizes the slashes below both eyes, the teeth marks on her eyelids and over her jugular vein; the gash was deep but spared the vein.

That night my grandfather announces he is giving Topsy to a farm four hours away. Once, my mother had been throwing rocks against the side of the coal shed to make her terrier, Scotty, bark at her. Topsy, ever protective, grabbed the animal in her jaws and shook the smaller dog until she was dead.

"He feels Topsy can be unpredictable, too. She could do the same, or worse," her mother says. "To you or to a neighbor child."

My mother pleads for him to change his mind, tells him Topsy, unlike Jack, would never hurt a child. But her father, a staunch, practical man, is unmoved. Two days later he packs Topsy into his Ford and heads off, tires crunching across the gravel.

My mother, eleven, is riding, her legs dangling, on a two-ton trailer behind the tractor Audrey is driving through the cow pasture. It's July, and she and her sister are helping their father transport the last load of hay into the barn before the dark clouds overhead open, the forecast calling for a massive rainstorm. This hay crop is doubly important, since her father's main source of income, his soybean crop, was wiped away by a big flood two weeks before. Later my mother will tell me that her father was an organic farmer before the techniques he employed were identified as such. He used the rotation system, green cover crops, and wheat-spread manure. He kept his own grain for seed, thus insuring that there were neither weeds nor herbicides. He was the first farmer in his area to plant alfalfa, and gauged its superior nutritional value by the shining health of his animals. Other farmers gathered to buy his seed and soon clamored for it until it became a standard crop. He was the first to farm soybeans, noting that this crop added nitrogen to the soil. His crops always looked twice as green and full as the fields of the farmers who used other methods.

Now my grandfather reaches his hand out and taps my mother's knee. Be careful, he tells her, pointing to the taller-than-he-is wheel just in front of her legs. "If you fall, you'll go under the wheel." But he isn't worried. Audrey, four years my mother's senior, stays close in the kitchen, helping her mother with the cooking and cleaning. It is my mother, blond-haired, blue-eyed, who follows him in the fields, picking peaches from the trees while he plows, often riding beside him in the tractor.

On this day a stray baling wire, looped on both ends, lies unseen in the pasture just ahead of the tractor. As they pass over it, one loop catches my mother's foot. As the other end of the wire vanishes under the rolling wheel, it pulls my mother, before my grandfather can grab her, off her seat and drags her under the trailer. My mother sees the wheel coming and throws her head out of the way at the last minute. The wheel pushes her body a few inches into the moist ground as it rolls directly over her chest. She struggles to her knees, unable to take in a breath. Ray, the hired hand who had been walking beside the trailer, reaches her first. Without waiting for instructions, he kneels, puts his mouth over hers, forces his hot breath into her crushed lungs, one breath, two breaths, three. Ray, her father, and Audrey wait for my mother to draw the tiniest sip of thin, ragged air, though her chest feels as if the weight of the trailer is still upon it. Then Ray lifts her, heading through the pasture toward the house as my grandfather runs to get the car. In Ray's arms my mother begins to pray silently over and over, *Please, dear God, don't let me die.*

My mother holds tightly to the hand strap in the backseat of her father's '41 bright blue satin-interior Chrysler New Yorker, where the year before she had thrown up pineapple soda during a whooping-cough attack. Now the road to town is almost inaccessible. Filled with ruts and ditches from a flood a few months before, each bump is an explosion of white fire in her chest. The pastures out the window are going in and out of focus, and the black, framing her periphery, is closing in.

"Am I going to die?" she asks.

"Not if you're a very good girl," her father says.

At the hospital my mother loses consciousness. The doctors tell my grandparents that her heart and windpipe have been pushed to one side, and one entire lung and half of the other are crushed. They say she will not live through the night. One doctor wants to operate; the other, a specialist from St. Louis, does not. The specialist wins—there will be no surgery—an outcome, my mother will later say, that most likely saved her life.

Outside her room, where her parents and sister hope for news that she has awakened, Audrey attempts to hug her mother and knocks my grandmother's only pair of glasses from her face. They shatter on the floor.

In her unconscious sleep, my mother whistles for her dogs all night long.

My mother spends the summer in the hospital. Benny Miller, who owns the drugstore in town with the soda fountain, gives her carte blanche for anything she wants. She orders only once: a cherry nut sundae with whipped cream and three kinds of ice cream. Sulfa drugs, the forerunners to antibiotics, have just been discovered, and my grandparents are told how lucky they are to have the miracle drug to keep infections at bay. Later my mother will say that even at that time she felt these drugs were unnecessary and merely polluted her body and no doubt contributed to her total loss of appetite. In the fall, the doctor instructs her to strengthen her lungs by blowing balloons or playing a wind musical instrument, so upon entering high school, she joins the band, choosing to play the same instrument as Audrey: the bassoon. The following spring, my mother performs Mozart's B-Flat Concerto for the bassoon, which she transposed note by note by ear from a recording, wins a statewide contest, and is chosen Outstanding Woodwind Soloist. Also that spring she has begun to notice unexplained headaches, a rash here and there. The doctor suggests chlorinated water is detrimental to the sinuses and recommends she stay away from the community pool. He administers a scratch test and determines she is allergic to berries, wheat, grass—a majority of basic foods. The doctor does not offer suggestions for alternative diets, however. It's 1944 and he doesn't know any. My mother, already uncomfortable in the water, is happy to avoid swimming. Her parents encourage her to wear shoes when she walks through the pasture, to avoid direct contact with grass.

My mother is thirteen when the Army Corps of Engineers, her family's ally through many floods, delivers the news that the United States government, through the power of eminent domain, has allocated most of her father's farm for the purpose of building a canal that will bypass the dangerous Chain of Rocks Reach. The acreage allocated for the canal amounts to two-thirds of the farm and will be taken out of the very middle of it. For remuneration, the government offers to pay my mother's father one thousand dollars. Moving to a new farm marked the beginning of an irrevocable separation between her and the world of nature, my mother would later write in private notes. Although her father continued to farm close to one thousand acres at various other locations, the new home farm contained only one hundred acres, which put my mother close to neighbors on almost all sides. Though soon, in high school, she discovers her new love, music and high school band, as she grows into a beauty and is elected May Queen her senior year. She is accepted to Lindenwood College, twenty-six miles away, where she majors in music and plays field hockey, wearing a special mask to protect her mouth for the bassoon. In college, her struggles with her health continue. She finds herself falling asleep at inopportune times: in her humanities class after lunch, and during orchestra practice, where she dozes off during the sixteen-bar rests, falling asleep while counting measures, a sixth sense waking her up just in time for entry. Her parents order tests, including a basal metabolism test that requires the wearing of a claustrophobic mask she has to breathe in and out of. No cause for her inability to stay awake is found.

My mother is twenty-eight and visiting New York City for the first time with the only friend we will ever meet from her childhood, Jean Bilbrey. Jean's fiancé owns the St. Louis Cardinals. He has a friend in New York, my father, who can show them around town. Without taking the time to meet them, my father puts them in the care of one of his producers, Ty Lubell, and goes off to Bermuda to fish. My mother is driven around New York City, looking up openmouthed at the skyscrapers through the open roof of Ty's blue Ford Thunderbird convertible. She will later laugh that while waiting at curbs to cross the street with Jean, she paces, misunderstanding the meaning of the NO STANDING signs.

Meanwhile, my father is battling a two-hundred-pound blue marlin. The fishing guide is young. He drives the boat too far to the left as the giant fish pulls the line under the bow to the right, torquing my father's shoulder, pulling muscle from bone. When my mother and Jean stop by my father's office on their last day to say thank you to Ty, my father is there, his arm in a sling, back from his trip a day early.

At five foot eight, my mother looks every bit what she is: a model and, as Miss Missouri, five years before, a Miss America beauty pageant top-ten finalist. On this day, her shining chestnut hair bounces at her shoulders. She wears dark red lipstick, a white cotton two-piece knit dress trimmed in red and navy that she proudly sewed herself, red high heels, and red stockings. My father, who had never believed he was good-looking, must have imagined himself with my mother on his arm. My mother, who will tell me she fell in love with my father's intellect, must have imagined herself living the glamorous life of a broadcasting executive's wife. For one year they travel back and forth cross-country. My father visits my mother's family's farm. She makes trips to his bachelor apartment on Fifth Avenue. In New York she proudly wears her home-sewn outfits from the *Vogue* and *McCall's* patterns she elaborates on with her own touches to produce stylish two-piece knits, knee-length skirts with gold-buttoned matching jackets. In New York she shakes off any last remnants of her Missouri farm-girl childhood to reveal the elegant being she has known herself all along to be.

They talk of eloping. The weekend before they are supposed to marry, my father calls my mother to tell her he is feeling unsure. She reassures him, "I'll come up anyway," since this is a visit they have already planned and she already has her plane tickets. She tells him, "No pressure," they can have their visit, a visit that doesn't have to mean anything more. A month later she learns she is pregnant with me.

My mother and father have been married for three months. They sit at Joe's, somewhere on the outskirts of New York, my father's favorite restaurant, facing each other across the square wooden table. Their laminated menus are lying open across their plates.

My mother has mentioned my father's working late on Tuesday nights. Once a week, on Tuesdays, Shirley, my father's only sibling, comes over to their small Fifth Avenue apartment for dinner.

Shirley lights cigarette after cigarette and fills my mother in on all the hometown Long Beach, New York, gossip. My mother listens politely as Shirley goes on about the Shuman family's garage sale, an eighty-year-old cousin's asthma, the neighborhood drugstore closing after four generations, and the Levys' new baby that weighed almost twelve pounds. Finally my mother stands, walks over to open a window, her head throbbing from the cigarette smoke.

"I think you feel guilty," my mother has just told my father, "about not really wanting to spend time with your sister. But I don't feel it's fair that you expect me to entertain her."

She has hit a nerve. My father responds, though she doesn't hear everything he says because as his voice grows more and more high-pitched, the diners at the small tables around them are beginning to look over at them.

My mother shifts in the hard wooden seat. He is pointing at her now, jabbing at the air, the thrust of each sentence, his voice tight and loud and relentless, matching each thrust of his arrow-straight finger.

"You-will-entertain-my-sister-it's-the-least-you-can-do-my-sister-raised-me-took-in-boarders-to-feed-and-clothe—"

My mother excuses herself to go to the bathroom. She leaves her coat, brings her purse. By the kitchen, she asks a waiter if there is a back door. He points down the hall. My mother slips out into the street, slick with rain, raises her hand, and stops a cab.

My father sits for a half hour before he realizes she isn't coming back.

Chapter 2

The keen is low but urgent and getting louder; it hurtles along a dark street, one of the thousands of streets that make up the vast and terrifyingly gargantuan sprawl of city outside our apartment. My bedroom, equally cavernous, with towering ceilings and two enormous windows like giant black eyes, is empty except for my younger brother Greg's and my cribs and one hard wooden rocking chair. Red-and-white lights flash across the ceiling and the siren's wail fills the room as Greg pulls himself to his feet. He can't yet walk, so he holds the crib railing, sobbing out his panic. I am not yet two, but this is something I am aware of: my brother is a worrier. Though I'm not in disagreement that the siren is too loud—I'm crying, too—as he shrieks, red-faced, his baby-fine blond hair sweat-dampened, with no sign of letting up, his terror seems bottomless. Now our mother, wearing only a thin sheath of a nightgown, fills the doorway. Greg is still standing and crying as she steps into the room, pads over to my crib first, then Greg's, lifting then carrying each of us, one in each arm, to the rocking chair in front of the windows. She sits back, holding our damp bodies against the dryness of her slip, our hot cheeks pressed to the cool skin at her collarbone, and rocks us slowly as the siren's screech recedes. As it goes, the ebbing scream traces an auditory grid of streets and avenues and boulevards that stretch away endlessly, reminding me that the world around us feels too big and that I'm a worrier, too.

Down at the other end of our Dakota apartment building, Alan Alda is laughing. I know he is important, like all the people at my father's fortieth birthday party mingling now in the museum-formal rooms where we are not allowed. I lie in my bed. Punches of laugher and bursts of exclamations drift down the city-block-long hallway of our apartment. Though I am five, I know from past experience that to be my father's daughter, the only girl and eldest of four, is a kind of spotlight. I have two choices, lie here unnoticed and uncelebrated, dutifully obeying our bedtime schedule, or go see if I can elicit some attention. It is 1966, and my father is head of programming at ABC. In the past few years, he hired Jim McKay and Roone Arledge and created *Wide World of Sports*, which, I will later understand, serves as the model for all sports broadcasting to come. My father's pioneering belief that sports are a story and need to be in every living room fueled his efforts to bring weekly block-buster football broadcasts, pregame commentary, and coverage of lesser-known sports to television. He was also a pioneer of the use of instant replay and of bringing the camera onto the field, under-standing that viewers wanted to feel closer to the action. More recently he has green-lighted shows such as *Batman*; the first soap opera, *Peyton Place*; and *Bewitched,* programs that, along with *Wide World of Sports*, are responsible for the fact that ABC is number one in the Nielsen ratings for the first time in history. He also put *That Girl* on the air when no other network would do so, supporting Marlo Thomas's vision and belief that a program about an unmarried career woman living on her own would have an audience, setting the stage for the cultural shift to come.

I climb out of bed, pad along our long rugless hallway. The rubber bottoms of my footie pajamas grip the long polished boards of hardwood, little *thwacks* in the now-quiet of the hall. Closer now, I can hear the low hum of conversation, the tinkling of ice against thin glasses, the occasional bark of a laugh or exclamation of surprise. I round the last turn in the hall and there it is, the living room, dark every other night, its furniture sharp-angled, silent sentinels, tonight lit white. I stop at the track along the wood floor, the runner for the doors as wide as the walls they slide into when this room is shut away. People stand in clusters, as tall as trees, their legs stilts. No one has seen me. I could go back to bed. I don't know, really, how I will be received.

"Christine!" someone cries. "Is this Christine?"

A rush of warmth. Marlo Thomas is perched like a pretty bird on the centerpiece of the large room, our blue velvet rotunda, under the marble bust of a Greek woman baring her white marble nipple. Marlo is smiling, reaching out her white arm. She doesn't stand; she waits for me to walk to her. Around her, legs part amid the rustle of fabric, the crackle of leather, the brushing together of stockinged thighs, murmurs of approval. Cigarette smoke swirls like totems. Someone touches my head. Marlo leans forward, takes my hand, and kisses my cheek. Her hand is warm and her lips are cold and pungent-sweet with liqueur. My father is standing in front of her. He is dressed in a dark suit and narrow tie and twists his feet to the right, his hips to the left. He is holding his elbows bent at his sides and is smiling with only one side of his mouth, the face he makes when he dances.

"Your old dad's pretty good, huh?" he says for me but also for the benefit of Marlo and whoever else is watching. He continues this sashay, hips and feet, the jitterbug. "I was quite a dancer in my day."

I already know, because he has told me, that he was a good dancer when he was younger. We have also been told of Marlo's affection for my dad, which is evident in the glow coming from her smile, her bright eyes.

"She says she is eternally grateful," my mother often says. "She is full of love for him."

My mother now stands in the opposite corner of the room by her Steinway grand piano, holding a short square glass and talking to a man with thick black glasses. She stands upright like the model she was, holds her head as if she is carrying a book on it. *Germans rule with the head, not the heart,* she likes to remind me, and this dictum seems to go with the formal way she carries herself, the way she nods and smiles to the man though her shoulders are braced and the smile on her face is wider than usual. Something else she has told me: she doesn't know how to make small talk. She doesn't like it when my father leaves her to "work the party," leaves her to fend for herself at these gatherings.

One month later our mother is crouched just inside the kitchen door, her arms outstretched. It's our bedtime, but she has just returned from a week with our father in the tropics. Tears run down her cheeks. Irma, the maid, puts Braddy, who is two, down, and the four of us run into her arms. She hugs us all at the same time.

"Why are you crying?" Jay, three, asks.

"They're tears of happiness," she says. I look more closely. I've never heard of this. They look like regular tears, though it's true she is smiling.

"I missed you children so much. It isn't natural for a mother to be away from her children."

"Irma, where is my shoehorn?" my father calls from the hall. He has been home for only moments, but his voice is high-pitched, the way it gets when he's angry.

Our maid, now washing dishes at the sink, stops, her gloved hands still soapy, and walks to the doorway between the kitchen and hallway.

"I don't know, Mr. Scherick!" she calls back. Her hands drip soap onto the wood floor.

My mother turns her head away from us to shout, "It should be on your shelf, Edgar!" Her voice sounds strained; she is pushing it so it carries down the hall.

"Which shelf, Carol?" His voice carries, too. My heart misses a beat. This is the way things usually start.

My mother stands up out of her crouch.

"I'm coming, Edgar!" she calls loudly.

The man with the thick white beard tells my brothers and me to lie down on the wooden floor of his New York apartment. My mother has introduced him as *Maharishi*. The foreign-sounding name goes with his appearance. He is wearing loose white clothing and his bare feet are at eye level. I am five. Greg is four, Jay three, and Braddy two. My mother stands in the entryway, smiling a patient, benevolent smile. Maharishi crouches and holds his hand a few inches over my stomach.

"Breathe," he says.

The wooden floor is cold under my back. I feel self-conscious with him watching me like this. I take a huge breath in, sucking in my stomach. Is this how I usually breathe? I suddenly can't remember.

"No. No. No," he says. His voice is smooth like cool milk and each *No* clips up at the end like it has a tail that he snaps up and out of the way. This is the man, our mother has told us, who taught the Beatles how to meditate.

"This is the incorrect way to breathe. This is how Westerners breathe."

My mother is nodding. Although she has never explained to us how to breathe correctly, it seems she has known this all along.

"Breath is prana; it is life force. You must fill your body with prana. When you breathe in, your belly should rise to *here*." He nods at his palm, which is still hovering over my stomach. "Try again."

I take another deep breath in. My stomach sucks in with the effort. This is harder than it sounds. I've been breathing my way, the way that seems to make the most sense, for all my life. This new technique is going to take some work. The Maharishi shakes his head. My mother is not smiling as broadly now.

"Fill your belly with your breath. Touch my hand," he says. His head is tilted over me as though I am a specimen he is examining, the representative for all children of my kind. Non–East Indian children. Children who don't know how to breathe properly. I feel suddenly responsible. Can we learn, or are we doomed to an existence of incorrect breathing? I don't want to let anyone down.

I take a third breath and push my stomach out as I do so. It feels like the opposite of real breathing—pushing out when I should be pulling the breath in—but Maharishi nods and sits back on his heels. From the doorway my mother is smiling again.

"Now you must practice," Maharishi says.

He pats my stomach and looks into my eyes. My mother sighs and folds her arms. I now know the correct way to breathe. The fact that I can't seem to actually take in any oxygen when I follow the Maharishi's instructions, the fact that the right way feels wrong, matters not.

The Maharishi moves to Greg.

"Take a deep breath," he says.

I feel some satisfaction as my brother sucks in his stomach just as I did, but also embarrassed. Does this Maharishi feel he is wasting his time with such ignorant children? Has he just remembered that he has better things to do?

"Fill your belly with prana," he says.

Greg tries again, taking in an even deeper breath. His stomach is concave with the effort. The Maharishi lays his palm gently on Greg's midsection as if bestowing a benediction. Then he moves to Jay, who miraculously, typically, has distended his stomach with his intake of breath. At three, Jay already possesses a kind of quiet knowing that Greg, Braddy, and I blunder around on the outskirts of. The Maharishi nods and lightly rests his palm on Braddy's stomach.

"They will get it. It will come." He stands.

The lesson is over.

My kindergarten room smells of just-cleaned-up afternoon snack, graham crackers and grape juice. Outside, the sky is gray and the large wooden-framed window that faces Fifty-seventh Street is dark and mottled with drops. I'm standing at the waist-high worktable, taking a break from tracing the letter K to watch these drops live out their life spans. Some have tails that are short; these drops disappear almost instantly. Others wind their way down the length of the window. I imagine myself like those bold ones. They seem adventurous and daring and kindred. I try not to think about the fact that all the drops on this window are dying almost as soon as they are born and the fact that they exactly resemble tears.

My mother has appeared at my cubby and is pulling out my galoshes. The day is over. Her black-and-white polka-dot raincoat is drawn in at the waist with a wide, stylish belt. She is wearing dark red lipstick; her shining, carefully curled chestnut hair bounces on the tops of her shoulders. Her smile as she greets Teacher is wide and dazzling. She is a beautiful, capable giant moving among child-size desks and tables and chairs, and I feel the familiar stab, the hot pain of my dependence on her.

After we leave my room, we gather Greg and Jay and their galoshes from their rooms. Braddy is at home with Tata, our nanny. This is the Child Development Center, a school my mother is proud to send us to because she says it is a pioneer in early childhood education. The school was recommended by our pediatrician,

Dr. Berenberg. When my mother brings all four of us to Dr. Berenberg's office, we arrive like a parade. At the Child Development Center, my brothers and I are given intelligence quotient tests. Though this is supposed to be a secret and our mother's plan was to keep our individual scores private, Greg tells me that he tested at the genius level, which doesn't surprise me. It was Greg who taught me how to tell time and tie my shoelaces in a bow, though I am older.

"You're my big helper, Christine," she says now. Our names are formal and Protestant, like my mother: Christine Carol, Gregory Edgar, Jonathan Jay, Bradford Roman. "William Bradford came over on the *Mayflower*," my mother has told us. My father's family is Jewish. She addresses us, with the exception of Jay, whom she calls "Jay Jay," by our full first names.

Outside, my mother asks me to hold my brothers' hands, and we wait on the sidewalk as she steps out onto the street to flag down a taxi. The wet streets and sidewalks are awash in light, reflections from headlights, taillights, blinking crosswalk signs. Still, the sky hangs low and the rain presses, the sea of umbrellas overhead creating a ceiling of black, everyone looking down. A checkered cab pulls up and my mother opens the door, unfolds one heavy jump seat, and sits down on it, holding Jay. Greg and I slide across the black vinyl seat, which is torn at the seams and losing its white stuffing.

"Broadway and Seventy-ninth Street, please, driver," my mother says. Her voice rings confidently. As the door closes and the cab light goes out slowly, it catches all the highlights in her dark hair.

The cab lets us out. The rain has stopped, but the sky is still gray. It's almost October and very cold in the shadows between buildings. Overhead, a rooftop incinerator spews a black plume that rises in slow motion and spreads, mixing with the clouds.

"Look at that." My mother's mouth is tight with disgust.

"What?"

"That building's incinerator pumping poison into the air. It's criminal, forcing everyone to breathe that pollution."

My mother pulls my hand as we cross the island that runs down the middle of Broadway, tugging at my arm as she steers me around the dusty-looking, Tootsie Roll–like pieces of dog feces that lie in the hard-packed dirt, where there are no cobblestones.

A cluster of bells tied to the door tinkles as we step inside Florsheim Shoes; the air in the shoe store is cool and thick with the smell of leather. The shoe salesman crouches at my knees and presses hard with his thumb at the toe of the brown Mary Janes on my feet. They're so stiff, his thumb barely makes a dent.

"I don't really like these." I eye an illustration on a poster by the door of a little girl on a swing wearing a pair of rubber-soled Buster Browns.

"They'll last," my mother says. "They're well made."

The shoe salesman crouches at Greg's knees, then Jay's. I practice walking and sliding along the store rug in my new shoes' slick leather soles until I shock myself when I touch the sales counter. I sit back down in a chair and swing my feet. Finally Greg and Jay have their new stiff shoes too, and it's time to go home.

Outside, the sky is clear but the sun has set. In the deepening dusk, despite the lit storefront signs, headlights, and taillights, Broadway is tinted blue. My mother leaves us on the curb again and hails another cab.

"Central Park West, driver. The Dakota," she says, after we pile inside, her voice ringing extra bell-like.

"How does he know where to go?" I ask.

"The Dakota is a very famous residence," my mother said. "Everyone knows where it is."

The cab pulls up in front of our building and Heinz, the doorman, steps off the curb to meet us, opening our cab door with one white-gloved hand.

"Mrs. Scherick," Heinz says, and nods.

All the doormen at the Dakota match in their long navy brass-buttoned coats and gendarme hats. But Heinz speaks with a German accent. I like the way his words sound like jabs and the way he smiles down at me when he sees me. Now he puts his gloved hand on the small of my back and, with a soft push, helps me onto the sidewalk. My mother, brothers, and I file past him to the wrought-iron gated entry, big enough for horse-drawn carriages to have parked and let out the building's inhabitants when the Dakota was built in the 1880s, when the Upper West Side of Manhattan was considered remote and was surrounded by empty fields.

Heinz goes back to his post beside his copper doorman's booth, his feet spread apart and his hands clasped behind his back. We stop in the dark paneled co-op office, which is located at the top of the marble steps, just inside the iron gate that closes off the Dakota's courtyard to outsiders. The office is a room of dark paneling and white-and-black speckled marble floors and smells of lemon Pledge and wood. Winnie is behind the desk, her reading glasses attached by a string of miniature balls that drapes behind her neck. She leans forward when she sees us, her middle-aged face alight.

"There they are, those beautiful children."

We are celebrities in this office, so I am used to feeling exclaimed over and important, though it is my brothers, especially, who are beautiful. Compared to Braddy's chubby cuteness or Jay's fragile blond-haired, blue-eyed beauty, I am clumsy and too big. Greg and I are mistaken for twins, but he is smooth-skinned and handsome, and important as eldest son in a way I'm not.

"You have such beautiful children, Mrs. Scherick," Winnie says.

My mother pushes my hair behind my ear with her finger, touches the top of Greg's head, pleased. We take the back door out of the office, head down the stone steps into the courtyard, which, surrounded on all four sides by ten stories of Dakota apartments, is very cold. We cross between the fountains. The copper man-size reeds and stamens—the fountains' motif is a water plant—are dry; the water has been turned off for the winter to prevent frozen pipes. Then we climb the stairs to the service entrance that leads to the back door of our apartment. This stairwell smells of furnace heat and dust. As our apartment is on the first floor, the cavernous basement is only one short flight down. My mother pushes open our back door, which leads into our kitchen. Our apartment, like Winnie's office, smells of dust and wood and floor wax. I head from the kitchen in my stiff new shoes, down the long, tall hallway that leads, eventually, to first my bedroom, then my brothers', then my parents', and beyond that, down another long, tall hallway, to the formal rooms of the apartment that sit too dark and silent and where I try never to go. As I reach my room, the stiffness of my shoes feels connected to the heaviness of our apartment; the towering ceilings and doors; the dark, cavernous hallways; the sharp angles and dense, closed-off atmosphere. My parents bought our apartment from a couple, two men, who, she told me, had painted all the wood black.

"Can you imagine? Black? Who in their right mind would paint over wood?" my mother spits whenever the subject comes up, though the wood she had painstakingly revealed is dark. I make a note never to paint over wood in her presence, but I also look into the apartment windows in the building next door and secretly long to trade our dark wood paneling and molding, our museum-quality, antique period furniture tacked down with plastic we aren't allowed to sit on, for the white walls I see in these other apartments. I long for these other comfortable-looking sofas and chairs, for the golden halos of lamplight throwing circles of intimacy and warmth.

After dinner the rain starts up again. I sit cross-legged on the radiator by the window in the kitchen that looks out onto the courtyard. I watch the raindrops fall into the puddle that always forms in the same spot on the aluminum roof of the walkway that runs around the perimeter of the courtyard. Every fall this walkway is carried in sections, man-high segments of glass and paneling, by workmen in coveralls, then pieced together to form a tunnel, shelter from winter rain and snow for residents as they leave their apartments. My nose almost touches the cold glass as I look out. The walkway's aluminum roof, the shadowy stone of the ten stories of building that rise up and surround this courtyard on all four sides, the small disc of stormy sky visible overhead, the puddle and the raindrops that fall into it, are all black. I am testing myself. Can I remain separate from the gloom around me? Is there a place deep enough inside me that it is impervious to the cold glass, the cold black raindrops, the low-hanging gray sky, the silently watching black windows of other apartments and towering walls of stone, the pointed Gothic spires that stab the heavy drape of clouds?

They are filming a movie outside our building. My mother points out the production crew and movie cameras on the corner. The movie is *Rosemary's Baby,* and the Dakota features prominently as the building where the witches and warlocks in the story hold their coven and Mia Farrow is forced to ingest blended green drinks with strange ingredients to prepare her to spawn an inhuman child. Though I know that some of the most famous people in the world live in the apartments around us, Leonard Bernstein and Lauren Bacall among them, as our mother guides us around the filming, I feel some relief that someone is recognizing the very thing I myself have felt, that this is a scary place to live.

My mother has bought a rug and rolled it out in the formal living room. As my mother is allergic to dust and except for the dining room, there are no other floor coverings in any room of our apartment, the arrival of this rug is an occasion. This new rug is white, and we squeeze handfuls of the soft piles, kneel on it, lie down on our stomachs, turn onto our backs and make snow angels. It's soft, softer than my bed, softer than anything else in this apartment, and despite the fact that it's down where my mother's rooms feel more like mini museums than someone's home, I don't want to leave. Maybe this is the first step, and our apartment can become like the apartments in the windows I look up into.

"Can we sleep here tonight?" Jay asks.

My mother sets us up with blankets and pillows and goes back to her bedroom. We lie in the unfamiliar night world of this room. The ceiling is lit with headlights that run from one corner to the other. The cough of the bus engines is louder here. I want to stay anyway. I plan on sleeping here every night from now on.

Braddy sits up first. Without a word he heads off. I hear him padding down the hall. Jay's next. He gets up and is quickly gone. The room feels darker and bigger with just Greg and me. I hold my breath. Maybe Greg's asleep and doesn't realize it's down to us.

"Are you going or staying?" Greg says. I look over. He's sitting up.

The thing is, even if I make it one night, tomorrow night, when everyone's brushing their teeth, I won't be walking back down here by myself. Nothing moves in this part of the house. It's so far from the kitchen, the laundry room, the bathroom, and the bedrooms where we spend our days, it seems to belong to another apartment. And if I can't make it a regular thing, why prolong the good-bye?

Greg is almost to the hall. I gather my blanket and follow him.

The rug is gone by the end of the week. The rug's departure makes more sense than its arrival in the first place. None of us asks about it again.

———

It's Saturday and we've been inside all day. We've played Battle-ship, Twister, Candy Land, Parcheesi, Sorry. Little colored wooden men go around and around, fighting to get into their plastic-domed homes while we want out of ours. I feel coated with a layer of grease, a combination of my own and my brothers' sweat from an ongoing wrestling match, from the invisible residue of artificial lights on skin, from animal dander, from furniture polish rubbed through my T-shirt each time I slide across the dining-room table and from floor wax rubbed through my socks from sliding down the halls. The small TV in the room by the kitchen, where the new maid, Rose, who replaced Irma, lives, plays cartoons while Rose irons my father's Hanes undershirts and white handkerchiefs. Twangy *boing*s and *eh, what's up, doc*s repeat like the endless loop of background cacti and desert mountain. I feel sick to my stomach just being in the same room with it.

Our mother is in her bedroom, leaning over her sewing ma-chine. This machine has traveled from her farm-girl childhood to our city apartment and has the appearance to prove it. Giant and bulbous, it looks like a relic, but when she unpacks and packs it, pulling off or setting spools on levers, threading and un-threading, her movements are slow and measured and reverent.

"When I was younger, I used to make all my clothes," she has told me.

Now large swaths of fabric are spread out on the floor and bed. "We have one month until Halloween and I need to get these done."

My youngest brothers are old enough to trick-or-treat and this will be our first Halloween. She is making our costumes. A few days ago she spread the Simplicity patterns on her bed and let us choose which animal we wanted to be. Jay chose the yellow duck costume, Greg a shaggy dog. I chose the gray mouse with long white whiskers and a pink nose, and Braddy, the black-and-white spotted Dalmatian.

I'm lying on her bed, watching her pump her foot on the pedal and feed the fabric through the needle that bobs so fast, it's a blur. Then she snaps a switch and the needle slows then stops; the hum of the machine quiets. She lifts up the arm, pulls out the material still attached by several threads, and holds up my gray mouse costume. She leans back and looks it over, seemingly glad to take a moment to appreciate her handiwork. The costume has a white stomach, a long pink tail. These are full-body costumes complete with fur paws, and they cover us from the tips of our fingers down to our feet. They even include fur hoods adorned with ears and whiskers. She's made them big so that we can wear them again next year.

"Braddy is walking into our game and knocking over the pieces." Greg, nine, appears through the dressing room that connects my brothers' bedrooms and my parents' room. The original one room that Greg and I shared, my mother has proudly divided (how many apartments in New York City have rooms that are so big—fourteen-foot ceilings—they can become four?) so each of my three brothers can have his own room. Greg and Jay, the oldest boys, have rooms on the second floor, accessed by ladder. Braddy's is on the ground floor, a fact he hates, next to the fourth room, which has a small guest bed and houses our toys. Our mother calls it *the playroom*.

Greg is wearing only a pair of cotton briefs. His naked skin is golden brown. He and Braddy both look perpetually tan, their skin smooth. It seems completely natural to me that I know my brothers' bodies as well as I know my own. Jay, eight, has the palest skin of all of us, narrow wrists and ankles, soft blond curls and light blue eyes, always flushed, feverishly pink cheeks. Both Greg's and Braddy's nipples are brown and round like copper pennies. Greg has a long body, long legs and arms. Brad has boxy toes, and his feet are square and slightly pigeon-toed. When he was a baby, he had to wear a brace between his baby shoes that held his legs so his feet would turn outward. He lay in his crib and screamed, his battles with the world beginning early.

"Bradford! Come play a game with Christine."

"No!" Braddy's six-year-old voice pipes from the bedroom.

"He won't leave us alone." Greg's shoulders are back, his chin jutting forward. He usually considers it our mother's responsibility to set his inconveniences right. Greg knows all the important things before I do. But right now, and often, Braddy is an affront he doesn't want to manage. The next step for Greg will be to use his fists and for Braddy to fight back, an outcome that is fairly regular between these two brothers born on the same day, four years apart.

In the other room Jay and Braddy are conversing. Jay's voice is low and soothing. I imagine his and Braddy's heads bent over the game pieces as Jay includes him in some manner, sensing in his fragile way that Braddy barrels in strongest when he feels most excluded.

"Bradford, will you find my handkerchief from Grandpa?" my mother calls. "You're my best finder."

Braddy's footsteps are instantly quick and loud as this distraction works, and he runs down the hallway toward the laundry room and comes back with a sheer white handkerchief, hands it to our mother, and crawls up beside me on our parents' bed. Greg has slipped back into the playroom to finish the game. The term will come later: *hyperactive*. Right now all we know is that most of us usually attempt to put distance between ourselves and the cloud of constant frenetic energy around Braddy. I compensate by sometimes stepping in to try to help when he and Greg butt heads. But mostly Braddy travels in a sort of bubble of isolation, attempting to relate to Greg and Jay, his older brothers, by annoying them.

Now my father's high-pitched voice travels down the hallway from the kitchen. I can't make out what he's saying but, home from whatever mysterious Saturday work goings-on he was engaged in, he's loud. Adrenaline instantly shoots hot from my chest down into my legs. His energy, like Braddy's, makes it impossible to relax. He chews gum too fast and talks too loudly, becomes angry when any clutter piles up on a countertop, when we leave a plate on the kitchen table or a toy in the hall. Right now I'm hoping he is joking with Rose, and this is the reason his voice is carrying. Braddy jumps off the bed and heads through the dressing room and into his room. I want to retreat to my room, too. But my father is coming down the hall now, his voice still strident, his leather-soled footsteps percussion strikes on the bare wood. He will hit my room, at the elbow of the turn in the hall from the kitchen to the bedrooms, first.

"Containers on every refrigerator shelf? Is it too much to ask for order?"

He is directing his attention to Rose in the kitchen, but his speed tells me he is bringing whatever problem he is having with him and will shortly unleash it upon this end of the apartment. I duck into the playroom at the last minute, just before he rounds the turn.

". . . five containers of rotting fruit . . . !"

I have an urge to hide in the closet. I crouch beside Jay and Greg's Battleship game instead. My heart is thudding against my rib cage—what have I left lying around?—but he strides past our door without looking in and enters his bedroom.

"Is there a reason we are saving *five containers of rotting fruit*?"

My mother's voice is low and I can't hear her words, but clearly she is attempting to calm him. What she won't say is that she doesn't like to throw anything away. She has told my brothers and me the story of her uncle Herman, who died trying to get the last bit of a gravel delivery out of a raised dump-truck bed with a stick. While scraping, he triggered the release mechanism and the bed of the truck fell backward and crushed him. It's a cautionary tale we don't adhere to. My mother wants to get the last drop of use out of everything, so our countertops are cluttered with items waiting to be needed: used notebooks, broken pencils and crayons, loose nails and screws, a pile of socks with no mates. In the fridge, her need to find a use for everything translates into shelves full of containers of mostly eaten food, which she will bring out with a flourish every time we sit down to a meal and attempt to coax us into finishing the last wedge of now-oxidized brown apple or the tablespoon of cottage cheese left at the bottom of the plastic container.

Now my father responds to whatever she is saying by maintaining his decibel level.

"Is it too much to ask to open the refrigerator and find *order*?"

"No, it's not too much to ask, Edgar, to open the refrigerator and find what you're looking for in it," our mother says stiffly. She's already had enough of this. We were having a nice enough time before he barged in.

His decibel level raises as he says, "It's *not* too much to ask to come home to a refrigerator where I can find something I want to eat. It's certainly *not* too much to ask for order in the kitchen."

Silence. I imagine her arranging her fabric pieces methodically. Like Greg, my father holds my mother responsible for his inconveniences. I know from experience that he will not let her off the hook regardless of her attempts to disengage from the confrontation. His decibel level quickly raises again, to an impossible scream I couldn't have imagined a man could make: "Goddamn it, this is *my* house, and I get to decide how things are around here."

The final tactic: escape. She is out of the bedroom and passes the open playroom door. He follows her down the hall, roaring, "I'm fighting for my life here, Carol!"

A muffled, angry tangle of voices from the kitchen. A bang, something being thrown. Another bang, a crash. My father's voice is at its highest pitch now. Then a door slams loudly and there is silence. He has left the apartment. I feel awash in cool relief. Then hot panic. It's so quiet now; is our mother all right? After a moment, she passes us in the hallway, walking like she is tiptoeing.

"I love you, children." She stands at the doorway in her thin nightgown. We look up at her. She looks pale, shaken.

"We love you, Mom," we chorus.

Then she is gone, heading back to her bedroom.

I wrap my index and middle fingers around a few tendrils of hair at the nape of my neck and pull. The tug, then the snap of hair as it releases from my scalp, feels satisfying. I hold the hair in the crook of my index finger and insert my thumb into my mouth, rubbing the hair against my upper lip. The hair balls up. This will be a good piece of *fuzz*, I can tell. Not too big, not too small. It is already compacting the way I like it, into a ring, one side of the ring solidifying, the other staying soft. I like both, the soft and the hard, against my lip. I flip the fuzz, taking turns with each side. My thumb is warm along the roof of my mouth; it fits snugly against the top of my tongue, follows the curves of my palate, fills in all gaps. I realize I'm not sure why I am awake. Then: leather-soled footsteps coming down the hall. My whole body tenses. I must have heard the door as my father reentered the apartment. I have an urge, as his footsteps get louder—it sounds as if he is walking straight into my room—to slide out of my covers and under the bed, but now his footfalls are receding as he heads for his bedroom, where my mother sleeps. I wait for her sharp protest, his matching high-pitched accusation, but I can hear only the dark, dense silence of our apartment at night, the whoosh and gurgle of the steam pipes, the Dakota's heating system, in the walls. *I'm not proud of myself when I lose my temper,* my father has told me. He must be apologizing. Promising my mother that it will never happen again.

It's Halloween night, and my mother is sitting at her sewing machine, cranking the foot pedal and sliding yellow fabric under the bobbing needle while my brothers and I lie in our underwear at the foot of her bed. Finally she stands up from her sewing table, triumphant. She bites the remaining attached threads and holds up Jay's duck hood, showing us where she has just finished attaching the orange felt bill. We jump down from the bed as she checks for pins in all four costumes then hands me and Greg ours, helps Jay with his, and dresses Braddy.

We follow her down our long hall. She opens the double front doors of the formal entrance to our apartment and ushers us through. We go out the front doors and pad with our mouse and duck and dog feet onto the cold white, with diamonds of black, marble of the lobby, which is dimly lit and empty and smells like our apartment, though the oily aroma of wood polish, of dust and wood, hangs thicker here. They are heavy smells, Dakota smells. Although there is an elevator—my mother has told us that the Dakota was the first building in New York to have one—she leads us to the staircase. It is rimmed by a carved dark wood banister and winds up to the next floor. I tilt my head back. From this vantage, the bottom of the stairway spirals up in perfect symmetry against the white underside, floor after floor, to a white ceiling, ten stories up. Swept up in the geometry, for a moment I lose my bearings—am I looking up or down?—until my mother nudges my shoulder with her hip.

"This way now, Christine."

She steps onto the first marble stair, holding Jay's and Braddy's hands. Greg and I follow. I slide my slippers as I go. Surrounded by stillness, it seems as if we are the only people to have ever walked these stairs. We reach the second-floor landing, approach heavy double front doors that look exactly like ours on the floor below. Everything about this floor is a replica of ours—black-and-white-checked marble landing, the door exactly the same—but also slightly off. The light on this landing isn't quite like our light, and this foyer leads to both the flight up and the flight down and doesn't have the extra expanse, as our ground-floor apartment does, leading out to the courtyard.

My mother knocks, then stands back. My mouse suit feels too hot, and I wonder if I can take off the hood without hurting her feelings. If it's true that there are many famous inhabitants living in the Dakota because of the gate and the security, people who don't want to be bothered, it doesn't make sense that she is so eager to knock on this door.

She knocks again. Steps back again. I'm just about to suggest we move to the next floor when the sound of dead bolts clicking rings out into the silence.

The door opens. A figure steps into the doorway, a woman with broad, masculine shoulders and a square jaw. She is very tall, and the dim white light from the sconces on the wall throw shadows around her deep-set eyes and around her mouth and cheekbones. I take a step back. Greg and Jay step forward.

"Trick or treat," they say in unison.

The woman smiles, but the shadows on her face remain and my mother has to reach back to pull me forward. I hold out my plastic orange pumpkin pail. The woman drops in two large-size Tootsie Pops.

"What darling costumes," she says in an unexpectedly gravelly voice. Her voice is deeper than my father's.

"Happy Halloween!" my mother says. "Can you say thank you to Ms. Bacall?"

My mother has told me the actress is very famous and very reclusive, which seems to explain, in part, her appearance.

"Thank you," we say in chorus as she smiles, nods, and closes the door.

We repeat this procedure on each floor, though I don't recognize anyone else famous. I've taken to pulling off my hood while we walk, then settling it back down when it's time to knock on another door. I'm not sure how I feel about Halloween if we're just going to go up and down this one staircase, though my brothers are smiling from ear to ear. We have been given more candy than we've ever held in our hands at one time: Milky Way bars, 3 Musketeers, Sugar Daddys, Tootsie Pops, Tootsie Rolls. Once we are back inside our apartment, my mother gathers up our pails.

"I will keep them separate, but I want to hold on to them," she says. "You'll get sick if you eat all this candy at once."

She gives us each a Tootsie Pop and unzips my brothers' costumes—the zippers run all the way down the back—then mine.

Down the hall my mother is bathing my brothers in the children's bathroom by the laundry room. I have the bathtub in the study to myself. This is the only time I like being at this end of the apartment. My mother poured in Mr. Bubble, and the froth and foam around me looks like millions of tiny round enclosures. I peer into the bubbles. Their walls shimmer with color and reflect the light from the sconces over the medicine cabinet. I imagine myself miniature, living inside these tiny, cozy, shimmering spaces.

"Ready?" My mother appears with a towel. I climb out and she wraps the terry cloth around me, helps me step into my footie pajamas.

My father is home and in the butler's pantry, by the dining room, scooping ice. I pass him on my way to the kitchen to get a cup of water. The rest of the apartment is quiet; my brothers are in bed. He kisses me on the cheek, his lips wet, his breath hot with the aroma of liquor.

"Hi, darling," he says, relaxed.

On the way back from the kitchen I peek into the butler's pantry again. The room is empty. I can hear the television down the long hall blasting from the study, where my father is most likely sitting in his favorite chair with his drink, watching the news. Where is my mother? I haven't seen her since my bath. I check in her room and bathroom. I walk back down to the kitchen and realize the door to the small bathroom by the maid's room has been closed since I passed it the first time. I knock.

"Mom?"

No answer.

Then I hear something muffled. It sounds like my name, possibly. I turn the ornate glass door handle and push open the door. My mother is sitting on the toilet, but the top seat is down, so she is just sitting. Her head is in her hands; her face is red and wet. She looks up, smiles, and wipes one eye with the side of one hand. She smiles again and tries to say my nickname, "Steenie," but it comes out as more of a croak.

"What's wrong, Mom?" I wonder if the costumes disappointed her or if she's upset because we got so much candy.

"I'm okay." She sits up, wipes her other eye. "Go to bed. I'll come tuck you in, in a minute."

"What's wrong?" I ask again.

"It's nothing. It's silly. It's just a day."

Yes, Halloween is just a day, nothing to cry over. Then it hits me. I was so wrapped up in trick-or-treating that I forgot.

"It's your birthday," I say, seared with guilt. "Happy birthday." She pulls me close. "It's not your job to remember."

She wipes her face with both hands now. She stands up. "Your father never remembers my birthday. It's just a day. It doesn't matter."

It's after bedtime. The piano notes travel down our long hall, reach me in my bed. My mother is sitting at her Steinway grand in the dining room. She plays first in the upper register—the sound is like a pinging of raindrops—then her fingers find the lower keys, and the notes are true percussion, pounding, like strong emotion. The tinkling resumes and the raindrops become a song, her favorite of late; she has been going to it at night after everyone is in bed. The theme song to the movie *The Sandpiper*, "The

Shadow of Your Smile." The sheet music with the photo of Richard Burton and Elizabeth Taylor strolling along a shoreline sits among her books of Bach and Mozart. Sometimes she sings while she plays. Though the song is sad—*now when I remember spring, all the joy that love can bring, I will be remembering the shadow of your smile*—I like knowing that she is sitting at her beloved piano. Knowing, as I drift off to sleep, exactly where she is in the apartment.

Now her playing stops, starts again from the beginning, stops and starts again. This time she plays the song all the way through, having gained mastery over a mistake only she can hear. I try not to think about the fact that music had been the focus of her life until she had us, that she was a child prodigy on the piano and that she began playing when she was four. When she plays sad songs like this, it seems like she misses that part of herself.

The piano playing stops for good. I am still awake. Blocks of light run across my ceiling, headlights from the parking garage outside my window. The rectangle with the square for a head, the three squares, and the triangle slip from the door to the closet to the fireplace, then run down the wall and slide through an invisible exit in the corner by my babyhood cradle. I am trying to match the shapes with possible names: *Rose. Geoffrey. Tom. Beatrice—Bea for short.* If I name them, I can make them familiar, instead of what they are, headlights from cars driven by people I don't know, coming and going from places that have nothing to do with me, more evidence of the vast and unknowable city outside our apartment. I'd rather they were my friends down here in my room at the far end of the apartment, where I sleep because I'm the oldest child and only girl. But the blocks of light don't stop to befriend me. They just continue sliding silently across the ceiling.

My mother is in her closet, getting ready to go out. She pulls out a shoebox from a wall of shelves filled with similar shoeboxes and opens it, bends down, and slips a shoe onto her foot. Most of the shoeboxes read *Ferragamo*. She has told me this brand of shoe is made well and fits her size-ten but very narrow feet. Most of her shoes are flats because, at five foot eight, she doesn't want to be taller than my father, who is six foot.

I pick up a small bottle of perfume from its place on another shelf and sniff at the cap. It smells like flowers and alcohol and other things I can't name. It's my mother's going-out smell, though the fragrance warms and softens when it's on her skin. In the bottle the smell is too strong, too sharp. I'm not sure how I feel about the smell anyway. I don't like it when she goes out.

"That's Joy," my mother says. "It's very expensive." She sounds proud.

"Where are you going?"

"To the Four Seasons."

"When will you be back?"

"You will already be asleep."

She slips on the other shoe. Black-and-white flats with gold buckles. Her legs are long; she is proud of them, too. *It's unusual to have long legs like this,* she has told me. She holds the doughnut roll of her stocking, tips her toes in, and pulls it up over her tapered ankle, her rounded calf, her long, lean thigh. She does the same for the other leg. There is a technique. She snaps the snaps around her garter. I am impressed, but the care she takes, preparing herself to go out, also tugs at me. How am I supposed to go to sleep when she's out wandering the dark, overwhelming maze of streets and sidewalks and alleyways of New York City?

"Don't let the bad guys get you," I say.

She pulls me close. A cloud of Joy engulfs us both.

"Nothing will get me," she says.

I want to feel comforted, but how does she know this? I look down at my own feet, barefoot and tiny on the wood floor. I feel suddenly weak-kneed. Everything comes down to her. She seems like a giant, tall, beautiful, and mighty, when she shows up in the doorway of my classroom and gathers my things from my cubby, stylish in her belted white raincoat and checkered Jacqueline Kennedy sunglasses. But now she is trusting and hopeful for the night ahead. The more I need her, the more vulnerable she seems. I imagine myself orphaned; maybe if I practice feeling self-sufficient, I'll be ready. But I can't imagine anything on the other side of my dependence on her.

It's the end of November and we are walking back to the Dakota from the rowboat pond, eating Cracker Jacks my mother bought at the concession stand. The trees are bare and Central Park is furred gray and brown. The puddles are frosted over with a thin layer of ice that cracks when I touch it with my toe. We stop at our favorite rock, the one with the worn surface that acts like a slide. I slip my sneakers into a crevice and pull myself up, climb to the top, and Greg follows me. My mother holds Jay's hand while he plays on the lower rock. Braddy is in his stroller. At the top of the slide I hesitate. Greg steps in front of me and goes down first. Our mother catches him with one arm, holds Jay with the other. She lets me slide down on my own, two of us already safe in her arms. On our way out of the park, we see police setting up white barricades along the sidewalk.

"What are they for?" Greg, interested in everything policemen do, asks.

"The Thanksgiving Day Parade is tomorrow," our mother says. "Remember the floats?"

The next morning we head out of our apartment, my father with us, cross the courtyard, and enter the formal lobby of another wing of our building, which, with its black-and-white marble floor and dark wooden stairway up, is an exact replica of our lobby across the way. We walk up three flights of stairs and knock on a door. A tall man with thick white hair and black square glasses opens it.

"Linda, our guests are here," he says over his shoulder.

"Can you say hello to Mr. and Mrs. Ashley?" my mother asks. "Mr. Ashley is a game hunter in Africa."

"Come in, dears!" Mrs. Ashley says.

My father gives me a push. I step through the threshold into an apartment that, except for the crown molding—though here the wood is painted beige—is nothing like ours. Instead, the room we enter is filled with animal skins: a zebra-skin rug, leopard-skin throw pillows, giraffe-skin footrests. There is a rhinoceros head mounted over the couch and a water buffalo head over the fireplace.

"Come sit by the window, children," Mrs. Ashley calls. I wonder if she feels guilty surrounded by dead animals.

To get to the window I have to walk across the zebra rug. I bend down to touch the hair. It is thick and plentiful. It seems strange that this zebra is dead but its hair is healthy and lives on, here in this room, so far from where it once roamed.

Mr. Ashley stands with his wife beside two semicircles of chairs positioned to look out the two large windows facing Central Park.

"Can these sweethearts have hot chocolate? We have snacks, too."

Mrs. Ashley indicates several trays laid out with bite-size pieces of bread smeared with cream cheese, miniature cinnamon rolls, and tiny hot dogs with toothpicks in them. I choose two miniature hot dogs. They are warm and slightly spicy.

"Here comes Snoopy!" my mother calls.

I had almost forgotten there was a parade going on outside. My mother hands me a napkin to wipe my hands with as Mr. Ashley pulls out a chair. Snoopy is coming down Central Park West in the nodding slow-motion waggle of arms and legs and head. The re-creation is good. They have his head and nose and eyes and paws right, but there's something off, something eerie about the movement. Snoopy doesn't move in slow motion. He isn't silent; his head doesn't nod the way the balloon's head is nodding.

"Spider-Man!" Jay calls.

"Smokey Bear!" shouts Greg.

My brothers are getting into this. Next comes Rocky and Bullwinkle. I am impressed by the balloons' enormity, amazed that an object passing so close could be so big, but there is something eerie to me in the slow-motion strangeness of these familiar characters, a strangeness no one but me seems to notice. In between marching bands and floats, Donald Duck, Mickey Mouse, Underdog, Popeye, Smokey Bear, and the Pink Panther bob slowly and enormously down Central Park West. After the parade has passed, my mother stands. We are not lingering. Mr. Ashley shakes my hand and my brothers' hands in turn.

"Can you thank Mr. and Mrs. Ashley?" our mother prompts.

"Thank you," we chorus.

"See you next Thanksgiving, dears," Mrs. Ashley calls.

"Isn't that lovely of them to open their apartment to tenants who want to watch the parade?" my mother says on our way down the staircase. She and my father are holding hands.

"We only see them on Thanksgiving?" I ask.

"The Ashleys' children are grown. It makes them happy to share their view of Central Park West with Dakota residents who don't have one," my mother says.

After the first snow, we walk to the sledding hill, in Central Park, across from the Dakota. We've been sledding for several hours. Greg is heading up the hill again, pulling his Flexible Flyer behind him for another ride. Jay and Braddy, each holding a plastic saucer, follow. My mother, dressed in her robin's-egg-blue parka with the fake-fur collar and matching hat, watches from the bench. I'm at the bottom of the hill, taking a break. It's dusk, and the opaque winter world is deepening to gray. My toes are cold, and as the sky darkens the chill spreads. I'm playing my old game of seeing how far I can get to the edge of the gloom without succumbing: the sight of the low-hanging clouds, the wet walkways like black ribbons through the snow, the bare branches, black fingers curled against the bleak sky, all add to my chill. But with my mother there beaming at us, and the newly strung white Christmas lights on the grape arbor at Seventy-second Street twinkling brightly against the gathering night, it feels safe to notice the winter melancholy. There is a beauty in it if I don't get too close.

That night, after dinner, my father's voice rises in a shriek from the far end of the apartment, where he has been reading in the study. My blood stops cold. I have been coloring by myself in the playroom, but now I freeze, hoping he's laughing. But no, he's roaring, and his bare feet pound the rugless floors. He's heading down the hall.

"Car—ol! I. Could. Have. Been. *Killed.* I don't play with your things. This is my chair—do you understand? Mine!"

My mother comes running out of her bedroom, where she's been finishing up a sewing project, a blue dress for an important function with my father, a month away. It's been giving her trouble because the fabric is stretchy. "I will never work with stretchy fabric again," she told me the night before, near tears.

"What is it, Edgar?" There's an edge to her voice. She sounds concerned but also impatient.

Overhead, my brothers scramble in their loft rooms, toys are dropped, bedposts creak.

My father's footsteps are louder.

"Leaned back on my chair. *My. Chair.* And the whole thing collapsed. My head missed the marble table by *inches.*"

I stay where I am on the playroom floor as he blows in, my mother right behind him, an avenging angel.

"*Get. Down. Here.*" Over my right shoulder, as I continue to color intently, heart pounding wildly, my father stands at the foot of the ladder, looking up. Braddy, having only the distance from his room on the ground floor to cover, is instantly beside him and stands as if in an army line, upright and at attention. He is wearing only a pair of white Fruit of the Looms. Jay climbs down the ladder first, Greg behind him. They are in their underwear, too. My father waits until all three boys are down and looking at him.

"I don't go into your rooms and play with your toys, do I?" His voice is suddenly calm and measured.

"No," my brothers say in unison.

"When you spun on my chair, the screw that holds it to the base unscrewed. I could have been seriously injured."

"Sorry, Dad," Jay says.

"I didn't know that would happen," Greg says.

"Sowwy," Braddy adds.

My heart is still in my throat. I breathe in anyway. My father is breathing, too. It feels like the whole apartment is breathing and waiting.

"Please stay off my chair," he finally says. "If you leave my things alone, I will leave your things alone." My father, for some inexplicable reason, when he really does have something to be mad about, is choosing to be reasonable.

"Okay, Dad," Jay says.

"We will," Greg says.

"I pwomise," Braddy says.

My mother crosses through the playroom, passing me, on her way back to her sewing. Crisis over.

My father gives each brother a kiss and exits through the adjoining dressing room.

I hear the low murmur of my parents conversing in their bedroom. I let out my breath, take in another. The low murmur continues and then the sound of footsteps as my father goes back down the hall to resume what he was doing in the study. Greg and Jay climb their ladders as quietly as mice, like they are walking on eggshells.

My mother tries to hide the patches of missing hair using her brush, but there's almost no hair left to hide it with. I don't feel like I've been pulling it out more than usual, but my father hires a psychiatrist to come to the house to speak to me. The psychiatrist wears a reddish tweed coat that matches a thin growth of gray-flecked reddish beard over his cheeks. He tells me I can call him Bernie. Bernie and I are in the den. I am on the gold chair, and Bernie is on the black leather swivel that almost killed my father a few weeks ago.

"How are things going?"

"Fine."

"Do you notice there are specific times when you need to suck your thumb?"

"I guess." I suck my thumb almost all the time.

"It's soothing?"

I know it's his job to ask these questions, but this is embarrassing. An eight-year-old who still sucks her thumb? I just crave the feeling of thumb in my mouth. My mouth wants thumb. After Bernie leaves, my father comes into my room.

"Bernie asked me if there was tension in the house. He said you were most likely reacting to the general tension. I told him I lose my temper sometimes. That I could be better."

It's Saturday. My brothers and I have gathered for a game of Giant Ladybug in the deep-red-and-fleurs-de-lis-on-gold-velvet-wallpapered dining room, the only one of my mother's formal rooms on the lived-in side of the apartment. In our game, the person designated as Ladybug must crawl on all fours around the periphery of the thick red area rug, the only rug in the apartment, which sits at the base of my mother's Refectory-style banquet-size dining table. The rug is the "grass" and the sections under the table legs are cave-like shelters. Not-It players get to choose what animal they want to be. Greg is usually either a gorilla or a giraffe; Jay is a wildebeest or a zebra. I always choose a horse. These animals graze and frolic in the imagined pastoral setting until they see the Ladybug coming, at which point they must scramble back to their homes, which act as base. The game lasts only as long as Braddy, who almost always ends up as the Ladybug, will put up with the humiliation of lumbering around and around the base of the table on all fours as Greg, Jay, and I scoot out of the way every time he approaches.

"I call I'm not Giant Ladybug," Braddy says, his hands on his hips.

"The Giant Ladybug gets to eat up all the other animals," Greg says.

"I want to be a puppy."

"The Ladybug is the best thing to be," Greg adds. This appeal usually works. "She's the meanest and biggest and scariest."

"I don't care." If Braddy is figuring this out, our days of playing Giant Ladybug are numbered.

"Jay, be Giant Ladybug," Greg says.

"Uh-uh," Jay says.

"Greg, you," I say. Greg is the quickest of all of us. This would add a dimension to the game I'm not sure I'm up for.

"No way," Greg says.

"Can we go to Candyland?" Jay says.

I feel a pang. This is a game I thought up out of the sheer desperation of excruciating boredom, but it comes with a price. The last time we played, Jay ran straight to Braddy's Steiff teddy bear and took a bite out of its shoulder, coming away with a mouthful of fur, and I've been feeling guilty ever since. At the time, I quickly explained that objects in Candyland are candy until we touch them, at which point they revert to their original states. I waited for the question: *What's the point of a world made of candy if it doesn't stay candy when you touch it?* But no one asked.

"Okay," I say.

Jay, Greg, and Braddy follow me down our hallway and into my room, and I open the door to my closet, which I've told them is actually an elevator. We all step inside.

"Close the door," I tell Braddy.

Jay asks, "How long till we're there?"

One, one thousand. Two, one thousand. Three, one thousand.

I open the door. My brothers peer out cautiously. They believe we are stepping forth into Candyland, where everything that we see, although it all looks exactly the same as our apartment in every way, is actually made of candy.

"Duck," I say.

We stoop under the first invisible electric eye I have told them runs in the middle of my doorway, then step over another eye in the hall. This is a land of giants, and grown-ups, though they might look like our mother or father or maid, are actually spies for these giants, looking to give away our whereabouts. The game consists of our tiptoeing around the halls and ducking behind doors when we see an adult coming, all the while imagining that we are in a world where everything is deliciously edible.

My father's voice booms from the kitchen, talking to Rose. He has just arrived home. He is loud, though it doesn't sound as if he is upset about anything.

"I want to go back now," Jay says, almost whispering.

No one disagrees. It's one thing to dodge the maid while she's folding laundry or mopping the kitchen floor and hardly paying attention to us. It's another to navigate around our father.

We step over the electric eye in the hall, duck under the one in my doorway, file into my closet. I count *one, two, three*, open the door, and we're back just as our father is striding down the hall, heading for his bedroom.

"Where's your mother?" he says when he sees us coming out of my room.

"At the store," Greg says.

"What's she getting?"

"I don't know," Greg says to his back as he continues down the hall.

We quietly scatter to our separate rooms now, an instinct kicking in not to draw attention to ourselves. It's getting dark outside, the winter afternoon ending early. Too late to go to the park now anyway.

My father has set out two platters on the kitchen counter, whitefish and lox, each wrapped in shiny white deli paper. It's Saturday morning, early December. We are at our beach house in Point Lookout. In one of my mother's photo albums there is a black-and-white picture of me as an infant in a long white baptism dress in my father's arms on the steps of one of two churches in Point Lookout, one Episcopal, the other Catholic. A friend had told them about the Episcopal church, an hour from New York City, that would marry a Jew and a Protestant in 1960. My brothers and I would be baptized in this church, the decision made that we would be raised Protestant. Two years after the photograph was taken, almost three after they were married in the tiny unfamiliar town, my parents bought our little redbrick house at the dead end overlooking the ocean. Every summer we pack up and leave New York as soon as school is out, arriving in town in our red Volkswagen bus laden with four children, two Siamese cats, one golden retriever, two tortoises, an albino rabbit, and a macaw. On summer weekdays, my father commutes the short train ride back into the city. On weekends, he fishes. But now, in the winter, our house feels smaller; the cold seeps in. The town is quiet and gray, not at all its summer self when it bursts at the seams with sunshine and beach bustle. But we're all together, away from the city, and we're supposed to be having fun. As we line up with our plates, my father elbows me, hitting me under my rib cage.

"We'd have gefilte fish. And pickled herring. My mother made it Saturday mornings. She ordered the pickled herring from Norm's Deli." He elbows me again. "Eh, Christine? A delicacy." He shakes his head at the wondrousness of the memory, then says louder, to include my brothers:

"Who wants fish?"

He pulls open the paper to reveal smoked salmon in one package and half a gray-skinned fish, complete with a small white marble of eyeball, in the other. The last time he brought us smoked salmon, partitioned out between my brothers and parents and me, we ended up with around four slices each, which wasn't even remotely enough.

"Me! I do, I do!" my brothers respond.

My mother stands beside my father as my brothers hold out their plates. My father pulls open the paper and uses his fork to peel the thin gray skin off the fish on the second platter. The whitefish is also smoked but isn't at all the same thing as the pink, almost translucent slices of salmon, though I don't say so. I'm guessing we're supposed to be just as appreciative of the lesser charms of the whitefish as we are of the salmon. To be picky is to be spoiled. Sometimes my father talks about "the evil eye," which seems to be related to this subtle lesson about humility and appreciation.

"Too much awareness about one's success tempts the envy of the gods," he has told me, explaining the evil eye. "When mortals are too proud about their worldly accomplishments, they attract notice."

I will later learn that, because they live their lives underwater, fish are seen, in the Jewish tradition, as being free of the influence of the evil eye. I will wonder if there's a connection he might not have considered in the fact that he loves to fish. A love that began when he was six and walked to the pier at the end of his street in Long Beach, Long Island, the town he grew up in, just over from Point Lookout, with his pole and bait to catch dinner for his mother's table. It was the Depression, and his father had lost his job manufacturing boys' sailor suits and, for a month, told no one. Day after day, for a month, my grandfather dressed in his suit, boarded the Long Island Railroad to walk around the streets of New York City until it was the time he had always returned home. When he finally whispered to my grandmother in the wee hours of the night that at fifty-one he had been turned out of the garment factory he had worked in all his life, my father's father sat down in his living room chair and never got up again. "He just stopped," my father told me. His father also raged every day from that chair. "I've always been fascinated by people who just stop."

My father moves to the salmon now, using a fork to separate the diaphanous slices. I hold my plate very still, lest I give away my delirious eagerness for this food. Once we sit down with our booty, the salmon's salty, candy-clear flesh melts in my mouth so fast, it almost vaporizes.

I'm lying with my head on my father, his worn white Hanes undershirt a thin layer between my ear and cheek and his chest, which rises and falls as he breathes. We have finished our treat of smoked salmon and whitefish, and my brothers lie around him, too. We are upstairs in my parents' bedroom. This room, like all the rooms in our beach house, is compact, but it doesn't seem small, because one wall consists of a large picture window overlooking our sandlot, the two jetties that bookend the Point Lookout beach, and beyond that, the ocean. Our father is telling us a story, the next installment of *The Rock*, which he insists is the tale of his true adventures with this giant bird. My brothers and I enjoy this time with him but, despite our relaxed appearances, lying with him like this doesn't feel completely natural. There's part of me that holds myself ready in case things take a turn, and I'm guessing my brothers have that same part of them, slightly fearful, reserved for trouble.

"And then, lo and behold, the Great Red Rock grabbed me in her mighty talons and, pumping her mighty wings, lifted me into the air and flew me to her massive nest. She opened her claws and there I dropped, finding myself in a nest as big as this room, awaiting her young's awakening."

I notice he speaks a little bit like the Bible reads. I have learned about the Bible in Sunday School at the church where my parents were married, which sits at the edge of town.

"Lo and behold," my father says again. This must be part of telling a story, making it sound important and big.

"What do you think happened?" He lifts his head off the pillow and looks at us, and his lips are wet with spittle formed in the excitement of spinning this tale.

I can think of no way out of this mess for him. But my father is here in this bed, so he must have escaped. One thing I really like about this story is that the Great Red Rock is so big and powerful, it sounds like it should be a *he*, but my father calls it a *she*.

"The baby birds woke up and ate you?" Jay says.

"No!" My father reaches out and tickles Jay, who squirms and squeals.

"You found a vine and swung down like Tarzan?" Greg says.

"The Great Red Rock returned and dug her great black claws into my shoulder and lifted me high in the air again. She flew far, far away over the sea, and dropped me into the foaming waves."

Though this is the only story my father ever tells us, in installments when the mood strikes him, we know a few real stories about his life. We know that when he was born, his head was so big—*that's why Eddie's so smart*, his sister, our aunt Shirley, has said when she visits—he split his mother. I also know that as a boy my father passed out circulars for the local movie theater in town. His pay was a free pass to the movies playing there. On Mondays and Tuesdays the theater ran a double feature. He saw four movies every week. He loved *Captain Blood* with Errol Flynn

and *The Ten Commandments*. His favorite movie was *Shane*.
When it came to town, he saw it as many times as he could, a
1953 Western about a gunslinger cowboy who becomes a father
figure to a boy but doesn't stay.

It's Sunday night, and we will be heading back to the city in a
few hours. My parents have each opened a can of Schaefer beer
in anticipation of our lobster dinner. I stand in the middle of the
kitchen as my mother drops three lobsters into the giant black
pot steaming on the stove. At first, the sound of claws scratching
frantically to get out fills the kitchen.

"Why do you have to put them in alive?" I ask.

"They need to be eaten fresh," my mother says.

This is fate beyond imagining: What must it feel like to die in
boiling water? But once we sit down, the steaming, soft white
meat of the lobster is sweet, hot, and delicious. My mother passes
the bowl of melted butter she has made for us to dip the meat
into. We even have special utensils for this dinner, silver crackers to split the leg shells open and long, thin, needlelike forks to
pull out the meat, which takes on the shape and color, complete
with the pink nodules, of the shell that had encased it.

A few days later we pull up, my mother driving the Volkswagen,
to a cold, unfamiliar beach. Just beyond the dunes, people stand
around, fully dressed, amid canvas-backed chairs, tables of food,
giant lights on stands and bug-heads of movie cameras, their long,
spindly wide-set legs like spiders perched and waiting. We follow
my father to a blanket where Marlo sits, dressed in a little-girl
white dress, her stomach engorged underneath. It's a shock until
my father makes a joke—doesn't Marlo look good pregnant?—
and Marlo punches her stomach a few times, her fist bouncing
lightly off what is clearly a prop.

"Why is Marlo pregnant?" I ask my mother.

"Your father is making *Jenny*, a movie about unwed pregnancy and about the Vietnam War. Two very important topics." My mother sounds proud. I know that my father was recently offered the job of being the head of MGM, but he told me he didn't want to step into anyone else's shoes. He created his own movie production company, Palomar Pictures, instead. *Jenny* is his first movie.

"Quiet on the set," calls a man holding a walkie-talkie. My father points down the beach and whispers, "Watch there, Gregory," as if I'm not standing there too. I don't expect what comes next: an explosion in the sand. I jump. Then another. Contained detonations of orange flame, smoke, and flying sand as Alan Alda, dressed in camouflage, runs through the blasts. The sound of small yellow popping flames explode around him as he runs: one, two, three explosions. As he goes, he pulls off the backpack he is wearing, unlatches his belt, and throws them onto the sand.

"Cut!"

"Those are supposed to be bombs?" Greg says now that we can talk.

"There'll be music and special effects added in the final edit," my father says. "It will look more like war. The magic of moviemaking, Gregory."

We leave the beach and make another stop, enter a small theater with velvet seats and a big screen. It looks like a real movie theater in every way but size. There are at most a hundred seats. My father holds my hand as we enter. A woman and two men in open shirts sit in the back row.

"Can you say hello?" my father says.

"Welcome. We have hot cocoa," says a woman with thick blond hair and black glasses. "Sit in the first row, if you'd like."

"Third row," my father says. "They'll see better."

My father sits in back with the others. My mother leads us down to the third row. The seats are soft and velvety. The lights dim; playing on the screen is the scene we just watched being filmed. The filmed version of the explosions, which looked silly on the beach, look real and believable on the screen in front of us.

After a few takes of this same scene, the screen goes black and the lights around us come up overhead.

"What do you think, Christine?" My father cracks his gum from a few rows back.

"It's cool." I feel shy knowing everyone's listening. He doesn't ask for my opinions when we're at home.

"Pretty realistic, Gregory?"

"Yeah," Greg says.

I glance over my shoulder; our father sits back, popping his gum, arms draped around the backs of the chairs on either side of him, looking very satisfied.

Chapter 3

I am standing with my mother, father, and three younger brothers in the middle of a surprisingly short—considering the fact that we just landed on it—cracked cement runway. The air, after the cool of the Bristol-Myers (the company funding my father's new movie production company) jet, is so wet and thick with humidity, it's hard to breathe. Three ebony-skinned men dressed in brown shorts and matching short-sleeved button-down shirts pass our suitcases from the hold of the plane and pull them toward a small cinder-block building. Vines creep through the cinder block's cracks, splitting and infiltrating the building as if they are taking it over in slow motion. It's clear that a stronger, stealthier Mother Nature than the one I know in New York City is at work here.

"Dis way, please," one of the men says. When he smiles, the pink insides of his lips match the pink pads of his fingers. I have heard the lilt of this accent before. In our apartment, my father sings, *I must declare my heart is there though I've been from Maine to Mexico . . . I had to leave a leettle girl in Kingston town*, and swings me by my hand, in a rare moment when he's focused just on me. Now he's walking beside the official, happy and relaxed.

"Is this Green Turtle Cay?" Greg, seven, asks.

"We have to go through customs," my mother says. She is holding Braddy's hand. Jay trails after one of the men in brown shorts.

My mother looks as she always does: shoulder-length shining dark hair, deep red-lipsticked lips, tall and poised and elegant as if she makes this sort of journey every day, traveling from our apartment on Central Park West to a three-mile-long, half-mile-wide island in the Caribbean that was once a stopover for vessels during rage seas in the Whale Cay Passage. Though her smile looks slightly forced, it has not wavered since we got off the jet, and she gives no other indication that she is terrified of the ocean, terrified of the feeling of putting her head underwater, terrified of the idea of any of us in the sea.

"After customs, we'll get on the ferry," she adds. "After the ferry, we take a motorboat, and then we'll be there."

I am eight and have found that an experience that starts off feeling scary usually feels scary all the way through. I have developed a system: if I can catch a thread of something comforting when exposed to a new experience, I am usually able to connect to that comfort when I need to. The flat sandy landscape of palm trees and dry feathery pines around the runway seems friendly. So far so good.

My mother calls it a ferry, but the boat we are helped into has seen better days. I'm leaving the friendly trees behind and am now looking for something reassuring in the worn yellow patches of fiberglass where the vessel has bumped too many times against a dock, the worn fiberglass bench seats, the worn blue paint, the fact that this small craft is riding so low in the water that every time someone steps into it, the boat tips and water splashes in over the side. In my world, when something looks this old, it is replaced. But the two ferry captains who load our suitcases, maneuver along the inches-wide walkway between the cabin and the edge, their feet clinging to the sides as if they are sticky with glue, seem unconcerned. My mother has told me there are two reasons we are going to Green Turtle Cay. She lowers her voice as if she is protecting family secrets: so my father can fish, *his only form of relaxation*. And so he can fish undisturbed by the office. That we have to travel one thousand miles to get out of range of his office phones doesn't seem unreasonable. When he is on the phone in our apartment, my father behaves the same way he behaves off the phone. The decibel of his voice rises, as does the urgency of what he's saying: *I'm fighting for my life here. I'm dying here. I'm telling you.* When his tirade is not directed at her, my mother will sometimes tiptoe into our rooms and whisper, "Your father has a lot on his mind," sounding shaken but also proud. It's not a huge stretch to see how shouting and being important might go together, and it feels completely unrelated that I continue to pull my hair out at the nape of my neck where the tug feels good, and suck my thumb with the hair. Jay stopped sucking his thumb a few months ago by whispering stories to himself at night after we were tucked into bed. I am both very impressed by this—he is two years younger—and a little sad for him because I can't imagine life without the snug feeling of my thumb in my mouth when I need it.

An inch-long slice of horizon has begun to thicken, a short dark worm along the otherwise unbroken blue line. On our earlier ferry ride, we never lost sight of land, but in this second, much smaller boat, a Boston Whaler, the same kind of boat my father has at our beach house in Point Lookout back home, I can see nothing but eggshell-blue sky and turquoise sea. We ride low in the water, and everything—our hair and clothes, our suitcases, my face and arms—is wet with warm salt spray. I sit on the worn fiberglass bench at the rear, everyone's backs to me because my brothers fought for the front seats, and trail my fingers in the thick bathtub-warm foaming folds where the motor churns the sea light green and leaves a long V of wake behind us.

As we make our way closer, the inch of horizon continues to

thicken until it is a flat, green, solid-looking piece of land. Walter, the caretaker of the cottages we are traveling to, swings the motor and the boat turns toward it. Soon coconut trees come into view. The motor grinds into a downshift as we round a promontory, motoring close to a forest of low, bent trees. The half-submerged roots are gray and waterlogged, their bark peeling; they look more like entwined limbs than plants. As we proceed, waves from our boat wake continue on in neat lines, slapping against the edge of this swampy tangle, then pushing through to crest and die between branchy elbows and knees. I wonder if we will be spending the next two weeks on an island made of roots.

"Don't suck your thumb, Christine," my mother says as we pass over an underwater lawn of sea grass so dark, it feels like the sun has gone behind a cloud. Though we are easily in twelve feet of water, at this slower speed the sea is so transparent, I can see the short sharp blades of grass below, tar green, speckled black. We leave the grass and glide over sand stamped in endless rows of repeating ridges that remind me of the roof of my mouth when I rub it with my tongue. Despite all the forces at work—wind, waves, storms—the pattern repeats itself perfectly, nothing out of place.

Walter makes another grinding turn and we are in a lagoon. At the other end sits a light pink boathouse and matching pink dock nestled amid the green. As we pull up to the dock, a fish, striped neon red and blue and yellow, so electric that it looks plugged in, hovers by one of the dock's seaweed-covered pilings. It pauses long enough to be admired, then zips out of sight. Walter jumps out of the boat and loops a thick brown rope around the middle piling.

"Go on, Christine," my father says, as if I have been holding everyone up.

Walter reaches down and grabs my upper arm and pulls me onto the dock.

Walter carries our suitcases, hoisting them into the back of a small rusted jeep. My father helps him with the heaviest bags, but Walter is moving so fast, my father has to step out of the way. Once the bags are loaded, Walter swings me up on one hard bench, Jay on the other, then he climbs into the driver's seat.

"The cottage is just a few steps down the path," Walter, whose ancestors are from Scotland, says with a slight twang, and turns the ignition. The jeep starts up, kicking and vibrating and rumbling, spewing a cloud of oily exhaust into the feathery light green foliage. I've never been in a car with no roof, no sides, and no back. I dangle my feet as we bounce along the sandy path, my father and mother following with Greg and Braddy behind. We pass a corrugated lean-to with tools hanging on pegs over a low workbench, then a wooden tower that my mother later explains functions as the water catch for the cottage. At the end of the path is a small neat sign, painted pink: SEA STAR 1. Walter downshifts and turns the jeep off the path, switches off the ignition, and begins carrying our bags into a pink stucco cottage. Instead of panes, the cottage's windows are lined with narrow slats of glass that flare out like eyelashes. The inside of the cottage smells like salt and beach. Sand crunches under my shoes. I take them off. A gray lizard clings, head down, on one wall, its tiny fingers spread.

My mother unpacks. The night descended quickly just a few minutes ago. Crickets have begun to chirp. They are so loud, she has to raise her voice to be heard.

"Smell the night-blooming jasmine?" She is dragging the big suitcase, the one with my brothers' and my clothes and the toys she brings to keep us entertained—Silly Putty, Play-Doh, a bag of SuperBalls, Colorforms—into the room that will serve as our bedroom for the two weeks we are here. I want to tell her that of course I smell it; the heavy honey that fills the room is as dense as the thick night that has settled around our cottage. I'd peel back both and step out from under them if I could, but I'm still trying to look for something to feel good about. My mother pops another suitcase open and begins transferring our shorts and shirts into the open drawers of the low dresser against the wall. A second lizard, this one black, clings with green toe bulbs to the crack that runs along the plaster wall just at the corner above what will be my pillow. The biggest moths I have ever seen fling themselves at the single overhead light, their worm bodies thumping loudly as they hit the glass. Smaller moths flutter in a desperate cloud; the ones that work their way inside the light's globe sizzle against the bulb then join the desiccated carcasses collecting at the bottom of the fixture.

After she unpacks, my mother tucks us in, sideways on the one grown-up–size bed, so we all fit. The sheets are thin and soft. My brothers are quickly asleep. My parents are quiet in the next room. The only evidence of civilization is the hum of Walter's generator, though Walter has gone back to the village on the other side of the island, and the hiss of the green light on his shed just beyond the sand path. The honey of the jasmine, the spearmint of unseen plants, and the sticky, salty air; the thrum of crickets and the rhythmic roar of the ocean, wave after wave gathering and crashing just on the other side of the thin hedge that rims the cottage yard, keep me awake. We are on a nearly empty island in the middle of an unfamiliar ocean. Of the six tiny cottages on this side of the island, ours is the only one inhabited. Only a hook-and-eye closure holds the warped wooden door shut on the screened-in porch. All of my friends' families go to hotels on their vacations. When, later, I ask why we don't, my father says, "You can be anywhere in a hotel. You don't get the feel of a place."

My father's fishing guide, Marcel, keeps his boat floating in the knee-deep shallows just off our beach. It's still morning and Marcel has motored around the point from the village. In our cottage my father thumps him on the back, as if he has known him all his life, and calls "Mar-cel," in his high whine although

Marcel is standing right next to him. Marcel's skin has a deep red hue and his hair is wavy brown; his facial features are strong; he has a large round nose, a prominent square forehead, though it's his feet I can't stop noticing. The bottoms are cracked and white, a thick sole of tough dead skin. How could he ever tuck those toes and that thick sole into a shoe?

"He probably has no need for shoes here," my mother says later when I ask her. "He's probably never had a need."

No shoes means never leaving this island. It certainly means never going to New York City. Marcel probably loves being barefoot, as I do. But at a certain point, and this seems like something everyone needs to know so they can monitor their barefoot time, his feet had toughened up and it was too late to go back to shoes.

After my father and Marcel head off to fish, my mother pulls boxes of cereal, two packages each of Chips Ahoy!, Oreos, Nilla Wafers, and Ritz Crackers from the food suitcase and sets them on the Formica countertop as we lie on the daybeds watching. She unpacks Lipton tea bags, packs of Kool-Aid, Jell-O, strawberry and chocolate Nesquik, Cream of Wheat, Sun-Maid raisins, Aunt Jemima pancake mix, and packs of Juicy Fruit and Wrigley's spearmint and peppermint gum. She cooks up some Cream of Wheat and adds brown sugar and raisins. Braddy takes the bowl onto the screened-in porch, sits down on the daybed, swings his feet, and eats.

Jenny, a woman from the village, has come to help, her dark shining skin in stark contrast to the white-and-red flowered dress she wears. She stands at the sink, chopping vegetables on a cutting board. Beside the vegetables sits a conch shell shaped like a horn, as shiny as ceramic, awash in the colors of a sunrise, speckled with black. Jenny touches inside the swirled recesses with the tip of her knife, and a tannish slippery something that had begun to protrude recedes quickly, gone in a flash back inside the shell.

"What is that?" Jay asks.

"Da conch." Jenny pulls something from her apron, a blade, but unlike the knife from the kitchen drawer, this blade is curved like a half-moon. She slips it into the shell and with a few flips of her wrist, pulls out the tannish something from its hiding place deep inside the shell and lays it on the cutting board, and before either I or the creature has a chance to consider what's happening, begins to chop. In moments the conch is reduced to tiny white cubes, which she scoops and drops into a bowl of diced tomato and onion. She squeezes lemon juice into it.

"Who wants da conch salad?" she asks.

Jenny hands Braddy a bowl. He scoops a healthy spoonful, pauses to examine it, then puts the whole thing in his mouth and helps himself to another. Jenny hands me a bowl next. The conch is firm, slightly slippery, chewy. It's hard to tell if it's the conch that tastes good or whether anything mixed with lemon, onion, and tomato would be this palatable. I feel sorry for the conch, but that doesn't stop me from finishing my bowl.

Later we kick around in the warm gentle shallows as our mother stands knee-deep in the water, watching us. Before he left with Marcel, my father told her to stop hovering, to go sit down on the sand and let us swim.

"Let them play," my father said.

"A wave might come up," my mother said.

"No wave is going to come up," my father said, his voice suddenly tight, loud. "What wave, Carol? This is the gentlest beach on the planet."

Now the faint hum of a motor. My father and Marcel, still a speck out in the dark deeper water by the two uninhabited neighbor islands, No Name Cay and Pelican Cay, approach. Soon the boat pulls up a few yards out and Marcel drops an anchor into the water. He flips a ladder over the side and my father climbs into the water, which is chest deep, and wades to shore. Marcel wades behind him, holding a burlap sack above the water.

On the sand Marcel opens the sack and lays out six bloody fish.

"What kind are they?" Jay asks. I wonder if he feels as sorry for the fish as I do.

"That's yellowtail, this is swordfish, and that's snapper," my father says, pointing at each one in turn.

Marcel pulls a knife from his pocket, snaps it open, holds each fish by the tail, and scrapes. Thumbnail-size scales, invisible when they were flush with the fish, gather slimily on the knife until Marcel flicks them onto the sand. After he's done scaling, the tip of his knife disappears into the fish-with-a-yellow-head's underside, slips easily from tail to gills. Marcel dips his finger into the slit and pulls out a pink-and-purple tangle of insides. He throws this over his shoulder into the water, then walks to the shore and rinses each fish. Finally he strings them on a line through their gills and hands the string to my father.

That night Jenny fries each fish whole in a pan; the eyes turn into tiny white marbles as they cook, and the tails curl up and crisp. We have one fish each on our plate, nothing else, with ketchup if we want it, for dinner.

"Watch out for bones," my mother says. "I'm trying to get them all, but I might miss some. You'll choke."

"They'll be fine, Carol," my father says, his voice high and tight again. "A few bones won't hurt them."

The skin is hot, crispy, and oily, the meat inside white and flaky. It's strange to eat a whole fish, and only that. My mother pulls off her fish's jaws, sucks the eyeball, then scoops out the soft material inside the skull.

"Eww, you're eating the brains," Greg says.

"They're delicious." My mother's eyes are half closed as she chews.

My father leans back in his seat, pats his stomach, then takes a toothpick from a holder on the Formica table and sticks it between his bottom front teeth. "Not often you get to eat fish caught an hour or so ago. That's as fresh as it comes. How much healthier can you get?"

The next morning, our bay is transformed. Sand fleas rise up in clouds from fishy-smelling tangles of seaweed stranded from high tide. At the water's edge, instead of the gentle lap of tiny turquoise waves, the sea has rolled back a quarter of a mile to reveal shiny, wet gray sand and lawns of black-green seagrass.

"Watch your step now," my mother says.

Wearing the thick rubber-soled terry cloth slippers she has brought especially for this walk, we follow her off the familiar beach and onto the newly exposed seafloor. The sand is grayer than I would have expected and dotted with mysterious pinholes. This is where we usually swim, suspended in this bay's shallow, glass-clear water. When I float, three feet over the sand, I feel like I am keeping my part of an agreement: I won't bother you from up here if you don't bother me from down there. But now Braddy pokes at a sea cucumber rolling, slug-like, in the warm shallow water. Jay crouches to examine a string of tubular slime. He touches it and it winds into a tighter spiral. Greg picks up a disc-shaped jellyfish, as firm and clear as plastic. Imprisoned by its own anatomical limitations, it offers no defense. I touch nothing. Are any of these creatures noticing us?

As we head out toward what is usually deeper water, the sea is still only inches deep and the grass begins. It is for this grass that we have our shoes. *If you step on a sea urchin,* my father has told us, *all you will see of the spine is a small black inky mark on the sole of your foot. The remaining four inches will be buried vertically in your flesh.* As there is no one on the island who can medically handle such an injury, a losing encounter with a sea urchin means our vacation is instantly over.

"Don't step on it," Jay says.

We have taken only a few steps over the crunchy blades, but already here is a sea urchin, a baseball-size orb of witch's black spindles, hidden inside a green-black tuft of grass. The urchin seems to bring its own shadow with it, and it takes me a moment to see that its long black spikes are actually moving in slow motion, each spike taking its turn propelling it forward through the grass. After a short journey, it settles again in another tuft, almost completely camouflaged. As we continue on, I don't dare put my foot down without making sure I've found a good place to land. As we get closer to the darker, rougher water ahead, I consider. How deep does it need to be for a shark to feel comfortable enough to swim through this tentative barrier of shallow sea? The fact that all the usual distance between us and the serious creatures of the darker, rougher part of the real ocean is growing shorter the farther we walk out is not lost on me. The water is at my kneecaps now. The tide is coming in. I have a vision of all the larger sea creatures rushing back in with it. My mother, who is terrified of the sea, will, nevertheless, do anything for a lesson and is still pointing out starfish. She proceeds slowly, with a forced smile, as if this wild place is here for our educational purposes, a neat and tidy classroom with boundaries no harm can cross.

On our way back to shore, an octopus the size of a grapefruit swims by Greg's ankle and squirts dark gray ink at his white shoe before continuing on wherever it is heading, vanishing from sight.

It's almost bedtime, and my brothers and I sit on the daybed in the screened-in porch, gathered around my father. He is reading "The Adventure of the Speckled Band."

"'Oh, my God! Helen! It was the band. The speckled band!'" My father closes the book.

"Wead more," Jay says.

"Tomorrow night," our father says.

There is no TV on the island. This is our third Sherlock Holmes story. He stops at the best part and opens another book, his *Oxford Book of English Verse*, which he carries around with him, tucked in the crook of his elbow like an old teddy bear, when we are at home.

He begins, *"The road was a ribbon of moonlight over the purple moor."*

One by one my brothers climb off the daybed and head to our bedroom until only I am left. Our mother is in the kitchen, helping Jenny clean up from dinner.

And still of a winter's night, they say, when the wind is in the trees,
When the moon is a ghostly galleon tossed upon cloudy seas,
When the road is a ribbon of moonlight over the purple moor,
A highwayman comes riding—
Riding—riding—
A highwayman comes riding, up to the old inn-door . . .

Darkness cocoons us inside one circle of lamplight; the crickets are so loud, he raises his voice to talk over them; the air is thick with the smell of night-blooming jasmine. My father reads with flourishes, pausing, enunciating, waving his finger. He holds the words in his mouth before speaking them, enjoying their feel. I want to tell him that I love words, too. That he and I are alike in this way, but I can't think of how to say it. When he finishes, he snaps the book's covers together with one hand.

"Bedtime."

The white fish with a yellow tail lies motionless on its side. We dip down a turquoise wave, and hot seawater, once clear, now pink with blood, rushes under my bare feet, across the brown patches where Marcel's small fiberglass boat's floor has worn thin, into the hold, to cover the fish's dry, sticky scales. Its wide, staring nickel-shaped eye glares at the sky through the thin sheath of water. It's my turn to go fishing with my father, and I have remembered, too late, how it feels to watch a fish wide-eyed and staring, its body slowly stiffening as it suffocates in the bloody hold of the Boston Whaler. My heart beats hard with the thought, if I throw this fish back now, will it live?

"Fish have a different nervous system than we do," my father has said. "They don't feel pain."

I think of the stories my father has told us about fishing as a boy to help his mother. Here in a boat with a rod and reel in his hand, he's calm and happy in a way he isn't at home. So I don't save this fish or any of the fish I watch die in the holds of his boats. And I don't ask why, if the fish feel no pain, do they seem, so clearly, to be suffering.

At high tide we carry Styrofoam boxes from the cottage to the beach and float in them in the three-feet-deep water. The Styrofoam is so firm and buoyant as it holds my weight, my rear end tucked inside my box, my arms draped on either side, the sea so clear as my feet dangle in it, I feel like I'm flying. At this tide, the water in our cove is dark turquoise and spiked with little tufts of waves. I am reading *Dolphin Boy*, a book I found in a drawer in the cottage. With a mask and flippers, feet pressed together, I dolphin kick, arms pressed against my side for aerodynamics, over the sandy sea bottom. In the story, a scientific experiment gone awry causes an explosion on a remote island. The scientist and his wife are killed instantly, but in the blast their infant son is thrown into the sea, where he is found, before he can drown, by a mother dolphin that nudges him to the surface to breathe. As the child catches on, adapting his arms and legs as flippers and tail, he is able to keep up with his siblings and, in this way, becomes a dolphin himself. When the child, now a young man, encounters humans, he is forced to choose between his biological destiny and his adopted one.

He chooses the dolphins.

On some days, when my father fishes with Marcel in the Boston Whaler, puttering around where we can always see him, a dot floating in the distance, he picks us up from our beach and drops us at No Name Cay, a tiny uninhabited butterscotch drop of an island complete with a fringe of swaying palms that sits a few miles out from our island, the buffer between the dark, rough outer ocean and the quiet of our cove. The sand is yellow on this doll-size islet, thick and wet, as unspoiled as the moon. My feet sink to my ankles as I stand at the sloping shore. Just beyond my toes, in the clear, shallow water, a dark gray stingray as big as my brother swims silently past, lapping the island, gliding around and around, in its slow-motion pumping of underwater wings.

On this day my father takes us in pairs from No Name Cay onto the boat to snorkel.

"Marcel says there is a reef here," my father tells me when it is my turn. All I can see is the dark swell of sea beneath the slap of the boat as we bob up and down the navy-blue troughs. The water here is nothing like the shallows we play in by the shore. Dark blue. I am unimpressed. This is New York Harbor water, Long Island Sound water. Just sand and water.

Do I want to go over the side?

What about sharks?

They won't bother you out here, Marcel says.

I want to ask him how he can be so sure of this, but instead I slip on my mask and snorkel, my fins. I feel clumsy as Marcel's calm, dry hands hold me, my arms and legs flailing despite my best efforts to be graceful, over the fiberglass edge. Then he lets go and I drop the two feet into the thick sea. It is so deep here that the water feels different; it holds me up indifferently. The thick sea holds me thinly, like it has better things to do. I kick my fins to tread water. I am surprised by how hard I have to work to keep my head and shoulders above the surface. Then, because I have agreed to this after all, eyes open, I put my face and mask into the water.

I am suddenly sucking gulps of air through the tube of the snorkel, trying to catch my breath. Beneath my treading fins, dwarfed now, I am floating over a mountain range with peaks so towering, so lush and green, I feel as if I am hovering over a rain forest. At the base of the peaks, far below me, acre-wide sweeping meadows of lavender-colored fans sway with the movement of the sea. I recognize the twisted white football shapes of brain coral and the orange treelike stinging corals we've been warned not to touch, clinging in alpine clusters to the slopes. Fish as big as me, neon yellows, blues, greens, purples, flick around this coral, nibbling here, darting there. Not far from me, I recognize the long, thin, slightly arched shape, the jutting jaw and silver flash of a barracuda. If it has seen me, it doesn't seem bothered. It swims lazily among a school of neon-red and -blue penny-size fish; they scatter then regroup as if only because it's expected.

That night I stand barefoot on the concrete porch in the hot, dark air, looking up. The stars are fat chips of light hanging low and wet, almost close enough to touch. They are no longer scary; this is how the stars are supposed to be.

My father comes out beside me. "That's Orion, the hunter. See his belt?"

Where's he been? I've known that for years. Still, I'm proud he's come out to stand with me. My brothers are too little to appreciate the sky.

It's morning and we're packing to go home. The air outside the cottage is wet and heavy and salty, as it has been every day. The sun is already hot. My mother has laid our shoes out; I haven't seen them in two weeks. I am walking around outside the cottage in the crabgrass, along the sandy walk. I want to soak in the last moments of being barefoot. I can't believe that tonight I will be back in New York City.

Chapter 4

"He's so handsome," my mother says. Her eyes are bright, her mouth soft. We are in our Dakota kitchen. It's Sunday.

"Who?"

"Your father and I had lunch with Sidney Poitier." She beams. "This will be another important movie."

We have a framed photo of my father and Mr. Poitier on the set of *For Love of Ivy*. I agree he is handsome. I don't really understand how a movie can be important, though; it's just a movie, not real life. In real life, we pass Vietnam War draft protesters holding HELL NO, WE WON'T GO signs, shouting the same on the street corner as we head up Central Park West on the bus from the Dakota to my elementary school, Walden, on Eighty-eighth Street.

"They don't think they should have to go to war and die if they don't want to," my mother says.

"Why do they have to go?"

"It's the law."

In real life, Martin Luther King Jr. is killed. My parents watch the news, their hands clasped in their laps, shaking their heads. My mother is crying.

"Why would someone kill him?"

"He was trying to do good things. There are people who don't like that. It's the good people who are killed."

There's a banner slung across the Central Park West side of the Walden building announcing the Andrew Goodman Memorial Fund. Andrew Goodman was a Walden student who graduated before I arrived in first grade. I'm only in third grade, but I have a general sense that Andrew Goodman was killed doing good things, too. I will learn later that he was murdered by the Ku Klux Klan for trying to register African Americans to vote in Mississippi.

It's early June. We are at our beach house, in Point Lookout. The television blasts from our small living room. My mother sits on the couch and cries again. Robert F. Kennedy has been assassinated. I go outside and kick a rock around in our yard. It's the start of summer, but it feels like the world is ending.

My mother isn't feeling well and has decided Greg and I will spend the summer at sleepaway horse camp so that she will only have Jay and Braddy to take care of. She buys me a small pillow filled with pine needles that smells like a forest.

"If you miss home, you can smell this wonderful smell and remember to be happy."

But the pillow doesn't help at all. The ache that had begun in my sternum when Greg and I stepped off the bus into the grassy-smelling green meadow, which had moved up into my chest as we toured the paint-chipped dining lodge and the weedy tennis courts, and had finally settled in my throat to bulge, hard and relentless, against the back of my eyes when Greg was led off to the boys' camp and me to the girls', has suddenly tripped some emergency warning system I didn't even know I possessed. Now I stand gulping air, desperate to catch my breath as, outside my cabin, the sky is red and heavy with a woodsy humid sunset. Girls I barely look at quietly brush their teeth in the long bathroom with five sinks, unpack pink and yellow shorts and tank tops into the small pine dresser beside each bed, lay out their pajamas. I try not to breathe in the sweet stink of our cabin counselor's strange perfume, to notice the pores on her face, the faint black fuzz of hair on her upper lip. I need someone to like.

I am homesick for six weeks. I packed The Chronicles of Narnia, my favorite books. I read and reread them as I walk along the banks of the stream by the horse trails, praying urgently for a doorway into Narnia to open up and let me in. Whenever girls' and boys' camper activities intersect and Greg and I see each other, my throat aches, tears spill.

"Stop, you're going to make me cry," he hisses.

"He's coming!" my cabinmates squeal.

It's week four out of eight, and we are in our bunks after lights-out. A few days ago I made the mistake of mentioning to my friends that I think the archery counselor, Randy, is cute. Black curly hair, compact body. I like the way he wraps his arms around me when he shows me how to hold the bow.

But a crush from a distance is as far as I've planned for.

The cabin door bangs open. I sense him blow in, as cocky and confident as a breeze. I scrunch down under my blanket, wishing I could disappear. Covers to my chin, I stare straight up at the wood slats of the cabin ceiling. Maybe if I don't acknowledge him, he'll go away before whatever is about to happen, that I already know I will hate, happens.

He stops at my bed, which is on the top bunk, closest to the door.

"Hey, Chris." He's at eye level, looking at me, smiling kindly, but also bestowing favor. I continue to stare at the ceiling as my entire body, head to toe, flames with embarrassment and something else I don't understand. Wouldn't most welcome the visit of a crush? But I don't like him at all now. I just want him to go away. After a long moment he reaches out and touches my nose with the tip of his finger.

"Good night, Chris."

"Whoo-hoo!" my cabinmates catcall after the door bangs shut.

I never look at him again.

Six weeks in, I see the light at the end of the tunnel, and longing for home has been replaced by the longing for food. Everything we eat at camp is white. We have cereal for breakfast, mac and cheese for lunch, and spaghetti for dinner. The thing I have noticed about white food is, it doesn't matter how much I eat; I am never full.

"What's the first thing you're going to have when you get home?" My cabinmates and I are lying in our bunks, taking turns naming the foods we miss most.

The thing I'm looking forward to eating most when camp is over never changes. I don't just think of steak whimsically; it intrudes on my every waking moment, though the idea of rare middles surrounded by crisp, marbled fat feels like a faraway dream. Tracy, whose lower bunk is closest to the door, receives a care package from home once a week filled with, among other items, Slim Jims, which, at first, mean nothing to any of us. Thin sticks of Spam-like product wrapped in plastic? Ho hum. Then, on an impulse of generosity, Tracy shares. I peel back the plastic and bite into explosions of fat and salt and peppery knobs of sinew, decidedly not white. As close to meat as any of us are going to get for weeks to come. We begin asking for handouts all the time until Tracy puts the hammer down.

"No more. They're mine."

I have never stolen anything in my life, but it seems like a good idea, when I present it to the rest of the cabin, to raid the box she keeps pushed as far back as she can shove it, under her bed, while Tracy is at arts and crafts. For the ten minutes it takes to eat our fill, I am in heaven. Unfortunately, when Tracy finds her stash has been raided, she knows she doesn't have to look far for the culprits. As punishment, the camp administrators put us on outhouse cleaning duty. The smell of Lysol mixing with human excrement coats the inside of my sinuses and the back of my throat for a full week.

At the end of eight weeks, when my mother picks us up from camp, she is shocked by our appearance. Greg and I are as pale as the pasta we have been living on, and we have moons of black under our eyes.

"Malnourished," she will say bitterly whenever she thinks about what we looked like. "Living on pasta all summer."

I have been home from camp for a week. Our newest maid is standing by the door with her suitcase. She started just before Greg and I left for camp.

"I need dis job," she says in a musical West Indian accent. Most of our maids are from the West Indies. "But de baby. Too much work dat baby. Too hard. Too hard."

"Can you wait until I call the agency and find someone else?" my mother asks.

"I'm sorry."

My mother drives her to the train station. I go too; I like running errands with my mother.

"He has too much energy," my mother says on the way back from the station. I have never heard her complain about any of us. "I don't know what to do."

She starts to cry. Her face screws up. She begins to sob, the hardest I've ever seen her cry.

"I'm. So. Tired."

It's fall and the first week of fifth grade. I'm studying our teacher, Ray, and the rash of pink pimples that follows his hairline and clusters around the strip of closely cropped hair shaped in a miniature boot in front of his pink ear. White flakes of skin sprinkle among the short hairs of these narrow sideburns, and a few have dropped to the corner of his mouth, which is cracked, his mouth clearly dry with first-day-of-school nerves. Debbie Levine, my best friend, and Nate, the principal's daughter, have told me that Ray is new to teaching and to the school.

He leans over my page of fractions, his focus on my pencil marks.

"Good, Christine," Ray says.

Of course it's good; this fraction page is third-grade level. Maybe fourth. At Walden School we call our teachers by their first names, and in fifth grade the schoolwork hasn't gotten any harder. Heat prickles run up my neck as Ray moves to Terrence Lagonne's fraction page. Terrence folded and pressed the tinfoil that his mother packed with his lunch into a dragon with wings and a long spiked tail, pointed snout, protruding nostrils, in a few seconds after he was done eating his bologna sandwich at lunch today.

"Good, Terrence," Ray says.

My chest feels tight as the year spreads out before me, all of us locked in Ray's jail of too-easy fraction exercises.

It's spring and the air that comes through the towering windows, tilted enough to let it in but with too small an opening to let us out, feels warm and dewy and carries the smell of bus exhaust and gasoline from the jackhammers rat-a-tat-tatting on the corner, of hot pretzels and cool grass and the ever-present waft of dog shit. It's 1970, pre–doggy scoop bags, and Central Park—we call it Dog Shit Park—is an obstacle course of piles of excrement in various states of decay. The dried feces leave only a slight smell, a dusty mark on the side of my sneaker. But the fresh piles are deadly and will ruin the rest of the day, forcing one to spend it bent over the offense with a stick, trying to dig the yellowy-brown mash out of every sneaker crevice, the smell of rubber sole blending in with the steaming smell of shit: vinegar and putrefaction. Beatles music is playing everywhere, on every radio, on the bus, in our VW van, on radios carried by people we pass on the sidewalks. I sing along, *I want to hold your hand*; the songs are bouncy, simple, rhyming. This is music I would have chosen myself to be the soundtrack of my life. Listening to it, I feel how I like to feel, confident, cocky. These songs are easygoing, friendly, childlike. Other songs that also come from the radios around me are less so. At sleepovers at her house in New Jersey, Debbie Levine listens to music to fall asleep. I lie awake waiting for the automatic shutoff. Doesn't anyone else notice this music is terrifying? Psychedelic, drug-induced guitar weeping and wailing that make my blood freeze. I want to go home. I fight homesickness on sleepovers even at the best of times. A panic descends at nighttime. I'm afraid of the block of endless dark, when adults shut down, leaving no one stronger than I am to tend to things.

"Can I join your gang?" Stephanie, straw-dry strawberry-blond hair, nose so upturned that you can see into her pink nostrils, the thickness of knees and ankles visible even through the poly-ester of her powder-blue slacks—who wears *slacks* in fifth grade?—is looking up at me. It's recess and we're across the street in the park. I'm standing on a bench, taking a break from avoiding the piles of poop. I didn't even know I had a gang, though it's true that I beat all the girls in both classes and all but two of the boys in the sixty-yard dash two days ago. I have taken to wearing only boy's jeans and the white Hanes undershirts I pilfer from my father's drawer. I draw peace signs with on them Magic Markers and sing "We Shall Overcome" in the hallways, hot with indignation. It feels good to have something to fight for. The anti-war protesters we pass on the street corner scream their frustrations, and I go as many days as I can without a bath or a shower. I am also protesting Ray, who treats us like kindergartners and still talks in slow motion when explaining math. It feels good to be grimy; I like my hair greasy. Showering feels like washing off my me-ness. I am lean and boyish. My body does what I want it to do. This must be what Stephanie means. From the outside this must look like something's been decided. What's the harm in letting her into a gang that doesn't even exist?

"I'd like to take you, but we're full," I say.

"How much is that penis in the window?" It's skit day and I'm singing to the tune of "How Much Is that Doggie in the Window?" My classmates are tittering. Ray's lips are stretched in a smile, but the rest of his face isn't going with it. "The one with the curly red hair?"

Ray approaches and grabs my arm. "You need to go to Lynn's office." Even the vice principal at Walden is referred to by her first name.

My parents say I am acting out. I have been sent to the principal's office twice this week, and once last week after a few of us wrapped Josh Korda's father's bottle of Scope like a present in a box with a bow and I drew the straw to give it to Ray. In my parent-teacher conference, Ray tells my mother I display *leadership qualities*, which sounds to me like he is trying to kiss up. My father sets up a meeting for me in another part of the city with a psychiatrist who wears a tight bun and horn-rims and speaks unintelligible English in a heavy German accent. She takes notes as I speak and, after forty-five minutes, she leaves me on a hard wooden chair and talks to my mother behind a frosted glass door. I watch their shadows through the glass. On our way home my mother tells me the psychiatrist's diagnosis is that I have a crush on Ray. Cold horror spreads through me. Does my mother believe her? (*Do* I have a crush on Ray?) At home my father is reading child psychologist Haim Ginott and spouts Ginott-isms in a playful way around the apartment, as if he's not quite swayed by this new way of parenting. *Let the punishment fit the crime* is a sentiment he can get behind and quotes often. This must be the new way of parenting, employing techniques that make sense.

But as we leave the psychiatrist's office, my mother rubs her cheeks as if she wants to rid them of something.

"This woman is traditional, Freudian. Psychology is ridiculous. Everything is reduced to sex," she says.

It's fall and I'm the new girl at Columbia Grammar, at least a year and a half behind in academics. There are two sixth-grade classes but, except for Ingrid, whose parents also pulled her out of Walden after fifth grade, everyone here has been together since kindergarten. No one is looking for a new best friend. Alliances have been forged since the beginning of time. I like Ingrid, but since what felt like heartbreak, leaving Debbie Levine behind at Walden, I'm looking for a bosom buddy. I have zeroed in on Inga, but she is already best friends with Lorraine. I become a threesome to their twosome, which isn't how I like to do things. I definitely don't have a gang. Besides, I'm not the person I used to be. Over the summer my thighs thickened and my lower half widened in general, and I now have hips. These are parts of my body I have never given any attention to, and I am just as uninterested in them now. But they have a mind of their own, growing out from under me and taking my boy cool with them. My new classmates, stiff and formal with me like we are all made of glass, look at me with no recognition. They don't know my history. I am blank to them and I feel newly blank to myself.

My father stands behind me. I'm seated at the kitchen table. In front of me, a page of word problems. He is helping me, but his frustration grows like a cloud gathering in size and threat. He reads the problem to me as if I haven't already read it myself. This is no help. I already know what's on the page.

"Ummm," I stall. My heart beats harder than it should. We've only been at this for a few minutes, but I already know what's going to happen. He reads the problem again, more slowly, as if the issue was his reading too fast. I stare at the words on the page, praying the numbers arrange themselves so they make sense, so I can see the answer in them. But they've already started to freeze the way they do when I panic.

"Christine?" His voice is high and tight. My heart pounds against my rib cage and in my eardrums. It's too late now, I know it; even the parts of the sentences that don't have numbers in them don't make sense to me anymore.

He reads the problem again, shouting it now.

"Ten, twelve?" I offer, pulling these numbers from thin air. Please, God, just let me accidentally get the right answer.

"Do you see"—his voice is suddenly calmer; I've given him something to latch on to—"how if this answer is fourteen, the remaining numbers must be seven?"

"Yes," I lie.

"Write it, then."

I write fourteen and seven under the problem, and my panic recedes. It's over.

"Now let's do the second problem."

Oh God. I look at the second problem. With him staring over my shoulder, the words and numbers are frozen solid. I can discern no meaning.

He reads it to me.

"Six?" A blind guess. Let's get this over with.

"Close."

"Eight?"

"You're guessing." He pulls the pencil from my fingers and writes an equation. I take a deep breath.

"Do you see?" he asks.

I nod.

"Write the answer."

He's done most of the factoring, so I can see the answer is three. I write it under the problem.

Eight more problems to go. He begins to read problem three, which is still frozen like problems one and two were, but slightly less so. *Maybe I'm going to be able to relax and think logically.* The phone rings just as he gets to the first half of the setup.

He lifts the receiver from its cradle on the wall, then covers the mouthpiece with his palm. "Carol? Hang the phone up when I get to the den. Christine, we'll finish when I'm off the phone."

I have never done a page of word problems so fast. I speed through them, panting like I'm in a race. I'm finished by the time he gets off the phone.

"Do you want me to check them?" he asks, sauntering back into the kitchen, cracking his gum.

"No, that's okay."

"Let me look at them." He has a short glass filled with copper liquid in one hand. I can smell the sharp sweetness on his lips and breath. He doesn't drink often, but when he does, he is more relaxed; still, my heart pounds as he looks over the page. Miraculously, I've gotten most of them right. He makes marks by the problems that are incorrect.

"Check these again," he says, and heads back down the hall.

I follow my brother and father through a warehouse soundstage. My father walks with a spring in his step, he cracks his gum, and the people we pass part so we can make our way through them. Men laying down thick black cables, women and men adjusting cameras, screwing white screens in place over lights, and ladies in director's chairs, thumbing through scripts, look up.

"Good morning, Mr. Scherick."

We are living in London for a month over Christmas break, staying in a flat while my father makes *Sleuth* with Michael Caine and Sir Laurence Olivier. We live, my mother tells me, in the elite section of town, Eaton Square. We have a key to the park across the street, a square of grass surrounded by wrought-iron gate.

"Want to see something, Gregory?" My father beckons to us with his finger, a grin on his face, revealing his tiny teeth, ground down each night as he sleeps, so they're getting tinier. He pushes open a door. We step from a drafty warehouse and are suddenly standing in a large lived-in room with a winding staircase, a comfortable-looking couch. There are pictures on the walls, a chessboard, dolls on stands, and, in particular, a laughing sailor with a maniacal twinkle in its glass eyes.

"Are these toys?" Greg asks. I've forgotten for a second that we're not in someone's strange home.

"Laurence Olivier's character likes games. *Sleuth* is about playing a game.

"They did a good job, wouldn't you say?" My father opens the door, and we step out back into the warehouse and head toward a construction trailer with a set of doors. My father knocks. Michael Caine sticks his head out and grins at my father, who takes on the hum of happy energy I've noticed he has when he's around movie-business people.

For Easter we travel to Grandma's farm. At the airport, my grandfather is waiting. We all pile inside his old Chrysler: my three younger brothers and me in the backseat, my grandfather and mother in front. My grandfather pulls away from the curb. His pink scalp is peeking through neat gray rows of comb lines wet with Vitalis. Beside him, my mother's arm drapes across the back of the seat, her hand open and relaxed. It seems like a long time since I've noticed the familiar awkward bend of her elbow, the only remnant from her fall from the stepladder when she was very young. Soon the white two-story house comes into view, doll-size amid checkerboard pastures.

"There it is!" my mother says, and I am reminded that she is returning to her childhood home. The light gray gravel pops and crunches under our tires. My grandfather slows and I look back at the cloud of dust we kicked up. "See the alfalfa? And the corn?" my mother says. On either side of us now, tight rows of leafy plants grow in neat lines.

"Bunnies!" Jay points as three small brown rabbits duck into the briar hedge lining one side of the road.

The hedge gives way to the house. It's springtime in Illinois, and the magnolia tree in front of my grandparents' porch is snowing purple and white petals. We spill out of the car and out of our shoes. The grass, long and feathery, lighter at the tips, is cool between my hot toes. My brothers find our rusted red wagon and shout orders to one another as they take turns riding it down the grassy hill in front of the house. I walk over to the gate, stepping carefully over the gravel pebbles with my bare feet. The cows grumble and stomp in the pasture just beyond the trees. I climb the aluminum gate and it tips, top-heavy, with my slight weight. *One whole week here.* Trigger, my grandparents' dusty pony, grazes at the far end among the cows. At home I have a plastic landscape—a farm—with a knobby molded plastic dirt path that meanders through green molded grass and rises up over a molded hill. I place the triangle of farm in my lap and trot my toy horse over the path—plastic hooves striking plastic dirt in a *tick, tick, tick*. In New York the dirt is sandy, citified. It spills up thinly through the sidewalk cracks like leftover dust pressed thin from the weight of a city. Here, where the grass is upturned, the earth is moist, like dough wet with butter, and smells sourly of manure by the barn and sweetly of earthworms and moss by the canal.

"Can I ride Trigger?"

My mother is following my grandfather, who drags in our suitcases. "Not now, Christine," she says, sounding overwhelmed. I feel badly for bothering her. "We'll do all that later."

Bare feet on linoleum. I stand and take deep breaths of the sweet, musty smell of this house, race upstairs, taking the steps in twos. My room is my aunt's old room; it has gabled windows and rose wallpaper. I flop down on the double bed's feather mattress and sink endlessly. In the corner of the room, our Easter baskets wait, filled with green plastic grass from years before. The baskets are in my room because I am the oldest and the only one who knows that it is my mother and not the Easter Bunny who leaves the chocolate by our beds on Easter morning. My mother has confided in me that she is tired and preparing and hiding the eggs is too much for her. This will be our last Easter egg hunt.

At breakfast, my grandparents' kitchen smells of coffee and gingerbread. My grandfather sprinkles sugar on his grapefruit half. In New York we eat our grapefruit plain.

I suck a sugar cube from the box in the cupboard. One for me, two for the pony; two for me, two for the pony. The sugar cube thins, wedged between the roof of my mouth and the thick of my tongue, geometry intact until it collapses like sweet ice. This morning my grandfather called *morning glory!* when I walked into the room. The cinnamon nose on my grandmother's bunny cookies, in the blue-and-white cookie jar on the linoleum counter, bled pink when they were baked. The plastic flowered kitchen tablecloth sticks to the underside of my mother's forearm when she lifts it.

My father's voice cuts through the morning, loud and high. He flew separately because of work and arrived this morning. He is now on the phone in the other room. My stomach tightens into a knot, but after several exchanges he hangs up with no incident. He strides into the kitchen, helps himself to a cookie from the cookie jar, and bites and chews it too quickly, it seems, to be tasting it.

"Things going well, Eddie?" My grandfather scrapes the last bit of grapefruit from its rind, sets his spoon down on the tablecloth, and pushes the bowl slightly away from him.

"Things are going fine." My father's voice is still tight and high. He finishes the cookie, pulls a napkin from the holder on the table, and wipes his hands.

My grandfather takes a sip of coffee. Swallows as if mulling over my father's response.

"How's business, Ot?" My father takes another cookie and looks it over, bunny head to tail. Then he bites off the head.

My grandfather also sells farm equipment.

"Oh well, why, we're doing all right," my grandfather says.

My father eats this cookie as quickly as the first. My grandfather takes another slow sip of his coffee.

I slip out of the room, push through the screen door, and head to the pasture, where Trigger grazes by the gate. Butterflies entwine in midair. Birds flit from branch to grass and back to branch again. I climb over the gate and approach Trigger, stop and rest my hand on the top of his neck, hold the sugar cube the way my mother showed me, palm flat. Trigger takes it, and his lips are dry and bristly on my tender palm; they tickle. He crunches the sugar then goes back to grazing. I clutch handfuls of mane. Will he get upset? He continues—step, *crunch-rip-crunch*, step, *crunch-rip-crunch*—seemingly undaunted by my presence. I jump once, twice, clutch the thick hair on his back and use the momentum to pull myself up, swing my leg over. Step, *crunch-rip-crunch*, he continues, unfazed. Overhead, the sky is blue and the sun is already hot. Trigger's brown back under my bare legs is warm. I settle my head on his rump, dangle my legs on either side of his neck, and breathe in the musk of his sweat, the dust of his coat. It's just him and me. Step, *crunch-rip-crunch*. Soothed by his rhythm and the warmth of his sun-drenched hide, I close my eyes. I hope no one comes looking for me. I plan to stay here all day.

"Now you just wait a minute there," my grandfather says to me.

I've come in for a glass of water.

"Sit down on the couch," my mother says.

I sit. My brothers are with my grandmother, making sugar cookies. The rest of the house is quiet. My father must be taking a nap. Bud, my grandfather's foreman, knocks on the door, opens the screen, lifts off his billed hat, and scratches the back of his head with the same hand. He kicks his dirt-streaked leather boots on the stoop before he steps inside. The three of them—my mother, my grandfather, and Bud—stand looking at me. He holds something very small in one hand, holds it close to his hip, like he is hiding it. I catch a glimpse of pink. Bud looks at my grandfather.

"Sure. Why, go ahead," my grandfather says.

Bud holds what's in his hand out to me, and I see a tiny pink nose, tiny squinted-shut pink eyelids, rose-petal ears, four miniature cloven hooves sticking straight out, a curly pink rubberband tail.

"Oh," I say. My eyes smart, fill with tears. I swallow.

"Take it," Bud says. He steps forward, sets the little hairy body into my arms. It wriggles, grunts, pokes its nose against my T-shirt. Its tiny hooves press into my forearm and my palm. A pig. A very small pink pig.

"It's yours," my grandfather says.

"What will you name it?" my mother says.

I consider. What's the most beautiful name I've ever heard?

"Kathleen," I say.

"The piglet is the runt," my grandfather says. "Its mother will crush it if it stays with her."

I hold Kathleen in my lap. She is rough, scratchy, so small, so pink. *Charlotte's Web* is my favorite book. I can't believe I have my own infant pig.

My mother is sunbathing on the grass in front of the screen door. I'm holding a bottle, feeding Kathleen. The piglet suckles for a while then grows restless, breaks away, and trots around the grass before coming back for another suckle. After a moment she breaks away again, this time taking a moment to hop up onto my mother's chest and walk around on her. Greg and Braddy squeal with laughter.

"It's easy to climb on me," my mother says, "because I am so flat-chested." She has told me she likes having no breasts to speak of. "I can sleep on my stomach. Most women can't sleep on their stomachs."

Suddenly my mother sits up. Yellow mustard streaks run off her chest, her arm. The smell is worse than anything I have ever smelled: putrid, rotten decay. My brothers shriek. My mother stands up, dripping and laughing.

"What *is* that?" Greg screams, holding his nose.

"The piglet pooped," my mother says.

"It pooped. The piglet pooped on Mom!" Greg and Jay shout.

I pick Kathleen up, wipe her off with my towel, and take her down to the tire swing so we can be alone.

At dinnertime, my brothers, mother, grandmother, and grandfather sit around the table with my only cousins, who are slightly older than us. Chipper is eight; John-John, nine; Carol, eleven; and Leatha, twelve. They are visiting from Kentucky with their parents: my mother's sister, Aunt Audrey, and her husband, my uncle George. My father left after two days to return to New York City to work. We are having beef stew and grits for dinner. The pot sits in the middle of the table. My mother serves us with a ladle. My boy cousins have crew cuts, and all four speak with a pronounced Kentucky twang. Carol and Leatha, both with feathery blond hair and cornflower-blue eyes, spent the past two summers with my grandmother, which makes me envious. They call her *Grannie*.

My uncle reaches for the bowl of cornmeal paste. "Want some of our farm grits, Little Steenie?"

He smiles at me from his square, chiseled face, his blue eyes crinkling, his voice soft. I hold out my plate, happy to take whatever he's offering. For the next two days I find any excuse I can to stand near Uncle George. I want him to talk to me so I can hear him say my name in his soft way. It's enough to secure my affections that he is a large-animal veterinarian; his handsome gentleness is an added bonus. I imagine what it must be like for my cousins with this kind of father.

It's our last day visiting my grandparents' farm; we leave in the morning. My brothers are shouting to one another as they head outside, and the screen door bounces several times before it stops with a final bang. I'm passing through the dining room on my way from the kitchen to head upstairs. As I walk, the old wood floorboards creak loudly under the braided rug my grandmother has stitched from my grandfather's socks and ties. I stop walking and the creaking stops. In this room, the blinds are kept closed and the air is still and somber in the way that air remains when the sun never hits it. Various projects sit out on the coffee-ice-cream-colored tablecloth that covers the dining table: small piles of photographs to be put in the open albums lie beside the tiny colored glass beads that my grandmother strings together with a needle and thread to become miniature bouquets of beaded pink petals cupped by beaded bright green leaves. I reach into the armoire and take out one of her tiny bouquets. I am struck by how much time must have gone into stringing these bouquets. In my world, effort is spent toward being important in some way. My father is a television executive. My mother restored our prestigious apartment. What would it be like to live in a world where stringing bead flowers would be enough? Beside the tiny beaded bouquets, glass figurines of birds collect dust. Tarnished silver frames hold photographs of people, most of whom I don't recognize. This room is the repository of the lives of the people who inhabit this house. The celebrations, the milestones as life rushes by, lived in all the other rooms; this room holds their remnants, the silt laid in deposits as the river flows past. In one photograph, my mother is a tall, elegant young woman, dressed in a white strapless gown, perched regally in a wingback wicker chair. Around her, six little girls on either side, miniature attendants in their own white dresses, gaze up at her in awe. My mother smiles at them indulgently, a dazzling, white, movie-star smile. On the back of the photograph, I recognize my grandmother's small, neat cursive written in blue fountain pen: *Carol, May Queen, 1949*. Another picture shows my mother as a young girl holding her bassoon. Her sister's instrument, the instrument my mother took up after the accident to strengthen her lungs. In the photograph, my mother is holding a plaque. My grandmother's writing says, *Most Outstanding Woodwind Soloist, Illinois State Music Contest*. A third photo reveals my mother as a young woman, dressed in a white bathing suit. On a stage with a banner reading MISS MISSOURI draped across one shoulder, falling at her slim hip. My mother, seamstress, bassoonist, pianist, musical prodigy, beauty-pageant winner, the golden girl of her family, must have gotten used to impressing; she impresses her parents still, returning here like a celebrity, with her four children in tow, from her glamorous life in New York City.

The next morning, our grandfather waits beside his sedan, his hair again wet with Vitalis. I kiss the top of Kathleen's head and hand her to Bud. She will be rejoining her brothers and sisters and her mother in their pen.

"She'll be fine in there now," Bud says. "You did a good job. See how big she got?"

I don't want to ask what will happen to my piglet once she reaches her full size. Kathleen has no Charlotte to spin words into webs. This is not a storybook.

Driving back from the airport, nose pressed to the window, I pass the landmarks that mean we are definitely not on the farm anymore: the blackened smokestacks of Con Edison, the enormous crunching Godzilla sweep of the Triborough Bridge, lifting us, cement and steel, metal cables as thick as torsos, rivets and bolts the size of human heads, up and over Brooklyn and then

Queens, each borough as vast and dark and lonely below as an unfriendly country, before dropping us into the empty, dimly lit streets of the outskirts of Manhattan.

That night, home in the Dakota, my mother says she has to tuck me in quickly so she can go lie down.

"My ankles are bothering me tonight."

Her ankles look fine to me, but I also know she is wearing a nightgown with no underpants—though she tells me she buys only cotton, because cotton breathes and most women don't know how unhealthy it is to wear synthetic underpants—because she has been getting bladder infections. Sometimes her infection gets so bad, she can't wear any underpants at all; she can only wear dresses and slips during the day, even when she leaves the apartment.

"Come and see me later." I feel selfish making her promise this when she isn't feeling well, though it is precisely because she's not feeling well that I want this promise.

"I will. I'll be up later."

I don't ask her why she'll be up later. She has told me sometimes the incinerators and the street exhaust bother her.

"Something I ate is bothering me," she says now.

That's a lot of things wrong. I'm used to this feeling of worry, though. Sometimes it seems I'm the only one paying attention.

"I love you, Mom."

"I love you too, sweetheart."

Chapter 5

We've been home from my grandparents' farm in Illinois for one month. Three days ago my mother collapsed in the hallway outside her bedroom after returning home from a dinner party with my father. I watched as she was wheeled on a gurney through our apartment on the way to the hospital. Now she's due home any minute and my brothers and I are playing Battleship on the floor of the playroom, waiting for her. When we hear the back door open, we leave the game and head to the kitchen, where my father is helping her walk. He is holding her by the arm, and she is taking slow, small steps down the hall. She is always thin, but now she looks bony in an old-lady way. Knobby shoulders poke through her thin sweater, and her hands—big for a woman, she has always been proud of that—look even bigger in comparison to the rest of her. Her pants hang.

"Are you still sick, Mom?" Jay asks quietly, looking up at her back as we follow.

"I'm much better, sweetie pies," my mother says, looking only partway over her shoulder.

My father and mother enter the bedroom and we file in after, the four of us standing together, arms hanging at our sides, as my father pulls the covers back and my mother sits on the bed, then lies back on the pillows and pulls the covers up over her legs. She is moving slowly, like she will break if she isn't careful.

"What's wrong with you?" Greg asks.

"Your mother is fine," my father snaps. "She just needs a little rest."

"I had an allergic reaction to an aspirin," my mother says. "I'm happy to be home."

We're home from school. I have been in charge of taking my brothers the eight bus stops back and forth from Seventy-second Street to school at Walden on Eighty-eighth. I drop my book bag onto the kitchen table, then head back to my mother's room, where she lies, wearing her thin white nightgown, propped up with her sheet pulled and tucked just below her rib cage. After my day out in the world, she seems extra fragile and weak.

"When are you going to get up?" I ask. I have three Chips Ahoy! cookies in a napkin and I'm eating the fourth.

"When I get my strength back."

"How long is that going to take?"

"I don't know, Christine," she says.

After dinner, I am in my bedroom. My father's voice raises from down the long hall. Instantly I go cold. His voice is urgent, high, and whiny, but he's not yelling yet.

"Four weeks? It's been four weeks, Carol."

There's a pause as my mother replies, though I can't hear what she's saying. Then comes the murmur of his response, too low for me to make out, too. This is unusual. Things usually escalate. He is clearly making an effort to tone down whatever frustration he is feeling. I'm guessing that, faced with the bedridden, porcelain-delicate version of his once-robust wife, he is at a loss. We are in a new landscape. My mother is not okay, as she has always reassured me. The bad guys didn't get her; something invisible has. The too-big city with its unknowable outer reaches is not outside our apartment; it's somehow inside now.

"The books are multiplying, Carol." My father picks up the small stack from the side of the bed. *Let's Eat Right to Keep Fit, Let's Get Well, Food Is Your Best Medicine.* He holds them over his head like he's going to throw them.

"You think these crackpots know what the doctors who have gone to the best schools in the world and spent their lives on the cutting edge of medical and scientific knowledge don't?" My father's favorite book as a boy was *Microbe Hunters,* about the discovery of penicillin.

I'm standing just outside their room. I was heading in to see my mother but stopped when I heard my father's voice. I can see in through the crack in the door.

"Doctors don't know about nutrition. Adele Davis makes the correlation between diet and health, Edgar." My mother speaks slowly and evenly and calmly pats the sheets down that cover her hips and stomach.

"There's nothing wrong with you that a trip somewhere wouldn't fix." His intonation lifts at the end in a slight plea. "This craziness doesn't have to take over the house."

He hands her the books. She takes them and he turns and walks out of the room, passes me without acknowledging me.

My mother has just returned from a doctor's appointment and is climbing back into bed. She slips under the sheets, tucks her feet in, then slides down, her arms behind her, arranging the pillow against the ten-foot Louis XIV headboard.

"Stupid doctors," she says.

"What did the doctor say?" I ask.

"He said there's nothing wrong with me."

My heart leaps. This is the news I've been waiting for. But as she pulls the sheets up around her neck, I feel a familiar sinking feeling in my stomach. She's not going anywhere.

"What did you tell him was wrong?"

"I told him my symptoms. Doctors only know what they know. They don't know how to think beyond their limited understanding of health."

A week later I return home from school to find her spooning wheat germ from a jar on her bedside table into a glass of orange juice on the tray in her lap.

"I had four babies in four years. When I asked the doctor what I should eat to fortify myself before having you children, he said I didn't need to take anything special. Nothing! I used to eat entire boxes of Lorna Doones when I was pregnant with Bradford. No wonder he has the issues he has. I can't get mad at myself; I didn't know any better."

The tiny square brown flakes swirl and spin. I've never heard of wheat germ before. I know my mother had never heard of it either before she read about it in her *Let's Get Well* book sometime in the last few weeks. It's late afternoon. She's just returned from a doctor down the block—walking distance from the Dakota—who has been giving her B12 injections, something I've also never heard of.

She finishes stirring. "When they make white bread, this is the part that's taken out to refine it. Anytime you refine something, you're taking out the vitamins. The healthiest part of the wheat is the germ. Do you want to try it?"

"Plain?"

"You can mix it in some orange juice if you want."

"That's okay."

I take the dry spoonful she hands me, put the whole thing in my mouth. It's a large dry mass on my tongue and I feel myself start to gag. Can I get this down? But the saliva starts to come and the mass slowly moistens. I chew. Swallow a portion, continue to chew. It tastes nutty and sweet but also too strong, like something that should be cooked. But overall it's not terrible. If this is going to be the extent of the fallout from her collapse, B12 injections and wheat germ, things might not be so bad.

"Your mother's breakdown isn't physical," my father says in a low voice.

We are in the hall, and I am heading back to the kitchen. My mother has asked for her raw egg and orange juice, something else she's eating these days besides wheat germ. He is going in the other direction, dressed in only an undershirt and boxers, scripts under his arm, clearly heading to the study to read.

I stop. This doesn't feel like information to just throw at someone and continue on.

"What?"

Is he saying she's crazy? My brothers are nine, eight, and six. I know suddenly and completely that he's not going to ever say what he's saying to me, to them. But ten feels too young to hear this, too. I want to tell him that so much of the information she's sharing with me makes sense: about *low blood sugar*; that milk is fit for the calves nature intended it for, not humans; that red food dye causes hyperactivity in children. But standing here, alone in the hall with him, none of that seems right to mention. And of course there's the question I can't answer: If these new things she's reading about are true, why doesn't anyone else besides the authors of my mother's books, *crackpots* as my father calls them, think they're important?

"Never mind, Christine. Go back to doing whatever you were doing."

I'm not going to tell him what I'm doing: running to fetch yet another strange concoction for my mother to ingest. I continue toward the kitchen without elaborating. He continues in the other direction.

My mother's cheeks are flushed when I get home from school

a few days later. She's been in bed for more than two months now. She's in bed but she's dressed in street clothes, jeans and a sweater. I have regressed. I miss my mother during the day when I'm at school, not just at night. I feel homesick, the way I felt at camp, even when I'm home.

"Are you going somewhere?"

"I took the train to Boston today to see a new doctor. He treats with food, not medicine. Something he could be put in jail for, practicing medicine without a license. Can you believe that? He's saving people's lives, which threatens the powers that be. Dr. Bilotte says he's never seen a case as desperate as mine. He said he almost didn't take my case."

"Why not?"

"He's afraid I'll die and he'll be blamed."

I'm surprised to see her looking this pleased with news that sounds so dire.

"I haven't told your father. I'll tell him when the time is right."

The slab of raw beef liver sits dark red and shining on my mother's plate. She's sitting up against her pillows in her nightgown.

She holds the slab down with her fork and cuts a slice carefully with her steak knife, brings the slice to her lips. I stand by the side of the bed and watch her chew.

"Does raw liver taste good?"

"It tastes good to me. It's keeping me alive. I'd be dead without it."

My mother has told me that Adele Davis writes about desiccated liver powder, how strengthening it is.

"Did Dr. Bilotte tell you to eat raw liver?" I ask hopefully.

"Not specifically. I will share with him how strengthening it is when I see him next."

She swallows, and cuts another piece. Tendrils of tissue attach to this slice and hang off the fork as she brings all of it to her mouth, slurping up the hanging bits.

"It's helping me regain my strength. I'm very grateful for it."

My mother flips the strange block that sits on our kitchen countertop, then flips it again. It's covered in waxy paper and wrapped several times around with a string. She finds the ends of the wax paper, which fold together at the ends of the brick in triangle corners like a Christmas present, and peels back the paper like she is unwrapping something precious. But all that's under the wax paper is a wet-looking gray brick. An unfamiliar smell, sour, like someone's sweat, wafts into the kitchen. My mother licks her thumb as if tasting a delicacy.

"What is that?" I ask.

She peels back enough of the paper to stab half an inch from the end of the brick with a butter knife and slices in a downward sawing motion.

"Baker's yeast. I had to buy it from the black market. It's illegal." She sounds pleased with herself.

Illegal? Could she be arrested?

"Doctors are nothing but drug pushers. The medical profession wants us all to be tied to taking their drugs."

The end of the brick peels away, flaking slightly. A clear dairy farm bottle of milk, though the milk inside is gray, not white, sits beside the brick. My mother explains that it's goat's milk. I have never heard of anyone drinking goat's milk. She pours the gray milk into the blender, then plops the gray wedge from the brick in with it and turns it on. The yeast and milk froth into a gray foam. After a moment of blending, she pours the foamy mixture into a glass.

"Do you want to try yeast milk?" she asks.

I pray silently and urgently that this shake's taste justifies its strangeness. I tip the glass forward. But as the foam brushes my nose, warning bells instantly go off. The sour body-odor smell, mixed with goat, is overpowering, and my face wants out but it's already too late. Hemmed in on all sides by the glass, I have breathed in a cloud of sour gray droplets. It's on my skin, up my nose. Some of the foam has touched the tip of my tongue.

I put the glass on the counter and try to wipe the smell out of my nostrils with the back of my arm.

My mother, on the other hand, sips it once, again. Then again. Swallowing and sipping like she is drinking the most delicious milk shake imaginable.

Bernie, the psychologist my father hired to speak to me a few months ago, sits at the foot of my mother's bed, still dressed in his reddish-brown tweed jacket that matches his reddish-brown beard. I think of reasons to pass by my parents' bedroom door, cracked just enough that I can glimpse inside. He raises his hands, presses them together as if in prayer as he speaks, then lays them on his lap. Then he uses them to support himself on either side of his hips, raises himself up slightly, hands flat on the bedspread, then settles back again and lifts one hand to scratch the side of his beard. His voice is low and murmuring. If my mother is responding to him, I can't hear it.

"Your father thinks I need a *psychiatrist*," my mother says to me after he leaves, spitting the word. "No one understands how to treat the body with diet. So stupid. So *stupid*."

My father hires workmen. They come dressed in overalls. They bring ladders and build scaffolding; the sounds of hammering and high-pitched drilling fill the apartment. As they progress, they leave in their wake long rectangular silver boxes and shiny round silver ducts clinging to the ceiling, overhead tunnels that, when they are through, run the length of the apartment and turn out to be an air system. Our eight-foot-tall windows are sealed shut with plumber's caulk. We are not allowed to break those seals or open any window. Shades are drawn.

"New York City is filled with people all breathing the same air," my father says. "Look outside. They're not sick."

I come home from school to the silence of our apartment, the white noise of the air system, soothing but also a reminder of my mother still lying in her room, down the hall, waiting to be well.

It's midnight, and everyone is asleep. My parents have allowed me to set up a cot beside their Louis XIV four-poster bed, itself dwarfed under the fourteen-foot ceilings of our apartment, because my dread of bedtime has turned into a full-blown panic. In my parents' room, the air is humid and comforting and smells of my father's shaving cream, the white vinegar my mother uses to rinse her hair with, and the faint ever-present aroma of floor wax. On the cot, I can hear my mother's breathing. In my own room, I am afraid she will die while I sleep.

The next morning I peer into the oven, standing on a chair so I can reach. The tomato bubbles, its flesh lightening to orange as it cooks; juices run down its sides into the grooves where the skin has split with the heat. The fat on the lamb has browned, and the juices, too, pool and crackle. She's graduated from eating raw liver to this meal, broiled lamb, broiled tomato, and yeast milk, three times a day, nothing else. It's been a month.

My mother sits up in bed as I approach, pats the sheet and comforter down to flatten them into a table, spreads the towel she keeps with her for her meals in bed. I set the plate onto the towel, hand her a knife and fork.

"Don't you get tired of eating the same thing over and over again?" I feel sorry for her, though the lamb and tomato, at least, smell delicious.

"Dr. Bilotte says lamb is the easiest meat to digest. This meal is designed to give my body the most nutrition with the least amount of work involved to digest it. I can feel that this is giving me strength."

My mother is feeling stronger and we begin going to Point Lookout again on the weekends. As we leave New York, we pass through the city's outer rind. I am conscious for the first time how frayed New York City is around the edges: the overpasses tattooed with graffiti, chain-link fences woven with rusting cans, fast-food wrappers, smashed paper cups; the city's sloughing off dandruff and dead skin. In the car, my brothers sleep, my father reads the paper, my mother drives. No one else seems to notice how litter and loneliness both lurk on the outskirts of things, the places where no one's paying attention.

Chapter 6

My mother is up more and more, mostly to make trips in the Volkswagen bus to a shady establishment, in my opinion, on the outskirts of the city, a closet-size room lined with crates and a sawdust-covered floor that she calls *the health food store*. She slides the door of the Volkswagen open for the volunteers—this health food store is a co-op—all wearing aprons over their street clothes, to load in the food she has purchased: oatmeal-ish brick-hard dollops trying to pass themselves off as cookies; bags of dried apricots, two kinds—one shriveled and brown, the other plump and apricot-like, and apparently the plump version is the treat because the sulfur used to prevent the shrivel isn't good for us; twiglike sticks lumpy with sesame seeds—my mother calls them *sesame sticks*, and she's glowing as if they are the most exciting thing she has ever seen; unsweetened square peels of *fruit leather*—raspberry, grape, cherry, all the same color brown—all packed in the cardboard boxes we will be bringing these items home in.

There is nowhere for me to hang my legs as we drive back through the streets of New York to the Dakota. I busy myself by looking up into the windows of the apartments we pass, imagining myself living inside the rooms I catch glimpses of, playing my game: How close can I get to seeing, in my mind's eye, inside the seedy rooms with stained, torn curtains and not lose myself in that sadness? In the apartments we pass where the windows are clean and the lights glow velvety warm, I imagine soft rugs and oversize couches and chairs, lamps throwing golden halos that envelop and cheer, and feel my old tinge of envy.

When we reach the Dakota, my mother drives up the curb, without hesitation, into the arched entrance, and I am reminded that she has told us how she started driving when she was nine in her father's pastures and often scoffs at women drivers on the roads around us: *Most women can't drive.* She stops the perfect distance, just feet from the gates. Once, we arrived to several police cars and my father pacing out front. My father had called the NYPD because we had been gone so long.

"Where have you been, Carol?" His voice was high-pitched as I climbed over the boxes and out of the car. He, as usual, didn't seem to care that people, passing on the street, were staring.

"I was shopping, Edgar." My mother's voice remained calm as she turned to survey her cargo. Her hair fell loose and soft around her face, dressed in her favorite outfit of late, jeans and a sweatshirt; she seemed very capable and in charge again.

Now she hauls off the box on top, which is filled with cartons of unfertilized eggs, glass bottles of raw milk, and bags filled with rings of dried pineapple, and hands it to Heinz. She carries the next box herself and a service worker, who Heinz has radioed for help, grabs the third. The three of them make trips back and forth until all the boxes are stacked in our kitchen. Then my mother backs up the Volkswagen and pulls it around to the ramp under my bedroom window, which leads down to the garage under the building.

"Isn't she pretty?" my father asks. I am standing at his side, looking up at Cybill Shepherd. She is a towering princess, glittery, blond, shiny. We are in Miami for a week; my father is filming *The Heartbreak Kid.* He has brought Greg and me to the set.

Jay and Braddy are too young to be unattended, so they are at the condo with my mother, but Greg and I get to hang out all day. It's morning and we have just arrived. Every tourist in the hotel knows a movie is being filmed, and as we walk through the lobby, all eyes are on us. It's fun to feel this important. In between shots, we explore the pool deck and ride the elevators. I feel coated in sweat and grime in the same way I used to after a Saturday cooped up in the Dakota, but here I feel privileged and happy.

"Quiet on the set," calls a woman holding a walkie-talkie.

Standing in the hall outside the hotel room where the scene with Charles Grodin and Jeannie Berlin is being filmed, Greg and I duck the hot lights and straddle the thick black snakelike cables that no one seems worried we will step on accidentally. I make myself still so no one will ask me to leave. There are electricians and assistants and makeup people hovering in the hall; the closest we can get is just outside the doorway. I can't see into the room where the scene is being shot, but I can listen. At home, I'm good at being quiet, good at being in a room without taking up any space, a skill my brothers and I hone when the tension around our father feels like it is at a breaking point. This scene— in which Jeannie Berlin has a sunburn and wears smeared-in cold cream and lies in bed while Charles Grodin paces—has been filmed over and over, which is just fine by me. Cordoned off, we are in; most of the gawking world is out. I love the long day, bored and in sticky, sweaty love with everything around me. This is so much better than real life.

After a week, when the shooting is finished and we are back in New York, my father brings me to the cutting room, where he oversees and Elaine May edits. The small room is filled with her cigarette smoke. Twenty-three stories below us taxis and cars honk and red taillights light up the night. I am a fly on the wall and I soak in the banter between them, Elaine May's crackling charisma, the sense I have that we are high above the rest of humanity, literally and figuratively, this rarified world my father is a part of.

My parents have announced that we are moving to Long Island to get away from the city air. Plandome is close enough to the city that my father can take the Long Island Railroad in each day. My mother has found a house suited to her antique furniture, built around the same time as the Dakota—in the 1800s. My mother is proud she has found a suburban environment that matches the architectural splendor of the Dakota. She has floor plans drawn up on dining room table–size sheets of tracing paper that lay out the dimensions and location of every piece of furniture as they sit in the formal rooms of our Dakota apartment so the layout can be recreated in the new rooms of the Plandome house. An appraiser generates a list of every item being transferred. Pages upon pages list tables of inlaid wood, lamps and sconces, urns and vases and fire screens and mirrors, ivory busts and bronze figures; sofas, loveseats, and chairs made of damask and silk and velvet, from the French Empire, Victorian, Chinese Chippendale, and Renaissance periods. Like those in the Dakota, the rooms in this new house loom; they are made of dark, formal wood paneling higher than my head throughout, and dark wood floors. Also like the Dakota, our new house has a name. I find a stone plaque under the ivy in the front: SHORE GABLES. Our neighbors' houses around ours, my mother tells me, were once part of what had been a large estate. The neighbor to our right lives in the house that was our Japanese gardens. To the left, our neighbor lives in the stables. I wonder if it suits my mother that we are once again in the most exclusive house; though, as far as I'm concerned, this house disappoints. Here's our chance to live in the country, and our yard is a sliver of grass in the back. Whoever partitioned off the estate was concerned, as my parents are, with house over yard. I'm wanting wildness. My favorite books are *The*

Five Little Peppers and How They Grew and *Heidi,* books about poor children surrounded by nature.

I attend Manhasset Middle School, where an entire culture I knew nothing about has been thriving: belly-button shirts, bell-bottom pants, platform shoes. The day I finally give in and wear what everyone else is wearing, a previously standoffish classmate says, "You look nice today, Chris." Only I know I'm wearing a costume. There are drugs here, as well as a subculture of bused-in black students of lower socioeconomic status. I am stabbed with a needle one morning while at my gym locker, a hot, sharp pain, all the more of a shock because I feel as alienated as these bused-in kids do; the needle feels like not just an affront, but a betrayal. In another hallway filled with all-white students, someone thwacks my training bra. Michael Murtag, who lives two houses down, is in my French class. He's popular and I'm not, but I imagine a quiet connection even so. An unspoken understanding that beneath it all there is some kindredness, at least based on our shared address. I am walking beside the row of desks in class, the bell has rung, I'm heading for my seat. Michael bounces in, shifting his weight left and right as he waits for me to move so he can get to his usual desk at the back of the class.

"Get out of the way, dog," he says, then pushes past me, bumping me hard with his shoulder.

The morning after Michael Murtag's insult, my father pulls up in front of school and leaves the engine idling. I don't open the car door. Hot tears prick the backs of my eyes, and I rub my nose. I can't go back in there. Into that world where I am special to no one.

"I don't like it here," I say.

I'm crying, which is not good. My eyes will be red. I'll be prone to more tears if even something minor happens. But I know I have no choice. There is no plan B in place. My father is patient, but he has to make his train. He believes I will adjust to the Plandome schools, which is the reason he chose this town.

It's Saturday and I wander outside. In the next yard over, I pull myself up onto the first branch of a tree I've named Elsa. The bark is white with black thumbnail-shaped smiles, cold and hard under my palms, wrinkled like elephant skin. The grass belonging to my neighbors, people whose names I will never know, is brown and furry, dormant already in October. There are no leaves on any trees, and the sky is colorless though it's only noon. Past a copse that dips then rises into our side yard, is the large kitchen window of our new house. The cold sky is reflected in the picture window; I can't see anyone inside. No one is outside. I reach up and climb to the second branch. How high can I go? The branches of this tree are splayed like rungs waiting for me to use them. Breathing hard feels good. I reach and step, reach and step, and each branch takes me higher. I stop three rungs from the top—the remaining branches are too thin to hold me—and look around. I'm very high. The air feels thinner up here; the neighborhood is laid out below me. I feel powerful, capable. It's too bad that I'll have to climb down, that it's cold up here and I'm holding on for dear life. There is nothing I want, nothing I would have chosen for myself, down there.

My father unwraps the steak. It is the size of a violin. The butcher paper has been folded over many times and taped. He lifts the steak free of the paper, deep red, edged and marbled with white fat, which I imagine crispy and glistening, salty and hot, after it is barbecued. Though it's morning and I have to wait all day.

"Look, Christine."

He unwraps a second package. Pink ground meat flecked with white speckles of fat. He pours soy sauce on it and sprinkles way too much salt.

"Steak tartar."

I think of the rhymes he has taught me: *Jack Sprat could eat no fat. His wife could eat no lean. And so between them both, you see, they licked the platter clean.* And *One man's meat is another man's poison.* He smacks his lips with his fingers the way he does when he is happy about what he is about to eat, and eats one forkful, then another. He doesn't offer this to me, luckily, because I can see steak tartar is a fancy name for what is clearly only raw hamburger.

I want to get into the spirit of Thanksgiving in our Plandome house. I ask my mom to sew me a Pilgrim costume. I bring the turkey in on its platter, very heavy, set it down. Brown juices run in rivulets along the platter's grooves. We sit as a family at the long dining room table, which is filled with traditional Thanksgiving dishes. Sweet potatoes, stuffing, salad, and turkey.

It's the day after Thanksgiving, and my father is on a rampage at the top of the grand staircase. He's holding an armful of vitamin bottles and throwing them onto the entryway below. The first bottle smashes, shattering into a thousand shards, and vitamins spill across the cool stone, the sound like a sudden downpour of rain.

"How. Many. Vitamin. Bottles. Are. We. Going. To. Allow. To. Accumulate? We're all drowning in vitamin bottles, Carol. Can you see we're drowning?" He throws another bottle. Pills rain across the floor.

I am hiding in the room my mother calls the powder room, a tiny bathroom on the first floor with one small stained-glass window out of sight of where my father stands. I want to leave, but I don't want to be seen.

My mother screams back at him from the kitchen, "No one understands the role of nutrition in health, Edgar!"

He roars his favorite response: "The. Greatest. Scientific. Minds. In. The. World. Don't. Know. The. Cure. To. Cancer. And. You. Do?"

Another bottle shatters. Then another. Now footsteps—it sounds like he's coming down the staircase. I need to get away. My heart is pounding as I slip out of the powder room and head for the front door. The going is treacherous: shattered glass and vitamins cover the entryway. They have spilled into the formal rooms and even cover the rug in the study. I slide with each step like I'm on ice. I make it to the front door, open it, close it behind me. I run, duck down into our backyard, crouch in the bushes, where no one will know I am.

Chapter 7

"What do you want?" my mother asks.

It's a week after my father's last tirade and things have settled down. I'm looking through the pantry in the Plandome kitchen for something good to eat. The shelves are filled with unfamiliar bags and plastic packages. I'm not seeing any of our old staples: Chips Ahoy!, Ritz Crackers, Cap'n Crunch. She's obviously been replacing things when no one was looking.

"We have sesame sticks. We have dried apricots. I got carob-coated peanut clusters yesterday," she calls from the sink.

I pick up a brown loaf of bread that, in my opinion, shouldn't even be called *bread*. The slices are thick and hard, and they don't bend; instead they break at the slightest pressure. I lift the jar of peanut butter. It's heavy in my hand, greasy under the lid though it's yet to be opened. I see the telltale thick, oily yellow layer at the top that signals *healthy peanut butter*. Though my mother will cheerfully open the jar and mix the contents with a knife, the density and oiliness will remain. This oily peanut butter can satisfy in a pinch—I mix it with honey and spread it on the unbendable bread—but it's never what I really want. The cookies she buys are brownish-gray lumps that taste like they look: too hard, barely sweet, a mixture of strange flavorings, heavy on the orange peel. The first moment when tooth and tongue connect with a carob chip, I can't suppress the hope that springs eternal—maybe it's secretly chocolate? Maybe chips changed hands and, unknowingly, carob chips were swapped for chocolate ones? But once I bite in, my hopes are dashed. My mother says chocolate is a toxin and stays in the body long after we eat it, so the cookies in our pantry these days are always carob.

She sees me pick up a baggie filled with carob-covered peanut clusters.

"Try the carob! It's delicious," she sings as if I have never had carob before.

I decide to give carob another try. Maybe this time I'll like it. I know I asked myself this the last time I tried the carob my mother brought home, but *have* I ever really noticed how much it looks like chocolate? I open the bag and breathe in the aroma. I have asked myself this question, too, but *would* I be able to tell a difference if I didn't know? I reach in for a cluster, put it in my mouth. Glossy, chocolate-like coating, check. Maybe if I keep an open mind, this time the carob could be enough to vanquish this constant longing I feel for chocolate so I can be left in peace. And indeed, the coating starts to melt on my tongue and teeth in a chocolaty way. I chew that cluster and take another, though with the second cluster the fruity un-chocolate taste is suddenly more noticeable. Hopefully, I'm also just imagining that the dried-fruit taste is giving me the beginnings of a headache. I push on, chew a third.

Please let me like it.

The fruit taste has drowned out any semblance to chocolate now and I'm definitely queasy. This is how carob made me feel the last time, I suddenly remember. My temples have begun to throb. I put the half-eaten cluster back in the bag.

"Good?" my mother says.

Whatever I love about chocolate, it's clearly about more than look and texture. As much as I wish it could be, it's not easily replaced. My mother says chocolate is bad for me and I know she will never buy it again. Carob is a false hope, a tease like everything else in this pantry.

My mother has set four supplements on the table. The glasses are tall, the glass thick but not thick enough to hide what sits waiting. One tall, fat glass of tomato juice mixed with three heaping tablespoons of brewers' yeast flakes and three tablespoons of desiccated liver powder. Slices of orange wait beside each in a saucer.

"Supplement time!" my mother calls from the kitchen.

We are living in Southold, Long Island, in a rental house on a little bay, while my father films *Law and Disorder*, a movie with Ernest Borgnine and Carroll O'Connor. On the weekends, when my father is home, he shows us how to wade out in the sound to our knees then stick our arms into the mud to our elbows and pull up cherrystone clams. We fill our buckets and then he pries them open with a butter knife. We slurp the pulpy bodies, chewy knobs of muscle, swallow the bitter, salty juices. He shows us how to squeeze the lemon; the lemon makes the whole procedure more like eating and less like murder.

It's morning. My brothers and I file in around the table, cracking jokes in a whisper about excusing ourselves to go to the bathroom and dumping the contents of our glasses in the toilet or calling the dog and tricking her into consuming all four supplements, as we turn the full glasses around in our hands, working up the nerve for those first swallows.

"Just drink it down," my mother says firmly from the sink. We've been stalling for twenty minutes.

"You're just letting it get warm," my mother says. "May as well get it down, get on with the day."

What *would* be the harm in sitting here all day with this glass in front of me? But Greg takes a deep breath, lifts his glass, and begins. Braddy follows. I don't want to be last; plus, as awful as a supplement is to drink when it's cold, it's worse when it's warm. I hold my breath, lift the glass to my lips, and take my first swallow as Jay does the same. It's as bad as I expect: thick, warm sludge, more solid than liquid. I suck down the first, then another grainy swallow, already feeling the need for air. By the third gulp, my lungs are burning. Finally it's unavoidable; I have to breathe, but as I do, also unavoidable, there's the rushing in of taste, raw liver mostly. I slam my glass, only half finished, down onto the table as my brothers do the same.

"Eat your orange slices! Your orange slices!" My mother rushes from the sink and, one by one, slides each of our saucers of orange slices to us. I bite down. The cool sweetness helps but doesn't drown out the dead brown taste of yeast and liver now coating the roof of my mouth and that seems permanently lodged in my sinuses.

Half a glass left. None of us make jokes now. Bubble pockets of powder pop as I chug, small detonations of pure liver and yeast, spraying my tongue and the back of my throat. Four more swallows in, the Coke-rim bottom of my glass appears, streams of thick, pulpy red flecked with brown and yellow clinging to the sides. Done. I slam my glass to the table. My brothers do the same, panting and sucking our final orange slices, breathing through our noses until the last bit of orange pulp is ripped from the rind and the overpowering taste of liver and yeast rushes in.

I come home from eighth grade at Manhasset Middle School to find my mother pacing in the Plandome house. She is crossing from the sunroom on one side of her bedroom, striding across the expanse of cold rugless hardwood floor—my mother is still allergic to dust and there are no carpets in this house—heading for the matching sunroom on the other side of the room. I love these sunrooms. They are filled with light and the windows and the walls and windowpanes are painted white. All the other rooms

in this too-big house of thirty-six rooms are made of dark wood
paneling; dark, towering staircases; dark brown tile; cold wooden
floors. If, God forbid, I am sent on an errand into the basement,
a maze of silent, empty chambers, the largest of which my mother
calls *the rathskeller*—a ballroom-size room that we are using for
storage since this house was built before cars and there is no garage—the hair on the back of my neck prickles sharp pinpoints
before I am even halfway to the bottom of the staircase. I am
afraid down here. It feels like whatever we all try to avoid on the
upper floors, with their windows and views to the yard, has been
concentrated into these shut-off, silent rooms. As if the weight of
the upper, empty house has compressed the very air into something
solid. Another kind of darkness lurks down here, mingled almost
gleefully with the shadows. A darkness we will never as a family
talk about. Still, I will myself to walk, to not lose my composure,
as if sprinting will weaken the force field of protection around
me, an admission of vulnerability to the powers that be. But I will
never complete a mission in this basement without ultimately
running for my life, twisting through the cold, dark rooms, leaping the stairs in threes, wind whistling in my hair, gasping for
breath, tumbling into daylight.

"I'll be okay," she says as she passes me, heading back across to
the other sunroom again. I am still standing in the middle of her
bedroom. She doesn't look at me as she goes by. I realize that she
doesn't seem to be looking at anything. I feel a twinge, a hot needle begin in the softest part of my stomach. I consider the time.
My father is on his way home from work in the city, out of reach.
My brothers are off on their bikes somewhere in the neighborhood.

My mother heads for the bathroom. "The coffee enemas are
helping," she says.

Coffee enemas?

By the toilet a small rubber bag hangs from a wire coat hanger.
A thin white hose with a nozzle at the end dangles from the bag.
It looks like something that belongs in a hospital a hundred years

ago, not here in this bathroom. She wants to give herself another enema, she says. She says she has eaten something, she isn't sure what, and felt a reaction coming on. But the enemas are helping her purge the offending substance.

"Go on, Christine. I'll be fine."

I immerse myself in my American history homework. After forty minutes it occurs to me that it's very quiet in her bedroom, which is next to mine, just down the hall.

Her bedroom seems so still as I approach.

"Mom?"

I peek in. For a second it seems the room is empty, but then I look over at the bed. She is lying, covers drawn up to her chin, staring at the ceiling.

"Mom!"

I expect her to look at me, but she doesn't. Her eyes don't waver from the ceiling. I notice her arms are shaking. I realize she is shaking all over, her legs and feet through the covers. Her torso and shoulders.

"Mom! Mom?"

I pick up the phone, dial my father's office. His secretary, still in the office, calls an ambulance.

My mother's hospital room is dark. On the single gurney I see a thin tangle of sheets. As my father and I walk closer, I realize my mother is lying under them, so small and suddenly shrunken, I don't notice her at first.

"A half hour later and it would have been too late," the doctor tells my father. Too many enemas caused the sodium in my mother's body to become diluted. Her body's water levels rose, and her cells began to swell.

"It's possible to drown from the inside," the doctor says.

My mother has been home from the hospital for two months. Neither my father nor my mother talks about the hospital or the enemas. She got home and began taking care of us as if nothing had happened. We are spending the summer in Connecticut while my father films *The Stepford Wives*. Greg and I get to spend the days at the set. Jay and Braddy stay home with our mother. The morning is still crisp and cool. My brother and I come together, each other's touchstones, then move off again, like explorers, to see what will come our way. The foyer of the house the movie crew is using for this week's location is an obstacle course of tarps laid over python-thick black cables, sheets of Visqueen, panels of plywood, lights waiting to be turned on perched on man-size tripods. I mosey over to the makeup trailer, then past the unneeded-for-now teamsters; they have pulled fold-out chairs in a circle for a chat and a cigarette, their hoarse, phlegmy laughter rising with the smoke. One teamster, nicknamed Fast Eddie, with a combed-back black ducktail and a cigarette pack rolled up in his black T-shirt, drives us back and forth from our rented ivy-covered tree house in the woods to wherever the set is—the rainy neighborhood street corner, the tidy white-shingled house, the marshy field—for that day. There's a lot of waiting on a set, more waiting than I've ever known—waiting for makeup, waiting for electricians, and, after a take, waiting as the scene is played back to see if the director, Bryan Forbes, his gentle touch on my shoulder and pastel voice matching the drape of his soft oatmeal-colored linen suits, his pink, sky-blue, and Easter-egg-yellow chemises, wants another take. I'm not exactly sure of the time, another phenomenon that's new. I stroll to the stone wall that runs along the backyard, stepping across the dirt where the lawn ends and the extra cables lie, back inside, treading lightly over the electrical wires. No one has called me to breakfast or lunch or dinner, the usual time markers for the day. No one has called me to anything. Instead the hours have slid together. No schedule except getting the shot. Everything revolves around this: setup, shoot, takedown, repeat. The makeup woman's makeup has worn off; her lipstick and eyeliner are smudged. The electricians' shirts are untucked. The script girl's hair, so neatly coiffed at the beginning of the day, sticks up in back where she has leaned against her chair, and her bangs are pressed greasy and flat against her forehead. I stop by the catering table whenever I am hungry; the caterers restock the snacks as soon as they are depleted: doughnuts and bowls of doughnut holes (doughnuts all day!), bagels and varieties of cream cheese, slices of carrots and celery and cucumber, cookies, sliced meats, every canned soda imaginable. I heard one of the caterers say that Katharine Ross drinks only Fresca. Picking at the treats all day, I have had no appetite, a phenomenon that is slightly unnerving. If I don't crave anything, then when I eat it, I experience no pleasure. What a waste; doughnuts all day, and I barely care, though that doesn't stop me from trying. My hands and anywhere else I have touched on my body—my cheek, the side of my neck, the crook of my elbow—are sticky from powdered sugar and jam filling. I am sweaty, my hair is mussed, my clothes are untucked. It's its own uniform. By dusk I feel as if I am one with every person here. These are my people. This is my tribe. I never want this to end.

An assistant director's walkie-talkie crackles and suddenly everything shifts. "Bring in Miss Ross."

This intimate, casual messiness that I have decided has bound me to everyone around me on this set dissolves in an instant. Everyone cranes their necks to see the arrival. Katharine Ross is petite and delicate, not much taller than I am, but even so, the very air changes with her approach. It crackles, and all the comfortable, sleepy bonding I had been feeling vanishes. She is being led over the cables, guided safely to the fragment of real-world living room that has been set up, surrounded by cameras and lights and crew. Her double, small like she is, long straight hair, but without the crackle and the command, steps out of the circle, melting instantly in with us, the silent watchers, as Katharine Ross steps in to the lit-up space. All eyes are on her.

Bryan Forbes smiles, says something funny, nice, and encouraging. Katharine Ross brushes a strand of hair away from her face and smiles an *I'm ready* smile in return.

This is the reason we are here. The reward for all the long, dull sameness, the stretched-out hours: the shot, made possible only by the charisma of the *talent*, their own species of human. I feel important here; everyone knows my name. Greg and I take turns sitting in Katharine Ross's and Paula Prentiss's chairs, and Bryan Forbes's director's chair. These chairs are not the ornate furniture my mother has collected and displays in our museum-like rooms at home; they are only made of canvas and wood, but these seem more valuable. We will bring these chairs home; they will sit in our garage for years. Fall apart, decay. But the fact that we have them is proof that I am part of an elite world.

The actors are more important than my father, even. The entire set revolves around them. My father even comes alive around them.

Whose autographs do you have? my classmates ask. They are shocked when I say no one's. I don't explain that I have taken a stand in my mind that all people are the same. I don't say that to ask for an autograph is to acknowledge these people are somehow better than me, better than the electricians who light their shots or the janitor who will sweep up the dust and debris we leave behind when the shot is made and a wrap is called. I don't say if we are all the same, then I don't have to feel sorry for the janitor or feel despair for myself, that I may never shimmer and shine the way I want to, like these movie stars around me.

We are back from my grandfather's funeral in Illinois. My grandmother died two years before. My mother had put my grandfather on her diet of supplements and yeast milk to get ready for the gallbladder surgery he had needed but that his blood pressure was too high to have. After six months of following her diet, the doctors gave him the go-ahead and he was told that "he was healing like a twenty-five-year-old" after the surgery. But good health or no, he still sat in a chair and cried when he thought no one was looking. He missed my grandmother.

"He died of a broken heart," my cousin Chipper says at the funeral.

Now we are in the Plandome kitchen, just back from the airport, and my father is raging about the mess on the countertops. On the flight home, my mother talked about the fact that my grandparents' farm would need to be sold and the idea of that, plus my father's yelling, suddenly seems too much for me to bear.

I pick up a kitchen knife.

"Stop," I say to my father.

I take the knife and slowly, while he's looking at me, slice the palm of my hand. Blood spurts.

"Christine!" he roars, and lunges at me. I drop the knife and run, heading out of the house and down the street. It's night and the headlights from passing cars periodically light me up, so I duck into a neighbor's hedge. My palm is bleeding, but the cut isn't deep. I plan to stay there all night, but he comes looking for me, driving slowly down the street, his head out the open window, calling my name, not angrily, but worried, desperate. I want him to leave me alone, but I don't want anything else bad to happen.

I stand up, walk toward him. He opens the car door and lets me in.

"I'm not proud of myself, Christine," he says.

The next Sunday, I find an advertisement for the Dalton School in the back of the *New York Times*. I would be joining a freshman class of seventy-eight students. I see from the ad that the school places an emphasis on the performing and also creative arts, writing and drawing, which thrills me. I love to draw and I have been keeping a journal since I was nine. I beg to go and my parents let me apply. Miraculously, I am accepted.

In his office, the principal says, "You will be always on the outside because you live so far away."

I don't say, *I will be even more on the outside if I don't go at all.*

For the first month I hide in the library on the tenth floor and read all of *Tom Sawyer* during lunch periods so I don't have to sit alone in the cafeteria. I feel kindred with Tom, who has to guide his raft, has to know when to go with the flow of the current, when to fight it to stay afloat. Like Columbia Grammar, most of my classmates have been together since preschool. But this is different. I feel possibility. This mini universe, with its definable ten floors, sitting in the midst of New York, a world within a world, offers a context that grounds me. I am shy. I haven't regained my fifth-grade cockiness, but there are girls around me I want to be friends with. I pick up the little cues—a subtle comment about this one's lack, that one's inability to see beyond her own preconceived notions—that their best friends aren't already set. By the time spring comes, I have loosened up and I am having regular weekend sleepovers with Libby and Patty and Sasha and Jenny. We go for pizza, ride the bus to their various apartments, go to movies, move with freedom and ease around the city. I like this independence. I like getting around without needing my mother to drive me. I like beginning to feel I know my way.

Sometimes I take a taxi after school to Stars Deli a block away from my father's office on Park Avenue. I order bagel and lox, take the bag up the elevator, and eat my sandwich on the couch beside his desk. I love visiting him in the office. I study the movie posters on the walls, listen to him on the phone talking to directors and actors. His voice raises, but whatever emotion he's feeling has nothing to do with me, just the way I like it. When the day is done, we walk to Grand Central Station and catch the Long Island Railroad back to Plandome.

Chapter 8

"Where are we going?" Braddy asks hopefully.

We are in Point Lookout for the summer. It's our second week there, and my mother is loading us into the Volkswagen. I wonder if Braddy's thinking about the kiddie-size amusement park in the next town, with its two-foot-high roller coaster, spinning teacups, and airplane ride where the planes actually lift off when you pull up on the throttle. Once I had seen a boy, his head lolling, his eyes half closed, vomiting silently as his plane went around and around. The possibility of motion sickness notwithstanding, not a day passes when my brothers don't beg to go.

"We're picking up our Programs," my mother says in a tone that makes a Program sound as good as, if not better than, an airplane ride. We would come to be suspicious of this bright enthusiasm, but not yet. Since she collapsed in the hallway two years ago, and graduated from eating raw liver, she has been having her broiled lamb chop and broiled tomato meal with a tall glass of yeast milk, three times a day. Nothing else.

We pull up to a white house with a striped green-and-white porch awning. Several folding chairs have been set up in the living room beside a flowered couch. I try not to stare at the man seated in one of the chairs. His suit hangs loosely on a tall, skeleton-thin body. The skin peeking out at the ends of his sleeves, up his neck, is raw and red as if freshly scrubbed with sandpaper.

"Severe rosacea," my mother explains after the man has been called into the next room by Celeste, a square-jawed woman in a yellow-and-red dress. "Dr. Cursio will help him."

The dark-haired woman with the bent head and raincoat has MS.

"A Program will cure her, too," my mother whispers to us, as if these illnesses are mistakes these people have made because they don't drink yeast milk.

It's our turn to follow Celeste into the next room. A barrel-chested white-haired man sits behind a large wooden desk. Later my mother will tell us Dr. Cursio had been a professional wrestler. She will also share that because he had cured members of the Mafia of various maladies, Mafioso now stood on the street corners of the various client homes he used to see patients, keeping watch. "It's against the law to practice medicine without a license," my mother explained. Though Dr. Cursio was treating with food, he had been put in jail several times.

Now his shirtsleeves are rolled to his elbows, and he grasps a gold fountain pen between a grizzled index finger and thumb. Up close he has the thickest nose hairs I have ever seen. With a nod in my mother's direction he puts down his pen, lifts my hand, and presses his thumb to the pulse at my wrist. I can hear the air whistling through his nose hairs as he breathes. His eyes, slightly glazed, look down at the desk. Finally he lets go, picks up his pad, and rips off a fresh sheet.

His cursive is feminine, the letters even and tall, with a slight lean: celery juice, blended salad, and two egg yolks. Celery juice, blended salad, and almonds. Celery juice, blended salad, steamed vegetables, and rice. Breakfast, lunch, dinner. A Program, it turns out, is a prescription for a daily diet. But is he kidding? Where is the *food* food?

After I am done, Dr. Cursio silently feels my brothers' wrists, one by one, then silently rips off a sheet of paper and silently scribbles a month's worth of nuts, seeds, and egg yolks.

"Isn't he a genius?" my mother says on our way out the front door.

In the car ride home I examine my Program more closely. The celery juice and blended salad begin each line as the first portion of every meal of the day. On Tuesday Dr. Cursio has filled "almonds" in the lunch blank. On Wednesday, cashews. On Thursday, filberts. On Friday, two ounces of unsalted, raw-milk cheese. On Saturday, almonds again. And so on, week after week for one month. I feel a sudden hope.

"What happens when we finish this Program?" I ask.

"We go back and get another one," my mother says. "What protein do you get for tomorrow?" she asks in an *Isn't this exciting?* tone.

"I get cheese," Jay says as if raw, unsalted cheese has suddenly become a delicacy.

"I get almonds," said Greg.

"Dr. Cursio says if you're still hungry after dinner, you can have two egg yolks."

For the first few days my mother watches us closely for a headache accompanied by a white coating on the tongue, indicators that our bodies have begun cleansing. When we cut our finger, she points out, our bodies will heal the cut. Similarly, the entire body will regenerate its own tissue if given the chance. Blending makes food easier to digest. This is the power behind the Program. It re-creates a state of fasting while feeding us at the same time.

It takes a week, but finally, falling into line one after the other, my brothers and I, when checked, all produce eerily greenish-white tongues.

Apparently we are under way.

———

Our tiny beach house kitchen is filled with crates stuffed to the brim with vegetables, all the vegetables that don't fit in the fridge that is already stuffed. One crate holds stacked celery heads, freshly picked and still smeared with dirt; one holds loose lemons; another, tightly packed heads of romaine. None of this was here yesterday. My mother, still in her nightgown, her hair held loosely back in a clip, is standing in the midst of all the produce with one hand on a gleaming silver machine: her new Acme juicer, which comes with a lifetime warranty. It's only 8:00 A.M., but she is already making juice, and the hum that comes from the machine fills the room, as does the smell of celery, tomato, and cucumbers. There are two boxes of as yet unpacked additional Acme juicers by the cucumbers. Clearly she has come to this day prepared.

"Sit down and I'll bring you your celery juice." She says *celery juice* firmly. She's trying to sell me on it, but she's also not offering another option.

I sit. The juicer screams as she feeds the celery stalks through the square opening at the top, one by one, then pushes them down with the bright red plastic depressor onto the blade deep in the body of the appliance. Then: what sounds like disaster. The juicer rattles with an unbearable loudness, like it's coming apart at very high speeds. It jumps and bumps across the Formica. My mother catches it, leans onto it harder, flips the switch off, leans hard until it calms. This, I later learn, is what happens when a chunk of vegetable misses the blade and in the spin of centrifugal force throws the entire machine off-balance. As the juicer loses speed and calms, my mother twists off the wide, heavy top and slows the spinning carriage with her open hand, the sound of metal on metal, her gold wedding band sliding on stainless steel. Once the juicer is still, she walks over and sets down a glass of vegetable juice on my place mat. It's light green and frothy. A pink dollop of tomato juice bobs on top of the green.

"Drink it slowly," she says. "Digest it in your mouth first."

I take a sip. The juice is watery and foamy at the same time. It seems like a mistake, like the foam and water should have somehow blended into a pleasant consistency. I mix them with my spoon, but all I get is water mixed with foam. The foam is already beginning to turn brown, and as the juice settles, the thicker greener liquid is separating from the thinner yellowy liquid. I take another sip. The tomato is sweet; the celery has a banjo-twang hit of aftertaste just as it does when eaten. I have an idea.

"Can't I just *eat* the celery?" I ask.

"Juicing removes the pulp, so your body gets the nourishment without having to do the work of digesting." My mother scoops the pulp from the stopped carriage with her hand and holds out the mash for me to see, a light green snowball. "The genius of the Program is that you are fasting while you are being fed."

She drops the pulp into her plastic compost container for the garden. Finished scooping, she clicks the metal top back into place and turns the machine on again so she can make my brothers' juices. According to Dr. Cursio, each juice combination does something different in the body. Greg gets cucumber and tomato; Jay, celery and carrot; and Braddy, cucumber and celery. The hum again fills the house. Although it's early, the June day is already warm and all our windows and doors are wide open. Our house, like all the others in this square-mile town, sits very close to the wide, usually carless street. It's small and made of red brick, with only a narrow strip of lawn between it and our next-door neighbors, the Ragusas. Francesca, the Ragusas' only daughter, and I once punched holes in the bottom of two paper cups and knotted a string through each hole, then strung the "phone" between our two bedroom windows. We were surprised to find the vibrations of our voices carried along the string and we were able to talk without our brothers overhearing.

I wonder what Francesca and her family are thinking this morning about all this racket.

My mother is cutting vegetables and placing them in the blender. Yesterday she showed me the ingredients for a blended salad. One peeled lemon, one tomato, one quarter of a bell pepper, half a cucumber—no skin, and three leaves of romaine. A stalk of celery is used to push everything down as it blends. She turns on the blender; both blender and juicer are now going at the same time. I glance outside, but there is no one on the street. I have the same feeling I have when my father yells, that we are a loud family. How far is the sound of all this machinery carrying?

My sleep-tousled brothers wander in one by one and take their seats at the table. My mother sets a glass of juice on the place mat in front of each of them, then sets a bowl of blended salad with a spoon beside each of our juices. Braddy reaches for the spoon and scoops a spoonful into his mouth—the blended salad is a reddish-brownish-greenish liquid flecked with dark particles of lettuce tip and pink granules of tomato.

"Drink your juice first, Bradford," my mother says as if she has known these rules all along instead of having just learned them last week when we picked up our Programs. "Dr. Cursio says we have to follow the Program *in order* because our bodies will digest the juices first, the blended salads next, and our protein last. We always start with the easiest food to digest."

I'm taking too long to drink my juice. The brown foam floats in the warm celery juice at the bottom of my glass. I'm noticing that celery juice at room temperature is even less pleasant than it is freshly made from cool-from-the-fridge celery.

"Finish that last sip," my mother says.

I down the last warm bit and shudder.

"Now drink your blended salad before it oxidizes," my mother says.

I lift the spoon. The blended salad, too, is already starting to warm. I scoop a spoonful. It sits coagulating, wiggling like Jell-O, a convex skin across the top holding it all together, on the spoon.

I spoon some into my mouth, hold it in the middle of my tongue, swallow. Like the juice, the blended salad consists of two distinctly separate parts—solid and liquid. Also like the juice, I wish these two parts worked more in tandem. The longer the blended salad sits, the more it separates. This leaves me with no option but to get it down as quickly as possible.

"Digest it in your mouth first," my mother calls again from the sink.

I swallow another spoonful. The bowl still looks so full. I've barely made a dent. In each spoonful, I taste all the ingredients at once: tomato, lemon, cucumber, pepper, lettuce. Spoonful by spoonful, I finish it. Now my mother brings me two eggs, their smooth brown shells hot and steaming, in a small cup.

"Like this." She shows me how to tap a spoon along the top third of the egg and take off the head. Inside, the white is jiggly and not all the way cooked. The deep yellow yolk sits wriggling in the midst of the jellied whites. She reaches in with the spoon and comes out with a scoop of runny yolk.

"Can't we cook it more? Can't I eat the whole egg?" I ask.

"Egg whites take B vitamins from our bodies," my mother says. "The yolk is very strengthening. It has lecithin, which our bodies need. Dr. Cursio says if we cook it too much, it loses enzymes."

She spoons first one egg yolk into my mouth, then the other. At least the yolks are hot, but other than the temperature, everything else—the texture, the taste—is no different than what it must be like to consume a raw egg. I swallow.

I have finished my first Program meal. My mother clears my plates. Her cheeks are flushed; I wonder if she's feeling triumph. I try not to think about the fact that I will be drinking another glass of celery-tomato juice and eating another bowl of blended salad in only a few hours for lunch and then again a few hours after that for dinner, day after day, week after week, stretching into eternity, with no end in sight.

Out the living room window, I see Francesca go by on her bike. She is riding down the street to the dead end and back, her usual sign to me that she is available.

"Can I go out and play?" I ask.

"Yes, but take it easy for an hour or so. Let your food digest," my mother says.

Except for the two summers before this one, my family has spent every June, July, and August since I was three in Point Lookout. Now Francesca and I are fourteen. When she called on me the day we arrived, a week ago, I noticed that her breasts now tilted up perfectly under her striped cotton tank top. Her legs, extending from bright green shorts, were cleanly shaved and curvaceous. Though my body is changing and my thighs are fuller than they used to be, my hips are narrow and my breasts are barely noticeable in a T-shirt. I still look like a boy. I'm allowed no makeup and my hair, parted in the middle, falls messily.

At lunch I once again face down my glass of celery-tomato juice and my bowl of blended salad. My *protein* is a banana, which doesn't even remotely feel like a real lunch. By the time my father gets home for dinner, we've already had our third juice and salad along with the plate of steamed vegetables and brown rice that constitutes dinner. It has been slow going for all of us today, slogging through the Program. My brothers and I have devoted much more time sitting at the table than we are used to, just trying to get everything down. Already I feel like I've been eating this way for more than just one day.

My father sits down on the couch in front of the television—the Mets game is on. My mother brings him his juice and salad. My brothers and I settle in various chairs around the room, pretending not to watch.

"What's this?" he says.

"Cucumber-tomato juice," my mother says extra-casually. If

the Program doesn't help my father's raging, she's out of ideas. "I can make you celery-carrot if you prefer."

My father takes a sip. He holds the glass out to my mother. "Celery-carrot."

She returns to the kitchen and we hear the loud hum of the juicer. She returns quickly with another juice. He drinks it like it's a glass of water.

"Digest it in your mouth first." My mother sets his blended salad bowl in his lap on a towel. The baseball announcer's smooth, practiced voice jabs, soothes, rises to a crescendo, then buzzes steadily behind the crack of a bat, the roar of the crowd, my father's guttural howl reaction to a missed play. My father looks down at the blended salad and dips his spoon in, asking no questions. Greg, Jay, Braddy, and I exchange glances. He eats that spoonful, then another. We look at one another again and titter. When our father is oblivious like this, we can find him amusing. He eats a fourth spoonful, his eyes glued to the game, then continues until the blended salad is gone. He sets the bowl on the couch beside him.

"What else is for dinner?" he asks, and I realize he is treating the blended salad like an appetizer, completely missing the point. My mother now sets a plate of steamed broccoli, steamed slices of zucchini, green peppers, and several scoops of brown rice on the towel in his lap. He eats this, too, without comment. My brothers disperse. I have to admit this is anticlimactic. So far, he's treating this food like it's *food*.

By the second morning, I'm hungry. After my breakfast egg yolks, I want to know what else I can have.

"I'll cut you a nectarine, or you can have another egg yolk," my mother says.

I eat both but neither help. I want something to fill the gnawing emptiness this steady parade of fruits and vegetables seems to be exacerbating. With all these cold, thin foods on one side of the seesaw, I've begun to crave dense, warm, heavy food to balance it out. But the Program doesn't permit anything on that other side.

"Go outside and play," my mother says, shooing me toward the door like I'm being silly. "It'll be lunchtime soon."

Lunch is essentially the same thing as breakfast: celery juice, blended salad, four ounces of fruit, and two ounces of almonds— the two ounces of almonds being about eleven almonds, my only hope for satiation—feel more like a tease than a meal and only make me hungrier.

"Distract yourself." My mother sounds impatient. "Americans are used to using food as entertainment. Food shouldn't be entertainment; it's nourishment."

The only good part of this diet is that my thighs, which somehow ballooned out from under me during this past school year, are being whittled away. Every morning when I check, looking at myself in the mirror over my parents' dresser, I'm thinner.

On the beach, three days into the diet, I see Greg eating a Good Humor ice cream cone. He's with Mateo, Francesca's brother. I am surprised at the hot shock I feel, the pang of sadness for my mother. She's in the kitchen all day now, making our salads and juices.

"Where did you get the quarter?" I ask.

"Mrs. Ragusa," Greg says. His face is white; he looks guilt-stricken at being caught.

I turn away, leave him be. There's nothing to say. It will always be like this in the rare moments we see each other cheat. We know the searing guilt, the shame, the sense of having committed an indiscretion—it weighs heavily on our consciences. Already, in this short time, keeping us on the Program has become our mother's life. She is in the kitchen from sunup to sundown. Our father is away all day and the implications of these salads and juices she brings him at night haven't yet hit home. But we know, as the receptacles of all her blending and juicing and measuring and washing, what our adherence means to her.

"So what does the diet do?" Francesca and I are walking along the boardwalk, heading for the beach. I'm one week in. I'm almost used to the constant hunger, to the passionate longing I now feel for all the foods, pretty much everything, that are now forbidden to me.

"Um, you know. It takes toxins out of your body," I say. I realize that as much as I don't want word to get around about our weird diet, I don't mind if Francesca knows.

"Toxins?"

"Yeah. Chemicals, preservatives." I feel a little smug. Maybe I know more than I think. "They get stored in our tissues." As hungry as I am, the things my mother tells me about cleansing, the point of the Program, make sense. This is another reason we don't cheat. She has been drilling the idea of toxins into us on such a steady basis that we have become terrified of eating off the diet.

Francesca nods, takes that in. Suddenly she grabs my arm.

"Oh my God. Gilly Calaghan and Pat O'Keefe. Coming. This. Way."

Ahead, two clean-cut boys riding Stingrays along the boardwalk come toward us.

"They're part of the Beech Street Gang," Francesca says hurriedly. I clearly have a lot to catch up on. "Their parents created the gang. Now all the kids hanging out are second-generation Beech Streeters. Gilly and Pat are the leaders."

I feel a pang. Francesca has, by virtue of her proximity, always belonged to me. Our domains were the beach, our families, and each other. Now my awareness shifts to accommodate this wider social sphere. Truthfully, I wasn't really looking to branch out, but if she has made other friends in the two summers I haven't been here, I don't want to be left behind, either. Even before my missed summers, I had accepted the fact that Francesca was in the Point Lookout *know*. Her grandmother lives a few blocks over, all year round. Her grandmother and mother sit with the other town women in beach chairs all day long at the shoreline. My mother has always kept her distance from the rest of the town.

"I don't like other women," she has told me.

This puts me at a disadvantage.

"Gilly's going to Colgate next year." Francesca indicates the boy on the left now. "And Pat's going to Fordham."

The bikes are almost upon us.

"Act natural!" Francesca whispers fiercely. She glances around, taking in the ocean, the light blue sky above us, looking every-where but at the approaching bikers. I do the same. But as the boys reach us, I can't help but focus on Gilly. I notice his Popeye-prominent chin and light, ice-water eyes. He nods to us, his bangs falling over his face, then he flips his head and tosses his hair up and out of the way. For an instant his eyes are beams of blue, then he ducks his head again. I feel stunned by this partic-ular combination of chin and eyes, of knobby elbows and the tilt of head. Then elated. In a matter of seconds I have been released from all ties to the earth. I'm floating above my life, no longer living it.

"Hi, girls," Pat says with a broad, friendly grin.

And they are past us.

Francesca grabs my arm. "Pat O'Keefe said hello to us. He said *hello*. Do you know what that means?"

Still dazed, I shake my head.

"He knows we're alive. He knows we exist. Maybe now we can work our way into the Beech Street Gang!"

Even in my new euphoria, this feels unlikely, but I don't want to squelch Francesca's ambitions. If she thinks we are up to the task of joining Gilly and Pat's social circle, I'll go along for the ride.

It's the first Saturday since we've started the program, and my father is on the phone with Brown's, the repair shop on the other side of town. Last weekend, the Whaler's motor died while the boat was floating in the inlet, and by the sound of things—my father is asking the person at the repair shop when they think it will be ready—it hasn't been fixed yet. He has already gathered his rod and bait to walk along the beach and fish from the shore; the rod leans against the picture window, but this isn't the same as heading out into the ocean, motoring about at will. There's a cloud around him when he hangs up and walks to the kitchen, where my mother is cutting and chopping among her crates and boxes.

"Do we have to have all these boxes in the house, Carol?" His voice has an edge and, even at this early stage of annoyance, is already high-pitched and loud.

"I'll move them outside, Edgar." Her words are clipped, the sentence delivered in a nasal monotone. Even I can hear the wall that just went up.

My father's voice tightens and raises another notch. "Is it too much to ask on the weekends to have a little order, a little quiet?"

I detect a plea. He wants the boxes out, but he also, and maybe he doesn't even realize this, wants her to let him back in.

"No, Edgar, it's not too much to ask." More icy monotone.

I get up from the table, where I was waiting for my celery-tomato juice, and head down the short hall to my bedroom. I grab my journal from my bedside table, wishing it could swallow me up, and lie down with it on my bedspread. Opening the page to my last journal entry, I read: *I saw Gilly Callaghan walking his Schnauzer, Freddie, down Beech Street just now. I never see him off the beach. It's a sign!*

"How are we supposed to live like this? How many heads of celery do we need?"

I look out the window. Francesca's mother stands up from the plastic lounge chair on their porch and goes inside the house.

"How many boxes of tomatoes does one family need?"

A lot, I think, if they're going through them like we are. He doesn't see how many trips she makes to the health food store, returning with our Volkswagen bus overflowing with vegetables.

"How many boxes, Carol?"

Now the kitchen screen door slams against the side of the house. Someone has pushed it forcefully.

"I'll move them outside so you don't have to see them." Her voice sounds strained. I hear the sound of a crate being dragged across the linoleum.

"Leave them!" my father roars. "Leave the goddamn boxes."

He is battling an invisible monster that he senses but doesn't understand, the silent pressure that has begun, the tourniquet squeezing all of us.

Another crate dragging across the floor, and the screen door slams again. She must be moving them into the garage. He follows her outside.

"Goddamn it, Carol. Leave. The. Boxes."

I imagine that her back is to him. Maybe she has stopped moving crates. A long period of silence follows; I can't hear either of them now. Then the bang of the screen, and someone is in the kitchen again. The juicer starts up. It's my mother.

I tiptoe up the hall. My father is outside by the garage, one hand on the brick wall for support, his poles leaning beside him, tugging on his white Keds, stained rusty with splotches of fish blood. My mother finishes pushing a stalk of celery into the juicer, snaps off the machine, and pours juice into a glass, then walks with it outside. Through the window I see her hand the glass to my father, who has finished putting on his shoes. He takes it, tilts his head back, drinks the whole glass in one gulp.

Francesca and I run an errand for her mother, maneuvering our bike tires in and out of the sun-softened black tar cracks that marble the light cement of the wide block on our way to the deli at the other end of town. On the corner, we kick out our kickstands and leave bikes in front of the small shop with the large window overlooking Mineola Avenue, file in, and hop up onto the stools at the counter to wait as the man behind the counter finishes wrapping the order Francesca's mother has just phoned in. As he wraps the coleslaw, the freshly sliced roast beef, and the thick slugs of pickles neatly and tightly in shiny white paper, chats pleasantly about his sons, who are electricians on Fire Island, and asks after Francesca's family, I can smell every ingredient: the mayonnaise in the slaw, the sharp dill in the pickles, the spice of pepper in the meats. It's also hard not to notice the fact that when someone eats what everyone else eats, they are part of a web of connections: *How is your mother? Let me tell you about my sons.* Dr. Cursio never says a word when he's feeling our pulse or writing up a Program. No one who is normal is eating the way we are eating. We are alone, which is probably the way my mother likes it.

Afterward, unpacking the groceries in Francesca's kitchen, I feel like I am walking through a minefield of all the treats that are always there: the box of cinnamon crumb cake on the counter, the powdered doughnuts on the kitchen table. Two weeks into the Program, Francesca asks if I want a Ho Ho. Before I have time to think, I take it, bite in. The hard shell breaks off, separating in my mouth from the spongy cake, and the white marshmallow creme—for a moment so thick and sweet on my tongue—slides down the back of my throat. As soon as I finish licking the chocolaty smear off my teeth and my mouth is my mouth again, I realize what I have done: erased my hard work and all the purity I had accomplished.

Back in my own kitchen, my mother has lunch laid out on the table. Celery juice, blended salad, three ounces of filberts, an apple. She is cleaning the juicer, bent over the sink, scrubbing hard at the carriage with a steel pad.

"Your lunch is there, sweetheart." She stops scrubbing for a moment, turns her head, and smiles at me.

I sit down, begin sipping my celery juice like a hypocrite. It's one thing to enjoy the Ho Ho in Francesca's kitchen. It's another thing entirely to come back to my own house and face my mother's cheerful trust in me. Should I tell her? If I promise to myself never to cheat again, can I absolve myself of this transgression? If I'm perfect for two weeks, I'll be back to where I was five minutes ago and I will earn the approval I'm feeling from my mother. I can do that. I try not to think about the fact that I will always be two weeks behind and the fact that five minutes ago suddenly seems like a lost utopia.

On the first really hot afternoon of summer, three weeks into the Program, Francesca's father barbecues. We are eating outside in our yard around the redwood table with the umbrella. Our blended salads taste warm, slightly soured in the heat as greasy, fat-laden clouds of T-bone waft over the fence, settling around our outdoor table. I imagine the slab of steak on the grill; the browned, crisp outline of fat; the charcoal-darkened flesh casing the warm, wriggling, if-you-pressed-on-it-it-would-spring-back-and-release-sweet-and-salty-juices middle. After dinner I confess to my mother that I crave steak.

"Animals that eat meat have very short intestines," she says. We are in the kitchen. She is standing at the sink, cleaning the juicer. "Animal protein moves through them quickly. People's intestines are longer. Meat putrefies while it sits, then our bodies absorb that rot." She says *rot* like it's a word she hopes she never has to utter again. She isn't looking at me. I feel like the word. I feel like my confession has brought this unwanted horror into our kitchen. I wonder if she thinks less of me now.

"You won't want it anymore," she adds, "when your body is pure."

———

When it storms, the first rain of the summer, the sky and ocean outside our beach house's picture window touch at the horizon, opposing forces facing each other in a chalky opaque-green matchup. The vast, smooth surface of the sea erupts into spikes, small choppy waves that crest into foaming slices at their tips as if they are splitting at the seams from the mounting tension. When the rain finally comes, drenching Point Lookout's sunbaked streets, the smell of hot, wet stone rises with the steam from the concrete, and puddles grow to small warm lakes on the street. My brothers and I put on our bathing suits and run through this curtain of warm rain, each drop as big as a grape, arms outstretched, palms turned up flat to feel the hot, thick raindrops.

Our beach house dining room table is set for dinner. Blended salads and spoons, cups of freshly made celery and cucumber and carrot juice wait at our places on top of the paper tablecloth. Although we aren't supposed to drink anything with our meals except celery and cucumber juice—because drinking dilutes the digestive juices and juice must be sipped so it is digested in the mouth before swallowed—someone has set a clear plastic pitcher filled with lemon water on the center of the table.

In the kitchen, my father stands at the open refrigerator. For a moment I cling to the evidence of his frailty: the straggly prematurely gray hairs at the V of his thin, worn Hanes undershirt; the coffee-colored stains, fish blood, on his favorite blue shorts; his too-skinny calves rubbed hairless by a lifelong preference for tight calf-length work socks. He's pulling cellophane bags of vegetables from the fridge, piling them onto the counter, my mother's weekly supply of approximately forty-two cucumbers, fifty lemons, forty tomatoes, twenty-one peppers, ten heads of romaine, twenty-five thick green heads of celery (though most of the celery sits in a cardboard box under the sink): enough for three blended salads a day for six people for seven days. It *is* remarkable how much she can fit in one refrigerator.

"Who lives like this? Someone, explain this to me." His voice is

tight, whiny, and high-pitched. He throws three bags of tomatoes on top of the rows of celery, bags of lettuce, peppers. *"How. Did. We. Come. To. This?"*

He moves to the cupboard. *"Vitamin C. Vitamin C. Vitamin C, rose hips. Vitamin C, acerola chewable."*

He pulls the jars out, one by one, all shapes and sizes, pushes them like shuffleboard pucks—little round men gathering shoulder to shoulder in brown suits along the counter. My mother never buys just one of anything. *"How many vitamin jars does one family need?"*

My father has a Program, too. On weekdays my mother packs jars of blended salad and juice in a small lunchbox-size Igloo and he carries it on the Long Island Railway to work. On weekends she pats his head, brings him his blended salad three times a day on a tray, sets it in his lap, then gives him a kiss on the cheek. It's been two weeks. Up to now he's accepted these ministrations. Maybe he hasn't been paying attention or maybe he liked the extra affection; maybe he didn't think she was really serious. Clearly the reality of our new lives is beginning to set in.

From the couch, I scan our small living room: worn couch, TV, the short hall past the arch into the kitchen that leads to my bedroom. Have I left any of my stuff, his target for these rampages—shoes, shorts, wet bathing suits—lying around? I am frozen in our usual dilemma: to run over and gather my things, thereby making myself a target, or stay put and risk the consequences for leaving my belongings lying around. When he goes off like this, my brothers and I look at one another wordlessly, waiting for one of our parents to finally say it: *divorce.*

"Meanness is a sign of a sick liver," my mother says now after every tirade. This diet regimen that will eventually tear apart her marriage is also the one thing she clings to to save it.

Now my brothers are on reconnaissance, each making quick dashes from the couch to various parts of the room. Jay grabs his baseball helmet; Braddy his catcher's mitt; Greg picks up a wet beach towel left beside the television. My father is still pulling out bottles.

"*Vitamin B, Vitamin B6, Vitamin B12. Is it too much to ask for a little sanity?*"

At the table, my mother is sprinkling brewer's yeast on her blended salad. Pieces of soft hair loose from her favorite banana clip fall around her pretty, little-girl-shaped face. She reaches up to tuck them back, but they fall loose again. I silently beg her to answer him, but I can see in the brace of her shoulders, in her jerky movements as she dips her spoon into the bag of yellow flakes, sprinkles determinedly, then licks the spoon as if yeast flakes are better than ice cream, that she will not.

"*Am I crazy?*" His voice is at its highest pitch now. "*Goddamn it. Carol, am I crazy?*"

Sometimes she will say, *No, you're not crazy*, in a deadened voice. But tonight she only continues to lick her spoon.

I must really be cleansing. I feel queasy. My head is eggshell-fragile; I move it slowly to minimize the reverberating throb. I pull out my chair, sit down at the table, and face my glass of celery juice and its foamy bobbing dollop of tomato floating on top, the blended salad in the bowl beside it. It's one thing to eat something now and then. But three times a day, every day, meal after meal after meal, and it's a whole new world. The green, grassy smell alone is enough to nauseate me now.

Cleansing feels like sick. I am weak, headachy, perpetually queasy. During the day, out on the beach, my body catches a gear and moves out of this new state of sensitive fragility. Sitting here, facing the contents of this glass and bowl on my place mat, I feel the changes my body is going through, my organs of elimination hard at work: liver, skin, tongue, blood, urine, sweat, all eliminating the toxins. But I also have begun to notice a sweet pain on the razor's edge between hunger and satiation. It feels like love, this kind of hollow, like wanting, like floating. Since I have no choice any-way, I decide that I may as well see if my mother is right, if there is a brass ring that will be mine if I follow the Program exactly.

I sit down at the table and pick up my glass. The thin green aroma of celery, the sweet-sour pink tomato smell that wafts un-avoidably. I am not even allowed to chug.

"Drink it slowly," my mother says, reading my mind, standing at the sink. "Digest it in your mouth first."

I begin.

These are the new rules no one I know has ever heard of, much less has to follow: no salt, no pepper, no vinegar, no drinking water with a meal. Raw vegetables can be eaten by themselves, though my mother discourages eating anything that isn't part of the mea-sured, prescribed three-meal-a-day Program meal. Fruit should never be eaten by itself; we can only have it with blended salad. If we go to pick something up with the intent to ingest it, my mother will fly at us, flipping her hands and fingers up like she is shooing us and these intentions out of the room—"aaaaa, aaaaa, aaaaa"—causing us to spook and usually drop the offending ed-ible. In fact, nothing should be eaten by itself, except a stalk of celery or a slice of cucumber.

"Meat and potato culture," my mother says, spitting venom. "People are putting themselves into an early grave with food."

About the Program, she says, "It's threatening to people. They don't want to hear they have to change their diets. Most people are addicted to junk."

I crave roast beef, chocolate, black pepper. Sometimes I'm not even hungry; I just want salt. Actually, I want salt always.

I have a fever, something that is not unusual for me. My mother will later tell me she had been unable to breastfeed me and had given me canned formula as an infant. She will come to believe that my ear infections are a result of that early foundation of processed, dead food.

"A fever is merely your body's way of getting rid of toxins," my mother says now, when I ask for Aspergum, something that is handed out pretty regularly at school. "People panic, but a fever is a sign that your body is fighting; it's good. If you take aspirin, you are squelching the body's efforts; you are working against the body." I tell her I'm hungry and she says eating also works against the natural efforts my body is making now. "Your body is working very hard to rid itself of toxins. If you eat, you will divert it from these efforts. The old-timers knew this—*starve a cold*; they were on the right track. This is the perfect time to fast." She reminds me that our bodies, given the chance, will heal all maladies. "Digestion takes a lot of energy, so when we fast, we are freeing up that energy. The body will direct it toward healing."

Before the Program, in the Dakota, when I was little and had a fever, I found myself inexplicably craving a paper-thin slice of white cheese with a blue stripe down the middle I had once been given as a taste at the market down on Columbus Avenue. I was sick, and though she was periodically checking on me, my mother was busy in other parts of the apartment, taking care of my brothers. No one was going to go get me this cheese and absolve me of this craving, I knew that. The intense, feverish lusting for the sour, salty, pungent, moldy blue stripe was something I had to accept, like I had to accept the pinprick sensitivity of my skin; the raw, scratchy hot of my eyelids; the ache in my knees and hands. That afternoon, it made perfect sense to me that the wanting and the fever were interchangeable.

I'm sick and it's dinnertime, the hardest part of a water fast. Even the smell of my brothers' broccoli steaming downstairs stirs what feels like an ancient response. Forced to the outer reaches of the day's landscape with no nourishment, I feel cold, empty. I swallow gulps of water, lie back against my pillows, and cycle through more versions of hunger than I realized existed: food is warm comfort in this newly cruel, dinnerless world; food is food and I'm truly hungry; food is entertainment and I'm bored—eating passes the time and the day is three hours longer without it; I'm lonely, and my favorite foods feel like familiar friends. Food is also a tie to daily rhythm, to the normalcy of mealtimes, to the comfort and weight of the physical. By fasting, by eating the Program diet, I feel cast adrift from this comfort and normalcy.

My father has a cold and is supposed to be water fasting. But here he is, standing in the kitchen, crunching a stick of celery. The enormity of this transgression is lost on him; he chews carelessly, blithely. I feel shocked at this blatant disregard for the rules but also slightly superior. I am familiar with the stages of a fast. I know the importance of staying in bed so the body can use all its energy to cleanse. Eating in bits throughout the day, even if the snack is only celery, is *not* fasting. I understand suddenly that he will never feel the benefits that my brothers and I feel—against our wills, of course, but benefits just the same. Our mother's constant stream of strategically placed information is sinking in. I notice my beach friends sniffling for weeks. Three days in bed drinking water, and I don't think I'm imagining the renewal I experience. Though there is more to my allegiance. The enormity of maintenance required to keep this regime and our family going takes every bit of my mother's day. If she's not in the kitchen juicing and blending, unpacking groceries, or washing dishes, she's folding laundry, which sits in stacks that never seem to diminish. I try to help her, but I am free to do what she isn't—leave when I want to. So I listen about cleansing and toxins and B vitamins in the celery and what foods create mucus because what she is saying makes sense to me, but also because I am her ally in her mostly allyless world. But I can never quite shake the guilt I feel breezing outside and away from the groceries that need to be unpacked, the clutter that should be put away, from the suck of the dishes or the laundry. As the oldest child and only girl, her burden feels like mine.

My brothers play baseball at the end of the day. Two Little League fields sit at the end of town, where the Point Lookout pavement ends before the marshland begins. Gilly is on the pitcher's mound. I am on Greg's too-big-for-me bike. The ice cream truck sits in the dirt outside the backstop. I have a dollar in my pocket and gum isn't food. Gum is freedom and tart blue and red food dye. I bite into my gum, rip off a piece. Chew down. Guilt and pleasure. The release of sour-sweet artificial blueberry, banana, cherry, raspberry, lime, lemon, grape. The possibility of endless chemical flavor creations. The sun is warm but hazy. Blades of grass sprout thinly in the friendly, sandy white soil.

Gilly licks his fingers and adjusts his navy cap. I see what makes him, him. The inward slope of his thighs, the pronounced turn of his right foot. His face and chin, without the curtain of hair, are chiseled, older-looking than the other boys' faces under the other baseball caps. His blue eyes are so light, they seem to be the absence of matter, what would shine out if we weren't encased by flesh. Pure light. Beams of ice. Messages from an unsullied soul. And yet here he is in uniform like everyone else. I imagine him held down and forcefully clothed. His unwilling allegiance to something as ordinary as a baseball league.

Gilly throws a pitch. An easy toss, no windup.

"Steer-iiike!" The umpire brings down his arm, triumphant.

The July sky is white and pink with the beginning of twilight. The air, warm and cottony, smells of tomato plants and earth and dry summer grass. Crickets have begun to chirp. I feel as if all my pores are open, as if I am breathing with every part of my body, every inch of my skin.

I turn on the light in the bathroom and climb up onto the edge of the bathroom tub so I can see myself in the medicine cabinet mirror above the sink. I've lost my layer of winter fat because of the blended salads, from swimming in the ocean every day, walking everywhere. My stomach is flat, my thighs more streamlined. Though I'm hungry almost all the time, I'm not skeletal. The brown rice and steamed vegetables at night, the egg yolks, the unsalted raw-milk cheese, the almonds and walnuts have enough fat and calories to sustain us. Plus, I overeat the vegetables and rice at night, the one meal that isn't measured. It will take me decades to unlearn this compensatory eating, to learn the lesson that if I eat what I want, I don't have to overeat what I don't want.

I hop off the tub.

In my room, my toy-size clown night-light smells sweet, good enough to eat, some catnip-for-children ingredient mixed in with the rubber. I press my nose against the clown's belly, breathe.

I climb into bed. My sheets are cold. I push my bare feet down and lie still, waiting for my own heat to warm me.

The sun rises over the silver inlet behind our block; the first thin yellow rays, not yet warm, spill shafts into the spaces between houses. Across the sand, tractors trundle down to shore to begin the sunrise task of leveling the beach. The town's own background morning noise: the rhythm of a tractor motor climbing a dune, revving as it strains; the sound of release at a crest; the high hum as it dips into a trough, then gears up for another hill; the cry of seagulls; mourning doves on the telephone wires above the street, the wires that cross over our roof.

I steal, barefoot, to the inlet cove; scramble from jetty rock to jetty rock, toes and arch and heel, palms and fingers clinging to the rough, cold granite. Boulders the size of beach cabanas mix with the jagged remnants of old roads, yellow and white median lines still visible, bordering the last block of town.

I am in Giant Land, climbing among pebbles. I am the last survivor of a postapocalyptic world. I am an island girl deftly leaping the shoals in between the roll of foaming breakers.

I stop climbing.

Across the sand, two baseball fields away, I see a figure approaching with a small dog trotting at his heels. Even from this distance, I recognize the unmistakable tilt of his head, the slightly knock-kneed walk.

Oh my God.

Gilly?!

Coming this way.

I duck down, my hands pressed against the boulder in front of me, my nose brushing the stone. My heartbeats feel loud and warm in contrast with the cool stillness of the giant rocks around me.

After a moment, I peer over the boulders. He's closer. I can see his chin, the hang of his bangs, his blue T-shirt, the ravel of his jeans along the hem dragging in the sand.

If I run now, over the jetty rocks toward home, I will be seen fleeing. I consider appearing, only slightly less awkwardly, from the rocks as if I am on a stroll myself.

To walk together under this pink-and-yellow sky along the shining wet sand of the inlet shoreline?

What would we talk about?

Gilly: (peering through his bangs) Hey.

Me: Hi.

Gilly: (flashing his heartbreakingly crooked smile) How ya doin'?

Me: Fine. How are you?

Gilly: (smiling and nodding) Doin' good. Doin' good.

Silence.

What if that's all we have to say?

I can't do it.

I *have* to do it.

I duck lower. He is half a baseball field away. Then as far as second base is from home. They cut down to shore, dog and boy, strolling along the cool, slick, wet sand of the inlet shoreline.

I *want* to walk with him in the soft pink light of morning. Just him and me. The entire beach to ourselves. I'll even risk a bad conversation.

But he's turning around now. In a few steps, he's passed the boulders where I wait. A few steps more, he reaches the soft, dry sand. I watch him, the back of his head, his shoulders, his compact rear in his faded jeans, head off the way he came.

Just like that.

And this is what is suddenly clear: I will never talk to Gilly Callaghan. I will love him forever from afar. I am not up for anything more.

I am cold, crouched in shadow, pressed up against stone. He is far enough away. He hasn't looked back. I stand and head for home.

The town is packing. Awnings rolled up, windows locked, shades drawn. The all-year-round houses seem suddenly like lonely outposts, their tricycles, yellow plastic tractors, toy buckets, and shovels still strewn about in sandy driveways, as, all around, summer families stow away and sweep up, batten down the hatches of their dwellings to prepare for vacancy and the cold months ahead.

Though we've been living in it all summer, our house suddenly smells the way it did the day we arrived. Lemon Pledge and house paint: the smell of empty house. I wonder what's changed. My mother is loading peaches, cucumbers, bunches of celery, and bags of lemons from the refrigerator into her ice chests; our least-important clothes sit in suitcases in the narrow hall. But we're still *in* the house. We have two days left. I don't want to feel like this, like we are already gone.

Chapter 9

"You've enervated yourself; you need B vitamins, calcium, and magnesium." My mother hands me a glass of celery juice. "Celery juice feeds the nervous system."

Summer's over. I don't want to be here, back in our Plandome kitchen with its dark wood paneling and cold, dark brown, penny-tile floor, in our house of too many rooms with too many walls between me and the outside, surrounded by large, silent estates and endless, winding tree-lined streets. I want to be back walking the streets of tiny, knowable Point Lookout, with the sun overhead and the ocean over my shoulder, where anything can happen.

"Your nerves are shot. You overextended yourself this summer. You're feeling the effects." I can hear the scold in her tone, the message that I was reckless in my choice to unspool myself in the pure joy of summer, to let abandonment and feeling overtake the priority of feeding my nervous system.

I sip the celery juice. It's dark green. I'm guessing my mother chose these stalks purposely; the darker the green, the more minerals.

"Drink it slowly. Digest it in your mouth first." She hands me three calcium-magnesium tablets with another message: now it's time to reel myself back. I swallow the tablets, waiting for the feeling of loss to lift.

———

It's my sophomore year at Dalton and Greg is a freshman.

"Have you seen *The Exorcist?*" our classmates ask, when they see our blended salads.

In the recently released horror movie, blended salad–like vomit is sprayed on the walls. Though we hide in the hallway by our lockers to drink the blended salads—soured, despite the tinfoil my mother wraps them in, from their morning sitting in our lockers—and celery juice, it's impossible to avoid detection in the small school. Greg is easy in his body and funny; he and his best friend, Andrew Zimmern, who will go on to write and host a Travel Channel program called *Bizarre Foods*, draw small crowds in the hallway as they riff off each other in impromptu stand-up. But, despite having friends, I'm still feeling awkward and shy, and the stigma of our weird diet feels less easy for me to shake off.

I like classmate David Cremin, but when he passes a note in math asking if I want to go to a movie on Friday, I am flooded with the familiar hot embarrassment I felt at camp when counselor Randy visited me to say good night. I stuff the note inside my backpack and am first out the door when the bell rings. I avoid him at lunch and for the next few days until I feel sure he got the message. But what's the message? Can I like someone who likes me? Maybe, now that our lives are about deprivation, I only know how to want what I can't have.

"It's blond. Hardly noticeable," my mother says. I've asked her for a razor.

It's summer again. We are standing in our Point Lookout kitchen, looking at my lower legs, which are covered in hair that has seemed to appear overnight. I want her to be right, but as I look this way and that, the light hits an amount of hair that, blond or not, no other girl I know allows on her legs.

"It's noticeable enough," I say.

"It's lovely," my mother says. "Once you shave it, it will grow in dark." Her voice drops in warning: "You can never go back to blond."

This sounds dire; I don't want dark hair on my legs. I also don't want hair on my legs, period.

"Sexuality is our basest drive," my mother says. I've also mentioned I want to pluck my eyebrows. I will turn sixteen in July. "If you pluck them, the hairs just grow in thicker. Look at my eyebrows. Ruined. The girl at the end of the road sat me down in a chair and promised she'd make them beautiful." She shows me the long, wiry strands that came from that day, tells me about the girls growing up around her on other farms in Illinois. "They were bored. Girls who dress sexy and go looking for that kind of thing aren't using their minds."

The good news is that I put myself on an eight-day juice fast when we first got to Point Lookout, and it worked. I didn't mind being hungry. I fed off the high of knowing I'd see Gilly again. Each morning I woke up, walked upstairs to stand in front of my parents' mirror to find more and more of my winter chub seemingly rinsing away. My thighs are streamlined again.

"You can wax your legs," my mother says brightly. I have never heard of waxing. I'm certain no one I know has ever heard of it either. "Waxing pulls the hair up at the roots. It preserves the blond."

That afternoon in my bedroom, Francesca does a double take at my legs.

"I'm going to wax them," I say quickly.

"What's that?"

"It pulls the hair up at the roots so the hair grows back blond." I suddenly want waxing to sound like the cooler method of hair removal. "With shaving it grows back dark."

"Oh." Francesca sounds completely unconcerned that she has crossed an irrevocable line into battling dark hair growth.

The problem with waxing, I will find out, is the fact that in between appointments, in order for the waxing to work, I have to allow all my leg hair to grow back, which means for half the month, for a once-a-month appointment, I walk around with hairy legs. I don't get to fit in with what everyone else is doing, which somehow feels like exactly what my mother was after in the first place.

Francesca sets down the tape recorder and punches rewind. The tape slides in a high-pitched whine. She punches stop then start. Karen Carpenter's chocolaty silky voice begins crooning:

Why do birds suddenly appear
every time, you are ne-ee-ear?

We both chime in. We're making an audition tape of ourselves singing "Close to You" by the Carpenters and "This Guy's in Love with You" by Burt Bacharach to give to my father. It's Francesca's idea.

"Once he hears how good we are, he'll put us in movies."

I have the sense that if he were going to put us in a movie, he would have done so already, but I hold my fist like a microphone and pretend Gilly's standing right in front of me and I'm singing only to him.

I open the jar. Crouch down on the other side of the low brick wall that follows the sidewalk toward Point Lookout's beach then stops at the dead end. The late-morning July sun warms the brick. If I stand, I can see our beach house kitchen window, and through it, my mother at the sink. I crouch lower, then dip my finger into the oily marinade. This is the one thing I crave above all else. I have given in to it this morning, purchasing this jar at the deli on an errand with Francesca. One jar costs less than two dollars, so I don't feel guilty taking change from the basket on the table. Hot cherry peppers. I slide a pepper slice onto my tongue. And another. In my mouth, the papery skin peels from the soft flesh of the orange and green and red slices. Pepper by pepper, I eat slowly to the bottom then drink the juice, the pulpy, meaty, vinegary droplets inside the oily preserve. I turn the jar upside down and shake every last bit of salty liquid, then I wipe the glass inside clean with my finger.

It's the first week of July 1976. The Tall Ships have sailed to celebrate the bicentennial, and my father is upstairs on the phone.

In the small house we can hear everything. His voice is loud, high-pitched, urgent; almost, but not quite, the decibel he reaches when he rages. But today his focus is not on us. The air feels electric, as it always does for me around anything to do with his movies. From the couch in our living room I hear him say he knows exactly who to get to write a damn good script in two days. He'll write it himself if he has to. We're not entering this to produce *schlock*, his voice rings through the house.

He is racing against all other competing productions to make *Raid on Entebbe*, a made-for-television movie that dramatizes Israel's daring rescue of hostages held by Idi Amin Dada in Uganda, which happened last week. It's the first time one of his productions has this much urgency; there is no way to secure rights, so many companies are racing to be the first to produce a story of the saga.

Outside our upstairs picture window, I do a double take. Gilly is walking Freddie along the boardwalk just past our sand lot. He lives on the other side of town. I have never seen him over on this part of the beach. I watch him make his way down the path. After I lose sight of him behind the big sand dune, Braddy comes upstairs and flops down on the daybed tucked under the picture window, which takes up most of the wall.

"Gilly Callaghan gave me a message to give to you."

"What????"

"Gilly Callaghan gave me a message."

"How does he even know we're related?"

"I don't know. I didn't ask him."

"What did you say?"

"I didn't say anything."

"What did he say?"

"He said, 'Tell your sister to come out tonight.'"

Oh. My. God.

"Are you sure?"

"Yes, I'm sure."

"What else did he say?"

"Nothing."

"Did he say where he'd be?"

"No."

"What else did you say?"

"I told you. I didn't say anything."

He stands. He's had enough of my grilling, especially when he's doing me a favor. He sidesteps around me and jumps onto the first linoleum step leading downstairs. *Thump.* Then he jumps to the next. And the next. *Thump. Thump. Thump. Thump.* When he hits the first floor, he runs off.

Outside the window, the beach and boardwalk are deserted. *Tell your sister to come out tonight.* Why would he take the time to pass that message to my brother? Why would he walk Freddie on our side of town, so obviously out of his way? There can be only one explanation. He likes me. Gilly Callaghan likes me.

"He didn't say where he'd meet you?" I have run next door to tell Francesca what just happened. Francesca, bless her heart, is making it sound like a date. "How are we supposed to find him?" *We.* We're in this together. I am not alone.

————

I have been allowed out after dinner. My curfew is 9:30 P.M. Francesca and I cross the sand, our well-worn walk in the daytime, but after dark the gate to the beach is otherworldly, the bathrooms locked, the rows of shining bike racks empty. The night air, wet and thick and lit dark yellow from the streetlamp above our heads, presses down. My hair is curling, starting to drip moisture at the tips. My sneakers crunch, sand on cement. I can make out figures on bikes by the wall. I look for the tilt of a head, the stooped shoulders, the slight knock-knees.

For an instant, anything is possible.

But these are younger boys. Their voices, in conversation, jab out into the soupy cadmium night, then retreat. Then they regrip their handlebars, pull their bikes upright under them, step onto their pedals, and push off, swooping single file like swallows through the main gate.

Across the sand, I hear voices in the pavilion by the bathrooms.

We head over.

Away from the corral of lamplight, the sky extends to every horizon, a vast black suspended tent.

As we climb the pavilion steps, I feel the drama in the black waves crashing onto the beach only a few yards away. The dome of sky overhead is our theater, the raised cement a stage, our audience light-years away and silent pinpricks of light, but interested nevertheless.

But there are only three friends in cutoff jeans and striped T-shirts skateboarding up and down the stairs. Whatever we are looking for, this isn't it.

Off the beach, street corners are lit under streetlights. Midblock, the weed-cracked narrow sidewalks and wide, carless streets sit deep in shadow. Passing into the light, I feel obvious. Don't we have better things to do? Left to my own devices, I spend day and night with my horse books, reading about Pony Penning Day and wild horses swimming over razor-sharp shoals from the wrecks of Spanish galleons. Now I am trawling the streets, both fisherman and bait.

Two blocks ahead, in the spill of streetlight, we see a small gathering. Gilly and Pat on Steven Viola's corner. We can turn around still and not be seen; one more block and it will be too late. We hit the corner before Steven's. If we turn around now, it will look like we saw them, like we turned around because of them.

"Cross the street," Francesca says, panicking at the last minute. I'm already crossing.

We pass the corner across the wide expanse of Beech Street. I feel like there's a spotlight on us. I stare straight ahead, hot with embarrassment.

Francesca is looking out of the corner of her eye. "There's Gilly. There's Pat."

I can't believe we're doing this.

"What are you girls doing?" Pat calls across the street.

"Heading home," Francesca calls back, dimpling.

"Have a good night, then!"

Once we're far enough away, Francesca grabs my arm.

"Have a good night! Pat O'Keefe said have a good night! Can you believe it? He likes us. He definitely likes us."

The house is dark when I enter. It feels strange to be the only one awake.

I pass the small couch, pad over the living room rug, taken from my grandmother's farm, round and cozy and farmhouse old-fashioned. Hanging on the walls, gathering dust, are cotton nets, dyed blue, evidence of an attempt, long-neglected now, at nautical design. Some of the tacks have come loose and the nets have been left to droop where they've fallen. In places where the tacks still hold, thin blown-glass balls the size of volleyballs protrude from the thread latticework, fishing floats from the old days, my mother once explained, before Styrofoam. In the midst of nets and floats, a five-foot-long taxidermy barracuda holds center stage over the upright piano. We all know the story. How my mother, who grew up landlocked in her father's alfalfa fields and is terrified of the ocean, who still shudders at the feel of seawater on her shoulders, her neck, her face, somehow reeled in this fish on their honeymoon. I try never to look at it. The cheap shine of its shellacked silver scales, the black spots and forced arch of its body as if still in the mid-sweep of a graceful underwater turn, the stare of its glassy yellow eye, have always seemed to me to be the preservation of a mistake. The mistake of this fish arching across our wall when it belongs in the sea. The mistake of my mother in a fishing boat, the last place I know she would ever want to be, the hot sun beating down, my father's slowly stiffening day's catch dying at her feet. The mistake, though I will not formulate this thought until many years later: this trophy as symbol of their future life together, clearly foretold.

Gilly is in the pavilion. I see him before we are even across the sand. Pat O'Keefe is with him, plus Robert Manning and Marty, smaller Beech Street Gang players.

In the past week, we have seen Gilly here and there. Three days before, he rode up behind us on his bike—"Who are you? Oh, I know who you are"—then continued on. Now we climb the pavilion steps, where Gilly sits off a bit from the others, his face tilted *up*, toward the sky. The sun has just set; the sky is still white. "What are you looking at?" I ask, my heart pounding so hard, I wonder if he can see it.

"The star," he says.

Only four stars are out, but one shines down, the brightest of all of them. I don't tell him that ten minutes before, leaving my house, I had wished, *star light, star bright*, on this same star, as I do every night. *Please let Gilly Callaghan love me.*

But I do say, "That's *my* star."

He looks at me now. "No, it's not. It's mine."

"I saw it first," I say.

His eyes are transparent. "I'll give it to you," he says.

Nearby, talking to Francesca, Pat laughs at something, throwing his head back.

Gilly looks over at Pat, then back at me. He smiles, then looks down at his knees. His hair falls across his face.

"I gotta go," he says suddenly. He stands and brushes off the back of his jeans with the palms of his hands. "Hey, O'Keefe?" Pat nods at Gilly as Gilly heads down the pavilion steps. I watch him walking away on the beach.

"Gilly has to get some things straight in his head," Pat says, as if apologizing.

Francesca pulls me aside. "Pat says Robert Manning likes you. He thinks you have a great body."

"Are you sure he meant me?"

"Yes. He meant you."

I feel my image of myself shift slightly, though I wonder what it is he likes.

"Pat told me about Gilly."

My legs feel suddenly weak. "What about Gilly?"

"There's this guy, Roddy, who Wren likes back home. She's trying to decide between him and Gilly."

"Who's Wren?"

"Gilly's girlfriend."

Gilly has a *girlfriend*?

"They've known each other their whole lives. Everyone knows they're more brother-sister than anything else."

"Oh," I say.

"But he likes you, too."

"Gilly *likes* me?"

"Pat said that's why he left. He's trying to figure it out."

"So what does that mean?"

"Pat said you have to ride it out. You can't get too caught up in it. But Gilly is confused because of you. That's *good*, right?"

My father and mother are in California. We have a babysitter, who is asleep when I get home at night. I'm beginning to lose the urgency I feel to be home at 9:30 P.M. sharp. Point Lookout teems with teenage life after dark, and Francesca and I are caught up in the swirl of it all.

Every night I look for Gilly. It's been three days since he gave me a star. He is nowhere to be found.

In the cove, Stevie Sabelli—blond crew cut, white T-shirt, pale skin—and Peter Bekker, fringe Beech Street Gangers, share a six-pack of Budweiser with Francesca and me in the circle of black jetty rocks, then ride us through town on the handlebars of their Stingrays. My arms and legs feel heavy and warm; house lights and sidewalks and street corners swim past. I assuage my prickling of guilt by remembering my mother, at the beginning of the summer, telling my father that beer is healthier than soda. I tell myself that pot, which we tried two nights ago with Joe and Dean, members of the Bay Rat Gang who live on the bay side of town, comes from a plant.

I think I am rebelling, I write in my journal. *Against Gilly.*

Clearly, he can't like me that much, or he'd be around.

When my parents return from California, my mother finds Milky Way and Snickers wrappers filling the bottom two drawers of Braddy's dresser. He has emptied out his clothes to make room. There are at least a hundred. Maybe more.

"What's been going on around here?" my father asks.

I don't have an answer.

I am not allowed out of the house that night. Or the next. Or the night after that. They see something that I cannot. "I don't like your attitude," my father says.

"You girls pushed too hard," my mother tells me when I am

finally let out and a week goes by and I don't see Gilly. "Boys like girls who play hard to get."

At the bike racks, under the yellow streetlight, Gilly says he's glad we're having this talk; he wanted to before the summer was over. He says it's hard to talk about his feelings for someone else to anyone else. He says I probably can't really understand someone else's feelings and that maybe one day *he'll* understand. He says he loves Wren. He says he has felt so strongly toward her for so long that nothing could overpower that. He says he loves her and she loves him and they're finally happy.

In my journal, I write, *I'm so proud of myself. I didn't feel anything for him tonight.*

I don't mention that for the first time in my life I have lost my appetite. I swallow warm spoonfuls of blended salad, chew my eleven almonds, but it's all the same, before I eat, after I eat. The gnawing hunger, the brief fullness of a stomach heavy with liquid vegetables, the craving that quickly follows this false fullness, the body's sharp message that it needs *more* than egg yolk and nuts, have redlined to a constant, heavy, unwavering ache.

"If you look at a beautiful lake, the feeling you get is inside you, not inside the lake. You don't need anyone to make you feel a certain way. The ability to feel is inside you," my mother says, trying to cheer me up. I clearly don't have what it takes to be that enlightened.

A few afternoons later a skinny silver-and-black-striped alley cat follows me down our street, up our steps, and onto the porch. I open our front door and it walks boldly into the living room, trails after my ankles, into my bedroom.

"Its stomach is swollen. It's malnourished," my mother says.

It jumps into my open dresser drawer and turns around several times, like a dog.

"It's so tired," I say. "Look, it's already asleep."

"It must have fleas," my mother says. "If you feed it, you won't be able to get rid of it."

In the morning, six wet newborn kittens squirm and scratch amid my now blood-and-fluid-soaked T-shirts and shorts.

I think how maybe there's something to this. How, out of everyone it could have followed home, out of everyone in the whole town, this cat chose me.

When the fog rolls in, the day turns monotone steel, shades of gray and blue. My parents have been arguing. This fight is more physical than most: things are being thrown, objects that sound like baseballs slam against the kitchen wall. I can hear feet scuffling, my mother's voice, muffled, angry. Then her frightened, guttural animal moan.

I slip out of my bed and head for the kitchen. They are facing each other, close. My father seems to loom over my mother. His back is to me.

My mother sees me from over his shoulder. "Go on now, Christine," Her voice is impatient, *You're going to make it worse* tense.

Waiting in my room, it takes several moments for me to realize the house has gone completely silent.

I listen at my door.

Nothing.

I creep down the hall.

The kitchen is empty. I see a spatula on the floor. The seedy pulp of broken tomatoes bleeds and mixes with dripping, fist-size clumps of my father's non-Program cottage cheese on the wall beside the fridge. An open cottage cheese carton lies in one corner of the room, the lid in another.

I stand, feeling for them more than listening. A moment ago all hell was breaking loose and now the house is utterly still. Where is my mother? I push open the kitchen side door and descend the three steps into the driveway and our yard. The yard, like the house, is dead silent.

"Mom?" I half whisper. My mother never goes outside. She spends morning, noon, and night in the kitchen. We always know where to find her.

No answer.

"Mom!" I call.

I tug on the garage door, but it is heavy. It lifts knee-high and I crawl under. Maybe this was a bad idea. The light has been broken all summer. I can see almost nothing. If she were in here, if she needed my help, how would I know? I'm afraid to call out. Afraid to announce my own presence in the darkness. I should look carefully, under the beach umbrellas, the stacked outdoor furniture cushions, but instead I duck under the door and back into daylight. The yard is as still as before. Suddenly I feel completely calm. I don't feel surprised at all by the warm tranquility that has replaced my panic as I pull open the sliding door of our Volkswagen bus. The calm way I expect to see her feet, her legs and arms sprawled, lifeless, behind the driver and passenger seats, on the black rubber car mats. *He has killed her.* But the car is empty.

"*Mooooom!*" It feels purely practical now that I scream as loudly as I can.

I walk out into the middle of the street.

"*Help!*" I scream, standing completely still.

I feel like I'm looking down on myself, standing in my striped Danskin shorts and matching T-shirt, barefoot, my toes buried in the warm tar, my hair unbrushed and childishly tangled. I know this appears crazy, this choice I am making to stand here and scream at the top of my lungs, but inside I feel in complete control.

I want to do this. I want someone else to know.

"*Please-help-me.*"

A screen door bangs and I see Francesca's mother step onto her porch and spot me. She takes quick steps down the stairs, crosses her driveway, the tiny sidewalk, and reaches me in the street. She puts her arm across my shoulders.

"I don't know where my mother is," I say.

"Go back inside, Christine." Her voice is uncharacteristically gentle. "She's probably on a walk. Sometimes mothers need to go off by themselves. Okay? Go inside."

An hour later my mother opens the side door and steps into the kitchen, where I am standing at the sink.

My legs turn to water in relief. Her hair is frizzed from the fog. Her eyes are calm. She is barefoot, like a little girl. She is never without her clogs.

"I'm sorry if you were worried," she says without looking at me.

Still barefoot, she picks up the carton of cottage cheese, retrieves the lid, and puts both into the garbage can. Takes a rag and begins wiping off the walls.

"Ask the boys if they're ready for their celery juice."

It's the end of August, and Pat O'Keefe and I are standing knee-deep in the waves. Pat says he wants to see the kittens. He wants to try the blended salads everyone knows I drink.

Our living room is open and breezy. The late-afternoon sun slants through the open wood-framed windows. A thin layer of not-yet-swept-up sand feels gritty under my bare feet on the hardwood floor. Pat sits cross-legged on our comfortably worn couch, watching me with his Pat O'Keefe wide-toothed grin. I feel like a celebrity has dropped by.

I slice the peel from the lemon and skin the cucumber, cut the tomato in quarters, wash three leaves of romaine. Now, Pat has asked to be let in, to my house, to our diet—a blended salad, the emblem of all the ways my family isn't normal. This feels too big, but I don't know how to play hard to get. This is my house and I have nowhere else to go.

The vegetables have been in the refrigerator and, as I push

everything down with a stalk of celery, the liquid salad blends to a cool, foamy light green.

Pat takes a sip.

"Hmmm," he says. He takes another. "Not bad."

His grin is wide, happy, his eyes still on me. I have the feeling that I always have with him, that he is seeing right to the heart of me, where no one else has bothered to look. The living room suddenly feels cozier, friendlier than usual.

"It's like gazpacho," Pat says. "Cold soup. Have you ever had that?"

He's making the blended salad look good, and suddenly I want some. He hands me his glass. I take a sip. I can taste the sour of the lemon, the coolness of the cucumber, the sweetness of the tomato.

"Do you ever put spices in it?"

We're not even allowed salt or pepper. "No . . ."

"It doesn't need them really, does it?"

I consider the truth of this as he downs the rest of his glass.

My bedroom smells of milk and kitten urine. Dust particles float in the solitary beam of light from the doorway.

Inside the open drawer, the cat curls around her kittens. I reach into the moist warmth of silky, newly licked fur and slip my fingers under the biggest kitten. He's black, the size of my fist. I put the kitten in Pat's cupped hands. Its newly opened eyes are milky blue. We watch as it paws the air with claws so thin and clear, they look like curled hairs.

Francesca says Pat likes me. She can tell. He always wants to talk to me. We find out that Gilly left for college a few days ago. He didn't even say good-bye.

"He's changed," Francesca says. "He's not the Gilly we knew."

Pat rides me to his house on the handlebars of his bike. I sit on his bed while he throws T-shirts and jeans, hats, socks, sneakers, into several duffel bags, packing for Fordham. I wait for Maria or Jeanine, Beech Street Girls, to show up, to do what I'm doing, to keep him company as he prepares for the next stage of his life. But no one else arrives.

"You'd better write," Pat says. "Maybe next summer you can save your walks on the beach for me."

My room feels darker and colder after Pat drops me off.

I write in my journal, *I don't want to get hurt again, but I think I'm falling in love.*

I don't know yet that there will be no next summer. At the end of the school year we will move to California. It will be almost three decades before I set foot, accompanied by my own son and daughter, in Point Lookout again.

Chapter 10

It is 1977 and we are moving to California. My mother drives my brothers and me across the country in our VW bus, pulling out cardboard boxes of romaine lettuce, cucumbers, and celery; bags of raw almonds; and her tire-size wheel of raw, unsalted cheese from the back of the van to juice and blend all our meals at each motel stop, before packing everything up again the next morning when it's time to get back on the road.

For the summer, while my parents look for houses, we live on Sunset Boulevard, in hotel apartments not far from the new health food store my mother has found called Erewhon, which, Greg points out, is almost *nowhere* spelled backward. Bernadette Peters, the actress, lives across the lawn in the same complex that used to house movie stars in the old days of the Hollywood studio system. I see her sunbathing every day by the pool in a white bikini. I tell myself that if someone famous likes it enough to live here, we should like it, too. But my parents are fighting more than ever, and in the small space—my brothers and I are sleeping on a futon in the small living room—it's impossible to get away. I walk to the black wrought-iron gate at the bottom of the complex and look out over West LA. The apartments are perched on a hill, and I can see for miles and miles, all the way until the sprawl hits a hazy horizon. The seemingly endless stretch of houses and buildings and streets extending as far as the eye can see reminds me the world is vast and how far I am from New York. My friends, my life there has, seemingly overnight, become a memory. I try not to think about the fact that, come fall, my friends at Dalton will have their senior year without me or that it's July and Francesca is in Point Lookout right this moment, going to the beach every day, seeing Gilly and Pat, that life is going on in the places I love most, for everyone but me.

It's the beginning of September, and, at our mother's bright encouragement, we have signed up for surfing, which counts as PE at our new California high school, Beverly Hills High. On Mondays, Wednesdays, and Fridays at 8:00 A.M., we ride the school bus to Santa Monica. Whatever we imagined of California beaches when we were still in New York, this isn't it. Mornings on the beach in Santa Monica, it turns out, are freezing and foggy and cold. The sky hangs low and gray; the sea is thick and dark and foamy. Though my brothers manage, I will never, the entire semester, find a way to stand on the board. All surfing class in the morning does for me is ensure my skin feels slick with salt and my hair dries flat against my forehead for the rest of the day. My mother drives Braddy to middle school, so, on Tuesdays and Thursdays, my brothers and I ride bikes to BHHS. As most mornings are foggy inland, too, riding my bike, which I have named Red Flame, in the damp air ensures my hair is flat against my forehead even on the days that don't begin on a cold beach. Whatever confidence I had found in Point Lookout has quickly vanished. These kids drive BMWs and Mercedes to school, and I'm a senior, riding a three-speed that I pretend is a horse, wearing clothes that are stuck to my body with sweat or salt by the time I get to school. My brothers and I bring our packed blended salads in lunch boxes every day and meet in the halls to eat them. My brothers are tall and tan and curly-haired and blond and the girls flock. I am cooler, by association, than I would be otherwise, but I feel intimidated by all the easy, slinky West LA beauty around me. Unlike at Dalton, at Beverly Hills High, my brothers and I don't stand out in any way. We are in a show-business town that is unimpressed by show-business offspring, and no one notices our diet. But I'm in culture shock. There are names for groups of kids I have no reference for: Surfers, Jewish American Princesses, Stoners. There were so many Jewish kids in my New York high school, no one thought to call anyone else a princess or even a Jew. There were no surfers, and smoking pot was something almost all the self-proclaimed intellectual private school kids around me did. This is also the year the last Shah of Iran is deposed, and a third of the school is suddenly Iranian. The marble statues in front of the mansions on Sunset Boulevard, one of them belonging to the shah himself, have their pubic hair painted in black. Our new house on North Roxbury Drive sits across the street from Lucille Ball's and a few doors down from Jimmy Stewart's. Tour buses drive by every fifteen minutes. My brothers play a game with the buses, donning sunglasses and pretending to duck behind our front hedge as a bus rolls by, which they say causes the sightseers inside to sit up and strain to get a better look at what they believe are reclusive celebrities. My mother sits in the sun on the stucco deck off my new bedroom with peroxide combed into her hair, which is gradually tinting blond. She constructs an eight-foot-high mail-order aluminum pyramid in my closet, which she aligns to the east and sits under to meditate. She reads Aldous Huxley's Vedantic teachings and Carlos Castaneda's journals about his apprenticeship under a Yaqui Indian shaman. She tells me if she places an apple under a properly aligned pyramid, the apple will never rot. My father is tanned and wears tieless pastel-colored shirts with a few buttons unbuttoned and rubber-soled leisure shoes. Instead of a briefcase, he carries a soft leather bag slung across his shoulder. He acquiesces to blended salads and eats his Program meals at home. Our mother treats him, at least when things are quiet, like a work still in prog-

ress, encouraging him with pats on the head and kisses on the
cheek when she brings him his bowl. But once, when I am hanging out with him on a Sunday on a drive, he stops at In-N-Out
Burger for a hamburger.

"Want one?"

I say no.

"Don't tell your mother," he growls as he wolfs it down.

A month into school, my mother tells me she opened the door
to my father's office on the Burbank Studios lot, where she had
stopped by to say hello, to find my father hugging an associate, a
much younger female assistant.

"They were embracing," she says. "They pulled apart quickly
when I walked in."

If I have any reaction to this news, I can't find it. Nothing feels
the same in California, anyway, though I try out for softball and
make the team. During practices I crouch in a ready stance by
the mini oil rigs that pump away ceaselessly in left field, cradle
my mitt, and wipe away tears.

There is another social category at BHHS—Swimmer—and
the captain of the team, Mike Pullman, has been watching my
softball games. He has an on-again, off-again girlfriend, but he
high-fives me after my games and calls me Brown Eyes, though
my eyes are hazel. One night he asks me on a date, my first. In
the dark, we climb up over the twelve-foot-high chain-link fence
surrounding the Beverly Hills Country Club golf course, half a
mile from my house, and drop down onto the grass, still wet from
the sprinklers. He spreads a blanket and opens a bottle of wine
he produced from under his sweatshirt. He leans me back on the
blanket and kisses me. He has broad shoulders, a convex back,
and no butt to speak of. He's nice, but I can't find anything about
him that sticks to me in any important way.

After the date, when he drops me off at home and drives away,
my mother says, "You don't need a boyfriend."

Having a boyfriend sounds like a chore when she puts it that way. I can also hear her real message: *In the quest for purity, boyfriends get in the way.*

I can still feel his kiss on my lips, warm and wet, but neither it nor he are worth fighting for.

My father is making a television series about a Native American tribe, the fictional *Tales of the Nunundaga*, filming in Arizona. Like the old days, we get to visit the set, for me a reprieve from the heavy ache of homesickness, and a reprieve from this strange place we have landed in. In Beverly Hills the smell of honeysuckle and orange blossoms hangs thick in the air. I would have never thought that sweet and unhappy could go together. My mother has come upon turquoise in Arizona and now wears it in thick bracelets on her wrists, in large decorative pieces hanging heavily on her neck. She wears blue jeans, clogs. She says turquoise has healing powers. She spends time on this set, unlike my father's other movie sets. She tells me she feels a kinship with the Native Americans, who were forced from their lands, and reminds me that she was forced from her own land, her childhood farm, by the United States government. On the set, Dick Lundeen, the wrangler, as per my father's request, allows me to ride some of the horses that are being used in the filming. They are tricked out with Native American bridles and saddle blankets, no saddles, and when he gives me a leg up, he tells my father that I have a good seat. I am given carte blanche to ride any horse I want wherever I want. I choose a big half-thoroughbred paint named Lizard, and he and I wander the scrub, over hills and into canyons, no limits. When I return, my mother is sitting in my father's director's chair, chatting with the makeup ladies about the power of vortices, the energy forces that the Native Americans believed swirled in special places on the earth. Tucson was one of them.

For our first Thanksgiving in California, my mother invites

Dr. Cursio to our Beverly Hills house. He is seeing clients, thanks to her, in West LA.

"Dr. Cursio is making us a special Thanksgiving dinner!" She is alight with joy.

He cooks as my mother flits around, cutting and chopping as he instructs. She is laughing, giddy, light as a feather. Dr. Cursio shows how we can put vegetables on a platter and bake them, our first-ever veggie roast, which is a wonder to us. We can eat vegetables that aren't steamed? That are crispy on the outside and tender on the inside? He makes a soup with a light broth and large pieces of Swiss chard floating in it. He mashes yams and bakes russet potatoes. When we sit down around the table, my plate is full and everything tastes good, though I still miss salt. I try to shake the sense that the meal feels like a series of side dishes. I curse the label of the holiday. I'd probably be happy eating this food if it weren't for the fact that what we're *supposed* to be eating is turkey.

My father has invited me to go with him to the Beverly Hills Hilton for the Golden Globe Awards. *Raid on Entebbe* has been nominated. As we arrive and walk down the red carpet, it's like the old days, when just by being my father's daughter, I felt like a star. Inside, where the tables are set around the stage, we are surrounded by real stars. Richard Burton, Richard Dreyfuss, Vanessa Redgrave, Sally Field, Henry Winkler, Woody Allen, Carol Burnett. When my father's category, Best Motion Picture Made for Television, is read, I freeze. Then *Raid on Entebbe* is announced, and around us, everyone claps for my father as he takes the stage.

The next day my father is in the backyard with British stage and film director Tony Page and Tony's best friend, classical actress Rachel Roberts. I feel the enormity of having these gods descend to our patio. My father is happy and awake and energized. He is doing the jitterbug now on the outdoor tile. He grabs

Tony's elbow and pulls him over, twists his hand, forcing the gangly director to join him.

"Sir Tony," my father sings as they soft-shoe. Buckingham Palace conferred knighthood last month.

Rachel Roberts is perched on a stool, drinking water with a slice of lime. Our mother fills my brothers and me in: Rachel and fellow stage legend Rex Harrison can't live with each other, can't live without each other, though they've been trying some variation of one or the other for four decades. Rex, my mother says, brings out the alcoholic in Rachel and vice versa. She is on the wagon now, hoping to stay there.

"Ra-chel," Tony calls to her, drawing out the first syllable and reaching for her with his long arm. She clasps his hand for a moment, then lets go. His caramel-smooth Oxford British accent makes the angular slant of his narrow shoulders, his lisp, his balding head beautiful. He sits on our sun-bleached redwood lounge chair, one giraffe-long leg over the armrest. His shoes, which are soft and furry and have no backs, look like slippers.

Later that month, my mother will take in Rachel Roberts. She will feed her blended salads and talk about cleansing and about God, and about how addiction is caused by a clogged liver. Rachel Roberts will stay in my room and follow the Program for two weeks. After that she will leave her tortoiseshell Siamese, Daisy Mae, to go home and swallow a fatal number of sleeping pills. We keep the cat.

"I should be able to have a drink to unwind at night, Carol. Goddamn it. It relaxes me. It doesn't hurt anything." My father's voice is loud. I'm upstairs in my room and I can hear him clearly, but he's not screaming or out of control. He's trying to make a point. "One drink at night doesn't hurt anyone."

When I come downstairs, he has a glass filled with amber-colored liquid in his hand. He's sitting in the wicker chaise with it, watching the news.

My mother is at the sink washing the juicer for the night. Clara, our housekeeper, who arrives each morning with her cat-size poodle, Tiny, and leaves each evening, has gone home.

"Alcohol is a poison; it poisons the body and the liver. It's toxic." Her lips are parchment white as she hisses this so my father can't hear her. She is as angry as I've ever seen her. "If he wants to poison himself, so be it. What can I do?"

Later, after the fight, my mother tells me, "I dreamed about Bob Pettit." Bob Pettit is the basketball star she dated in college.

"Why didn't you marry him?" I ask.

"Oh, he wasn't interested in me in that way. He had so many women around him."

Does she notice how sad this is? That the man she is still dreaming about didn't love her enough even then?

She has begun talking about Pierre, a French art dealer whom she met at the West LA ashram. She tells me Pierre is gentle and soft-spoken. Her face glows.

In the spring she takes a trip by herself to France. She is completely out of reach, leaving us with our father and Clara for two weeks, something that has never happened.

"What kind of a mother just leaves her children?" my father says. "Chasing after a homosexual art dealer?"

Homosexual? This was something she had failed to mention. When she returns from France, our mother is pale and quiet. She doesn't talk about her trip and we don't ask. She never mentions Pierre again.

Chapter 11

My mother and I are on a road trip. It's time for me to apply to college. I like Berkeley because, from what I've seen in pictures, its ivy-covered stone buildings and grassy quads reminds me of how I imagine an East Coast school would look. I've decided I don't want to go out of state. I am the first to leave the nest—we've been in California almost a year—and the real East Coast, as much as I miss it, feels too far away. After the disruption of the move, it feels too soon to leave. I *just* left.

We arrive into town and, first stop, my mother locates the health food store a mile from campus. The familiarity of the store is comforting; it smells like every other health food store I've been in, like vitamins and hand cream and vitamin E oil, but the location is too far and I won't have a car.

"Look at this." My mother indicates a flyer thumbtacked to a bulletin board filled with other notices. *Acme juicer for sale: good condition. Yard work wanted.* In the middle of the flyer she is looking at sits a square-faced man dressed in red robes with a red dot between his dark eyebrows. *Meditate with Swami Muktananda.*

"Do you want to see what that's all about?" she says.

Outside the ashram, the air is wet, the sky gray with Berkeley fog. Without the glitter of sunshine to sparkle things up, every crack in the sidewalk is a wet vein, and the plaster side of the orange building is smudged and weathered as my mother pulls open the door and holds it for me. We step inside to a worn blue carpet where, just inside the door, pairs of shoes sit in rows. I try not to observe how, without feet, the shoes' ugliness, the creases at the ball of the shoes, the scuffs at the heels, the black inside where their owners' soles have ground in foot grime, is more noticeable. Too many things—the sidewalk, the chipped plaster, the gray sky—are melancholy here. My mother slips off her clogs without missing a beat; she is already heading through the small door. I untie my laces, kick off my sneakers that, without my feet in them, look as shoddy and abandoned as the shoes they are joining.

My mother stands at the chest-high front desk, where a white man and a white woman, both sporting dark red dots between their eyebrows, face her with blank smiles. My mother is leaning forward; she has laid her arm across the surface of the desk and grips the other edge as if she might pull herself up onto it and climb over the top to join them. The woman with the dot nods at her, clearly responding to something she has just asked, and stands, reaches to a pile of brochures at my mother's elbow, opens a brochure with one hand, and holds it up like a menu for her to read. My mother releases her hold on the desk and takes it, her mouth in a wide smile that looks suspiciously like triumph.

"The evening program is beginning in ten minutes if you'd like to head into the great hall," the man says. He has wide doe eyes with little crumbs of sleep crust in between his lower lashes.

"The evening program," my mother says, rolling the words around in her mouth. "Do you want to go?" This isn't a real question. This is a barbed arrow; there is no exit. She is already heading toward the double doors across more blue carpet. She has her hands together now, holding them palm to palm like she is praying, a gesture I've never seen her make, and bows, palms pressed, to each flowy-clothed ashram member we pass. A woman smiles and puts her hands together, nods in return.

We file in where people are already sitting cross-legged in

rows, men on one side of the room, women on the other. A blond man in a flowing shirt and equally flowing pants directs us down an aisle where pillows have been placed instead of seats. My mother files in and sits quickly, settling herself cross-legged. I follow. As I adjust my legs, trying to get comfortable on my pink pillow, an East Indian man in orange robes steps to the microphone, introduces himself as Swami Anantananda, welcomes us, then announces the evening program schedule for the upcoming week. As he speaks, I notice for the first time, behind him, an ornate wicker chair adorned with flowers sitting in the shadows on a slightly raised stage. I realize all the rows of pillows face this chair. Swami Anantananda moves from announcements to a brief introduction on how to meditate.

"Let your mind wander; it will. Don't pay too much attention to your thoughts; let them come and go. Focus on your breathing." He suggests two mantras, *Ham Sa*, which he says translates into, "I am that," or *Om Namah Shivaya*: "The lord who dwells within you as you." Then he steps down from the microphone and sits at the foot of the chair. As soon as the swami is seated, another man, also dressed in orange, begins to play a guitar-like instrument. The sound it emits is a long, low twang as *Om Namah Shivaya* appears projected onto the white screen behind the wicker chair. Everyone in the hall begins singing, matching their key to that first note, *Oh-oh-oh-oh . . . Ohhmmmm*. The next note is played, slightly higher, and the chanting responds, *Nam-ah-ah*. A third note is played, even higher, *Shiv-ay-ya-ya-ya-ya-ah*. My mother has joined in. After several rounds, when I realize this is what we'll be doing for a while, I join in, too. I'm mostly hoping to pass the time, but if there are benefits to be gained, I'll take them. After about twenty minutes, long after my inner clock has signaled it's time to move to the next activity, the twanging slows, the projector snaps off, and the lights in the hall dim.

Around us in the darkened hall, people settle in. Beside me, my mother settles in. It's time to meditate. I'm definitely picking up on the fact that the patience required for how slowly everything is moving might be part of the lesson of enlightenment for Westerners. At least, it's a lesson for me.

"Use the mantra," my mother whispers.

She closes her eyes and begins taking long, slow, deep breaths. I begin taking long, slow, deep breaths. In my mind I repeat the mantra, *Om Namah Shivaya*, but it's not easy, I'm noticing, to fit my breathing around all those syllables.

Om Nam-ah, breathe in. *Shiv-a-ya*, breathe out. I'm rushing it, attempting to fit everything in. My cheeks begin to tingle. I'm hyperventilating.

Ham, breathe in slowly, *Sa*, breathe out slowly. The tingling dissipates.

Ham Sa fits so easily with my breathing that it requires no concentration. I'm saying it in my mind as I breathe and thinking of all the other things I'm trying not to think about, at the same time: *Ham*, my hips ache. *Sa*, sitting cross-legged makes my right foot fall asleep. *Ham*, what will happen if I stretch my leg out? *Sa*, point my toes, flex my toes, point my toes. *Ham*, the two women sitting as motionless and upright as boards in front of me don't seem to notice my foot between them. *Sa*—

My mother taps my knee, sharply, with the tips of all her fingers.

I pull my leg back. I am not supposed to be feeling discomfort. If I were meditating properly—this is the message of her jab—I would have transcended the worldly naggings of pain and desire.

Across the aisle, in the men's section, a man with a moldy beard and a skinny neck begins to roll his head violently. Around the hall, more and more people do the same. Some begin to emit noises. In minutes, the hangar-size room sounds like a barnyard.

Grunts, squeals, barks echo off the ceiling.

"*Kriyas*," my mother will explain, once she has done some reading on the subject, "are a cleansing."

"A cleansing of what?"

"The mistakes of past lives. Unwanted karma."

She will talk about *ego*, the danger of following impulses that come from our *contracted* selves, and how Swami Muktananda, because he comes from a lineage of enlightened beings, can end the cycle of birth and death by taking away all desire.

"What if we don't want to end the cycle of birth and death?" I ask. I am thinking of orange sunsets with cobalt clouds, a crescent moon, the sound of rain outside my window on a December night, the chirrup of crickets floating in on a warm white summer dusk.

"The goal is self-realization," my mother says. "That's what we're here for."

My eyes are supposed to be closed, but I can't help looking around to see who else is restless, too, and who seems to be successfully achieving a quieted mind in this meditation session. Now a door opens and a round Indian man with white chalk marks over his eyebrows and a red dot between his eyebrows walks in slowly, his long orange robes flowing behind him. In one hand he holds several long peacock feathers. Walking among the rows of meditators, Baba Muktananda—I realize this is who has just joined us—raises the feathers and brings them down on people's heads or shoulders, harder than I would have expected. *Bop. Bop. Bop.* Eventually he approaches my mother and me. The bop is as hard as it looked; the feathers brush my hair, but the stalk part smarts where it hits the top of my head.

In these smacks, Baba is delivering *Shaktipat*, my mother will tell me, the energy from an initiated master that is needed to open our *Kundalinis*. The journey to *self-realization*, according to my mother, begins with this initiation. The rest is up to us.

The mewling and bleating, the wild swiveling of necks around us, is reaching a crescendo. I wait for the disgust my mother can so often go to, the thin line of her mouth, the upward tilt of her chin, when she finds herself in unwanted proximity with other people.

Instead she sits up even straighter and closes her eyes, her lips posed in a relaxed-looking smile.

I'm at UC Berkeley. I let my mother set me up, no questions asked, in Euclid Hall, a damp co-op with a bloodred rug and a Count Dracula staircase on the quiet side of campus, because she wanted me to have a kitchen to blend salads in. Homesickness sets in the moment she drives away. It turns out Euclid Hall is graduate student housing. All the other freshmen are in the dorms, making friends. There is only one student my age, a male, who I will make out with one night then avoid for the rest of the year. The inhabitants of this co-op represent yet another unfamiliar culture represented by dirty sandals and philosopher beards, by a language of sarcastic quips that I am no match for.

"Everything you need is inside you," my mother tells me in the language of the ashram when I call home, panic squeezing so tightly that I can hardly breathe.

I return from classes the end of the first week to find someone has baked brownies. They're still warm; the kitchen smells of chocolate and batter. Portions sit wrapped in tinfoil on the counter for anyone who wants them. At first I think I'm going to be okay. Just acknowledge them and move on. It's no different than it's always been; I'm used to wanting. But it *is* different. I'm hungry and my mother's not here to make sure I drink my celery juice and eat my blended salad before that hunger gets the better of me. I think of the Ho Ho in Francesca's kitchen so many years ago. Then, I was focused on summer fun and first love. Here, I am alone and missing home. My guilt at even thinking of cheating feels acute. Plus I am my whole family here. Who am I if I'm not eating the Program? I pick up a tinfoil square and smell through the foil. Smelling will be enough. Just to get a sense of it. What's the difference between eating and imagining I'm eating? Imagination has always carried me. I unwrap and breathe in the brownie.

A corner flakes off, into the foil. I pick up it up, mere crumbs. A mouse-size nibble. How could that hurt? Just to get the taste of it. It's the idea of it I want anyway. Before I can change my mind, I put the crumbs into my mouth. They sit on my tongue, sweet, granular. I flick them to the back of my throat and swallow. Too small. Crumbs don't count. Half a brownie is small, too. How could half a brownie hurt? I eat the half in two bites. If one half is too small, then isn't the second half just as negligible? In my mouth, the brownie liquefies, melts on my tongue. I take another bite, rub the pasty, sugary smear off my teeth with my tongue and swallow. I finish the entire brownie, suddenly exhilarated, liberated. I can do this: eat brownies like a normal person. The whole world has opened. I see myself balanced, eating blended salads when I want them but also brownies and cookies and cakes. It's flour. It's sugar. These things come from the earth. They are natural. Egg yolk is a Program food even. I can still consider myself healthy. In fact, I can eat another brownie *because* they are so healthy. I take slower bites this time. I see my future: my body robust and easy, taking food in stride, finding health in everything. I swallow, clean the last chocolate smears from my teeth, feel around with my tongue for more but there is nothing. The brownies are gone and I am suddenly alone with the consequences of what I've done. What was I thinking? White flour and egg whites take B vitamins from the body. Chocolate never leaves our system. I feel seared with sadness. The only thing I have is me and now I don't know who I am. I can no longer consider myself pure. In an instant, I've betrayed years, betrayed everything I've known to be true. Then a glimmer of an idea: If I water fast, I can clean most of this brownie out of my system, almost as if it didn't even happen. I can erase it from my body. I'll skip a blended salad and go to bed *now*. Fast for three days, the way we used to when we were sick.

———

One night, after my father has fallen asleep, a month after I leave home for college, my mother slips upstairs into my now-empty bedroom. He tosses and turns all night, she tells my brothers. He turns on the radio in the wee hours of the morning when he can't sleep. He is not considerate of her needs and she wants to see if she will sleep better alone.

Two months after her move upstairs my father tells my brothers he has found an apartment by the beach in Santa Monica. "It will be a trial," he tells me. "Your mother and I want to see if we are happier living apart."

"I'm starting a rugby team," Annika says. She sits next to me in Scandinavian Literature. I'm a year into college and I have one friend.

Rugby? I think I've heard of it. I imagine leather helmets, a muddy field in England, an oblong ball. But I could be wrong.

"Do you want to join?" It's January. We are walking down the cracked leaf-strewn sidewalk from Euclid Hall to campus. With Annika, I get glimpses of relief from my homesickness. "Goose Woman," the players on the men's team will call her, and the name will stick. She has a long neck, a small head, wide hips. When she laughs, she sticks her tongue out and her head jabs forward like she's pecking at corn. But she explains Kierkegaard to me and sits on a stool in the co-op kitchen while I blend my dinner.

"Yes," I say.

I first love rugby because it feels like I am back with my brothers, sprinting across the cold grass of our Point Lookout front yard. Practices on the rugby field, under the white lights of Strawberry Canyon, the froggy smell of mud, the horsey smell of crushed grass, catapult me from sadness into the crunch of rib cage and thigh, the grab of arms, the give of soft throats and bellies. Hard breath, wet hair, burning lungs. I haven't run this fast since I was eight. I run to get away, to score between the goalposts, palms flat, knees sliding across tufts of grass, sandpaper-rough mud and sand, to catch someone around her ankles, to bring her down, me and my brothers, and it's Kill the Guy with the Ball all over again.

Around rugby I feel noticed, like in the old Point Lookout days, when I was tan and thin from swimming in the ocean all day, all the pale, white, city uncool washed away and leaving me tomboy svelte, lithe and easy in my body. Rugby players like me and I like them. Frat boys' heads don't turn when I walk by, but I can't walk down a rugby sideline without feeling like there's a spotlight on me, and everyone I pass stops whatever he was doing to watch my progress. Feeling attractive lifts me from the sadness that hangs around like wisps of Berkeley fog, impossible to grasp and control, but always somewhere close.

I am bent over the small bathroom sink, holding my hair back with one hand, sticking my finger down my throat with the other the way my best friend and sorority sister has just taught me. Beside me, she is doing the same. I have permission from our sorority housemother to blend salads in the basement. Even so, I'm a sophomore and I'm finding it too difficult to live a lifestyle where I can take the time to blend salads before hunger is too pressing. I'm finding it too difficult to live shut away, removed from tempting foods, too difficult to go to bed for three days to fast when I slip up.

The food comes up, still warm from my body: Spicy tomato sauce, smooth white crust, chunks and strings of cheese. Too soon for stomach enzymes to have soured it, the purging is almost as pleasant as the ingesting. Afterward I feel high. Physical, endorphins perhaps, but also the triumph: This is so easy. For the first time I am having my cake and eating it, too.

———

"Mikey D likes the ladies," Molly says. We are sitting at the top of the stadium, watching the men's team emerge from the tunnel and run onto the field. "That's Fuzzy. Easy Money, Spare Change, they're brothers."

Molly plays hooker; she's as wide as she is tall, with a beak nose and freckles. We've only been a team for a month, but I wonder if one of these guys has already broken her heart.

"And that's Tim."

Everything slows as I watch him run onto the grass. His shoulder-length hair blows back; the muscles in his thick calves ripple. Long, soft strawberry-blond hair, a girlishly pretty face, narrow nose, cheekbones, Cupid's-bow lips.

"He's captain," Molly says, "been with his girlfriend, Louise, for four years, since freshman year. He doesn't sleep around like the rest of them. You guys play the same position. Outside center."

Except Lou stepped out on him while Tim was in the UK this past summer. Now, during our games, he strides up and down the sidelines, calling to me.

"Tackle at the knees! Take her outside shoulder!"

The final whistle blows. As the spattering of observers head down the hill, I find my bag leaning against the chain-link fence. Out of the corner of my eye, I see Tim linger, kick at a tuft of grass by the goalpost. He's been at my games for a few weeks, but we've yet to talk. Now he comes up behind me.

"What will all your boyfriends say?" he asks as he follows me down the hill toward campus and my sorority. I can't tell if he's kidding. I'm a fast runner, I like to tackle, and I'm blond from afternoon practices. Rugby has become the family I was needing. I'm feeling good about myself again, and I'm glad Tim thinks I'm popular. I don't tell him I've never had a boyfriend.

We go to get him a hamburger. He eats and talks. I listen. Stories of the night he and his teammates were rescued by helicopter from the national forest after a storm blew in and the rivers they needed to cross swelled to raging torrents. He is gorgeous, he is a star, he seems larger than life, like my father, only not like him at all. I feel awash in a calm kind of knowing. That unexplainable familiarity I've only had with a few people, all girlfriends, except for Tim. People I meet and just *know*, like déjà vu, that they are going to mean something to me. I have this sense that I can't explain, because I barely know Tim, that I've come home.

Chapter 12

It's 2:00 A.M. Tim and I have just come, last call, from McNally's, the pub near campus. We have been together day and night for two weeks. We are in his kitchen in the house he and his roommates call the Village, and I'm hungry. Tim rinses his hands over the sink, letting the cold tap water run over his roommates' empty glasses, plates smeared with the hardened paste of mashed potatoes, diarrhea stains of gravy, cereal bowls half filled with gray milk and spongy rings of cereal, miniature waterlogged inner tubes of pink and orange and green and blue. He stands slightly pigeon-toed, swaying lightly. His sneaker *thwacks* on the sticky floor when he puts out a foot to balance himself, as if he's lifted it from a strip of tape. I'm thinking: I have never been in a kitchen no woman has touched. I'm thinking: I'm drunk. The insides of my eyes, my stomach, roil as if each rides out its own set of slow-rolling waves. I'm thinking: no one knows where I am, this college frat house in the hills inhabited by men I barely know. I'm thinking: *I like this.*

Tim opens the fridge and pulls out a bowl of barbecued chicken, sets it on the counter. The skin on the legs and thighs and wings in the bowl is puckered, yellow in parts, charred brown in others. I feel detached from what I am about to do, woozy from the two beers I drank and woozy from love. Tim bites into a leg. The smell of barbecued meat fills the kitchen. Am I really doing this? I pick up a wing. It's shriveled and cold from the fridge but still smells of smoke. I bite the tip, rip it off, chew. Smoky, meaty, sweet, and salty: I haven't eaten a piece of chicken since before middle school, but the taste is like an old friend.

You won't want it when your body's pure, my mother says in my head.

I suddenly feel ravenous, hungrier than I can ever remember being. Tim comes up behind me. I finish the wing, move to a thigh, pull flesh from bone with my teeth. Tim presses against me with his stomach, thighs. He puts his hands on my hips, turns me so we are pelvis to pelvis, lowers his head until our chins touch, his nose pushing against mine. His lips, dry and firm, open my mouth, tongue probing gently. His skin and hair have, compared to the chicken thigh still in my hand, no smell. His breath tastes fresh. He takes my free hand and pulls me toward his bedroom. I drop the thigh into the sink as we pass. I can't throw up here, where Tim or his rugby roommates can hear. I can't fast properly because that requires three days of bed rest. This food will have to stay in my body and become part of me. Part of who I am moving forward.

Lying in bed, my first sleepover with a boy, our ankles touch. That night, in my dream, my mother is standing on an unfamiliar dock. A wind blows her dark hair; overhead the robust midday sun is hard and yellow. The ocean behind her is black-blue. She lifts her hand, palm and fingers flat, to wave at me. I wave back at Tim, who is on the dock now. My mother is gone.

It's July and Tim has driven down, a surprise visit, from his parents' house in Northern California, for my twenty-first birthday. We have been together four months.

That night I slip out the sliding glass doors that open from my bedroom and run, nightgowned and barefoot, across the driveway, climb the guesthouse stairs. In my life I wear boys' shirts and jeans. I still part my hair too far on the side and haven't yet considered even lip gloss. But Tim has been showing me things I hadn't known to appreciate about my body. Now I slip in beside him under the cool guest-room sheets. He is awake, waiting for me, shirtless, dressed in only his briefs. He pulls off my nightgown, presses against me; his chest is warm and smooth-skinned and muscled. A warrior tamed and tucked away in an empty upstairs room.

"I'm going for a run. Wanna come?" It's Saturday, 6:00 A.M. in Berkeley, and Tim is putting on his shorts. I groan. Doesn't he want to just sleep a bit longer? I don't like getting up this early. Still, this morning the fog will be threading through the hills. We will end up, as we always do, in a canyon or on a mountaintop, someplace I have never been. When I'm with him, the fog seems dramatic and beautiful, not dreary. Is an extra hour of sleep worth missing a Tim adventure? Whatever he wants to do, it's never something I would do if he weren't there, pushing me. It's the afterward, when I'm warm and dry, that I like most. The feeling of being tired and of accomplishment, the expanded way of seeing things. Left to my own devices, I'd do none of this. Should I stay and sleep? I throw back the covers.

Tim runs ahead of me on the uphill fire trail, like a deer, landing left and then right, dodging the greenery, ducking pine boughs, grabbing fistfuls of bushes and thrusting them away. I try to keep up, determined to show him I am equal to whatever test this might be of my abilities. My shirt and shorts are wet with sweat; my hands and face are pink with cold. My lungs burn, my forehead smarts with prickles of sweat, my bangs flattening the way I hate, even with the bandanna I tied as a headband. Trying to keep up but also trying not to notice the way his rear end, tight, muscled, pushes against the thin fabric of his running shorts. This run is fun, but I am also at the limits of my endurance; we've already been running hard, and mostly uphill, for what feels like a very long time. Fun and hard, I'm beginning to understand, is going to be a recurring pattern with Tim. Yesterday we launched a borrowed Hobie Cat in the bay and, despite gale warnings, I stepped into a wetsuit, peeled on the thick, warm rubber, and zipped it up the back. The wind was howling, and the sea-size basin was blown dark gray, dotted with explosions of tiny whitecaps. Crashing though the waves, when we hit our angle just right, the small catamaran lifted onto one pontoon, the sails singing a high-pitched hum, and Tim yelled at me to *lean back in the harness*, so I did, going against every instinct in my body, soaked and terrified and thrilled, as we sped on, suspended high above the windblown, unfamiliar waterscape. The weekend before, we drove to Tahoe, the rocky granite and pine forest terrain growing more and more majestic, to swim in the still-cold-from-snowmelt June glass-clear lake. In the book my mother read to my brother and me when we were little, *Where the Wild Things Are*, Max's room dissolves so he is standing suddenly in the great wide world. With Tim I have become a creature of movement and activity and wild expanses. I'm learning he pushes every boundary he comes to and lifts me outside of myself, which adds to the exhilaration of this new love and keeps me from sinking into my old sadness. Beers after practice, cold chicken from his fridge after beers, I make the salads, Tim barbecues the chicken, the steak. I feel like I'm tumbling in a warm, effervescent whorl of new feelings. My emotional allegiance has transferred from my mother to Tim and when I'm with him, I can eat Top Dog hot dogs, waffles at Denny's, 7-Eleven. It's—it's guilt-free. At 2:00 A.M. nothing counts anyway. I rip at the flesh with my teeth; blood runs down my throat. I imagine caves, tribal fires, and loincloths, an ancient past of violence and the heat of the hunt, the heat of freshly spilled blood, the heat of glowing embers to ward off a cold world. For the first time in my life I belong to the strong tribe. The dominant tribe. I am doing what everyone else does.

I'm in the back of Tim's pickup truck, lying on the bed, watching the sky as he drives through the tunnel that separates Berkeley from Lamorinda. On the other side of the tunnel the air smells warmer, sweeter. I sit up to see brown hills rolling by. *Oh,* I think. Like a pasture. Like farmland. I *like* it here.

Tim and I move into a rugby friend's mother-in-law's unit in Lafayette. The unit has no stove, so we cook everything in an electric wok, which sits on the countertop. It's surprising how many foods—pancakes, chicken-fried steaks, broccoli—can be made in its curved skillet.

We move from the condominium and rent a house that has linoleum floors and worn wood cabinets in the kitchen, old carpet, spiderwebs in the corners of the windows, and smells musty in a good way, like my grandmother's farm. A few months into living in Walnut Creek, we find a trail into the hills. Fourteen hundred acres, it turns out, of protected land: grass and mud and dirt and rocks, coyotes, squirrels, hills with one medium-size mountain in the middle. I open every window and let in the green smell of rain. I wade out into winter-dark skies; black mud; wet, knee-deep jade-colored fields; my sneakers and jeans soaked; my hair curling in the misty drizzle. These are my own real-life red dirt roads, my own farmy knolls, warm with the sunny, peppery yellow-flower smell of dandelion and mustard seed, my own Mary Poppins chalk drawing I have jumped into.

My parents are getting divorced. My mother is attending a jazz concert in downtown LA, where Jean-Baptiste Illinois Jacquet, an African American saxophonist who cut his teeth playing in bands with Lionel Hampton, Cab Calloway, Dizzy Gillespie, and

Count Basie, is performing his signature instrument, the tenor saxophone.

My mother will tell us that Illinois toured with the greats. His hit solo, "Flying Home," released when he was nineteen, was considered the first "crossover," a 45 that both whites and African Americans flocked to buy. Another first: In 1944, while playing at the Philharmonic Auditorium in Los Angeles, Illinois transposed clarinet fingerings onto his saxophone and pushed the instrument two and a half octaves higher than the tenor saxophone had ever been played. The crowd and the jazz world erupted and the saxophone was changed forever.

After the concert, my mother introduces herself, and as they talk, she and Illinois discover coincidences: Illinois taught himself to play the bassoon, the instrument that helped strengthen my mother's lungs after her fall from the tractor. My mother's family lived in Illinois when she was a child. She and Illinois also share the same birthday, October 31, Halloween. He has perfect pitch, as does she.

Jazz becomes my mother's new religion. It is the highest expression of music, she says, intellectually demanding, spiritually pure.

After Braddy finishes high school, my parents sell the Beverly Hills house and my mother moves back to New York. She tells me she was always cold in California. She helps my brother rent an apartment in Manhattan and she moves in with Illinois, in his redbrick house on a tree-lined street in Addisleigh Park in Queens, a neighborhood that was considered quite exclusive in the late 1940s, she tells me, when Babe Ruth, Count Basie, and Ella Fitzgerald were neighbors. Illinois's poor health has stalled his career, so my mother implements blended salads. When I visit, my mother serves them on a foldout tray and pats his head as he tucks his napkin around his shirt neck. Illinois and I joke about the Program restrictions. He is happy and healthy, but hungry.

In Los Angeles, my father is making television movies with Bette Davis, Jeff Bridges, Samuel L. Jackson. He marries Marge, an ex-scientist whom he met while living in his apartment by the beach and whom he tells us he reveres for her intellect. They move to a house in Bel Air, a neighborhood akin to Beverly Hills in affluence, and the house reflects it. Most of the flooring is marble, Marge has large paintings displayed on easels throughout the house, and there are bronze busts and statuettes perched on antique armoires and tables. When I visit, my father sits quietly watching his television with a smile as Marge lights up her afternoon cigarette on the couch.

"Modern medicine," he says. I have somehow left scuff marks from my rubber soles on Marge's kitchen floor and she's in the other room instructing the housekeeper how to clean them. He holds out his hands to show me the pills he is about to swallow, which include blood thinners, antianxiety, and blood pressure medicine. "What science has achieved." He shakes his head. "To consider that worthless?"

My father transitions into making miniseries: *Evergreen*, starring Lesley Ann Warren, "the story of America," he will later say, about immigrants in the United States in the early twentieth century; Ken Follet's *On Wings of Eagles*, starring Burt Lancaster; *The Kennedys of Massachusetts*. His 1983 documentary, *He Makes Me Feel Like Dancin'*, about a ballet studio in New York, wins both an Emmy and an Academy Award, a first for any production. My father gives Greg a position after college as assistant editor on the movie *Footloose*. Greg also writes a screenplay, *The Night Before*, which he sells.

I am standing in my father's Burbank Studios office. I've come to discuss the fact that I want to be in his business. This feels like a big moment.

"What do you like about this business?" he asks. He often uses the word *nepotism*, scornful of people who hire their relatives whether they are qualified or not.

Isn't the answer obvious? Movie sets, movie stars; the feeling of belonging, of being a part of something larger than life, of feeling singled out, chosen, lucky. I don't know how to say all this without sounding silly. I also don't know how not to hear between the lines of his question: *You're not in the club. Just wanting it isn't enough.* I have to be what he might think I'm not, crackling with charisma in the way the people around him are. Regardless, at twenty-four, I'm grown-up and his world isn't my world by default anymore. Now I have to earn it.

My mother's Ayurvedic practitioner, Dr. Joshi, a tiny man with a plum-colored robe and pale, bluish hands, holds his thumb to the pulse at my wrist. His office is quiet except for the sound of his breathing. I can hear a wheezy whistle at the tail end of each exhale as the room fills with the smell of mild poop. It's coming from his breath. I recognize, though also wonder at, the early-in-a-fast smell of cleansing. Shouldn't he already be cleansed by now?

In my mother's kitchen, blended salads have given way to *kitchari*, a warm yellow dal and basmati rice soup, the cornerstone meal of an Ayurvedic diet.

I have agreed, to make her happy, to this appointment. Dr. Joshi is touring the country, using various patients' homes as temporary offices to see clients who can't make it to either of his permanent headquarters in Albuquerque or New Delhi.

"He's going to be in Oakland the same week as my visit," she tells me over the phone while making her own plans to travel from her house in Queens to Southern California, to see my brothers, then me, her last stop. She will be with me for two weeks.

Now, alone with Dr. Joshi, I wonder if I ought to express a concern I could never share with my mother, who is waiting in the foyer.

"So . . ." I begin as he finishes with my wrist and, straightening his glasses, flips to a fresh page in the blue notepad on his desk. He pushes his glasses back against his nose again and looks up at me. He's a doctor. He looks to be somewhere near seventy. He's seen it all, right?

"I crave blood," I say. The newness of eating everything I want, my guilt dulled by the elation of my new relationship with Tim, has worn off, along with the high of new love. I'm back to Earth, and meat, once again, seems to ground me more than I want to be grounded. I am back to longing for the lightness. I'm also back to the searing guilt I feel when I eat meat. I've begun to notice that there are times when it's easier to resist, begun to realize that the one time my craving overpowers me is just before my period. In this part of the month, during ovulation, the longing is a force I can't seem to surmount. Surely, I think to myself, in his travels across his lifetime and across the world, Dr. Joshi has come across this before?

For a moment it appears as if he doesn't seem to know how to respond. He looks paler than he did a moment ago. After a few more seconds of silence, I realize he actually *really doesn't* know how to respond.

"There's something . . ." he begins. He doesn't meet my eyes. Is he embarrassed? Am I a monster to him, this gentle man who has easily eaten warm spiced beans and rice every meal of every day of his time on earth?

"There's *something* in you, Christine. . . ." He trails off, then stops. I wait, but he doesn't say anything more. It's the most he can do.

He looks down at his notebook and begins to write up the list of spices that need to be added to my *kitchari* and ginger tea. The personalized ingredient list that patients from across the country come to get.

"How was it?" my mother asks.

I show her the list of spices.

"He was great," I say.

Chapter 13

"Will you marry me?"

We are sitting at the Chart House on the cliffs near San Francisco, at sunset. Tim has orchestrated the proposal, the restaurant, the ocean view, the sunset. I suddenly feel my almost forgotten hot feeling. It starts in my feet and works its way up. I tell myself to take slow breaths.

"If I can go to LA, to work for a year," I say, and the hot sea recedes.

I'm visiting my father.

It's two o'clock and he is in his leather recliner in the den, watching football. Marge, sitting on the leather couch, lights a cigarette. Is it my imagination or has Marge's nose been shaped into a bob? I'm not imagining her room-size closet in this house, filled with St. John outfits and endless shoes. Or how easily she has made the transition from her science background into the role of Hollywood wife, a role my mother eschewed, to hobnob with Hollywood royalty couples like the Spellings, or befriend Marlo Thomas.

Now Marge takes several drags from her cigarette then places it on the edge of a black ashtray, unwraps a piece of a candy bar, and offers me a section. The smoke fills the room; my head aches from breathing it in. I think about my mother talking about the afternoon dip that can happen: *people's bodies are sick and are looking for a lift*. I want to like Marge, though her children are given privileges I can't imagine my brothers and me being granted. Her twenty-three-year-old daughter, Lori, lives in this house, for example. My father told us his responsibility toward his own children ended after college.

That night I lie on the blow-up mattress Marge set up for me in the den because the guest room is filled with boxes. I miss my mother. It feels cold here, no love. It occurs to me that the warmth we felt growing up, despite my mother's dictums, clearly wasn't coming from my father.

I have been working for a movie company, traveling back and forth between Los Angeles, seeing Tim on the weekends. Our wedding date is approaching. I don't want to lose this connection to the movie business, but Tim has a new job working for a brokerage firm in Oakland. He says he can't live in Los Angeles. The movie business is in my blood; I have always believed I would be famous, one day, like my father. But the day-to-day reality of traffic and the city and smog compared to the wild hillsides of Walnut Creek? The adventure of sailing Tim's Hobie Cat on the bay and weekend trips to Tahoe? When I imagine myself in LA, alone, even doing what I've told myself I always wanted to do, I feel that old panic, the old sadness that Tim vanquishes.

The next weekend Tim and I go for our usual run in the Berkeley hills. The fog rolls in, a thick blanket coming in off the sea. Its fingers reach into the nooks and crevices of the brown hills. I notice again that when I'm with Tim, the cold and gray of the fog doesn't affect me. Would I go back to feeling like I did those first months in Euclid Hall if I were alone? When I think about Euclid Hall, the fog suddenly seems threatening. The wedding is in one month. I make a deal with Tim that I will move back to the Bay Area, but to keep one foot in the movie world, my job will be to write screenplays. The idea fills me with hope. I imagine wings on my heels, step-flying across the tops of rows of strategically placed columns of plot points. Not sinking. The beauty of a script is that it isn't prose. Screenplays are distilled from the cream that rises to the top. I tell myself that the murky gray leftover, the medium through which the idea traveled on its trajectory upward, can be ignored. I'm also ignoring something else. The connection Tim and I feel for each other is strong, but each of us brings our own dysfunction to our union. I know how to want what I don't have. I still haven't figured out how to want what I do have.

Tim and I buy a house in Walnut Creek, farther inland from our rental, where the fog barely reaches, but writing is not going as I planned. I throw away screenplay idea after screenplay idea. This unweaving happens always about halfway through when the idea seems to thin and I lose the train of whatever had excited me in the first place. When I get into that place, I reject whatever I'm left with and begin an entirely new story. This rejecting of the old and beginning of the new happens over and over again, yet I tell myself it's not a pattern. I tell myself I'm just looking for the best story idea. Maybe this is what it feels like to write? Screenwriting doesn't come naturally to me; there is no room for the introspection I'm good at, the description of scenery that indirectly gives so much information. Screenwriting is writing stripped to the bare bones of structure and snappy dialogue, neither of which are my strong suits, but as the panic takes hold—*I made a mistake; I shouldn't have left LA*—I just push harder. Writing a screenplay is my way back to the movie industry, to my charmed life, where I was my father's princess instead of this nobody I've become in the nowhere place of Walnut Creek.

While in school at Harvard, Greg and Jay talk to one of their professors about Illinois. He is hired to teach a class on jazz. Though it's been thirty years since big bands were in their heyday, one of his students suggests he create his own. My mother acts as general manager, and she and Illinois start hiring musicians, using Illinois's basement as the rehearsal hall. This becomes their passion. They play at the Blue Note and the Village Vanguard, at Tavern on the Green in Central Park. They play at Carnegie Hall and at an annual gig closing the Midsummer Night Swing concert at Lincoln Center. Fans overseas book them gigs in Europe. Fashion photographer Arthur Elgort makes a documentary, *Texas Tenor: The Illinois Jacquet Story.* Under my mother's direction, they cut a record, *Jacquet's Got It!,* in 1988.

I'm pregnant, which brings a new awareness of how I am eating. I am eating for another; I have a new value. Though my craving for meat is through the roof, I don't feel the need to punish myself for what I eat. This growing life inside me needs nutrients. The usual worry I have felt whenever I sit down to any meal— will I be able to stay within the boundaries of how I think I should eat or will hunger and cravings drive me to the outskirts of what my conscience dictates?—has been lifted. I'm craving animal protein, and nothing else will do. "You're building a placenta," a friend reminds me. Flesh for flesh. The dichotomy of "this is good" and "this is bad" seems irrelevant. It all goes to the baby, so it's all necessary.

I have found a midwife, Yu-Yan Chen, who grew up helping her grandmother deliver babies in her village in China. I like the idea of blending old-school pre-technology knowledge with modern safety measures. Yu-Yan tells me that the doctors who rely solely on technology have lost something in their understanding of birthing. She describes how she can tell what's going to happen in labor just by feeling how the baby is sitting when she palpates a pregnant woman's stomach and by listening to the pace of its heartbeat. She describes how her grandmother would go in and physically shift a baby's position during birth to facilitate its passage through the birth canal, an art most doctors today have lost in their reliance on ultrasounds and electronic monitoring. I think of how my mother stripped the Dakota of all its modernity and brought it back to its original state, of her trust in Dr. Cursio and Dr. Joshi, men who have gone back to old-school knowledge and brought that knowledge into the present. When I tell her about Yu-Yan, she sounds very pleased.

I'm at the sink, washing the dishes, when I feel a hot wash of water drench my legs. Forty-eight hours later, I'm in the birthing ward of Samuel Merritt Hospital, being induced with a Pitocin drip hooked up intravenously so infection doesn't set in. Later I will learn that as Pitocin is a take-no-prisoners type of forced induction, its use usually doesn't go hand in hand with natural childbirth. I am only at six drips per minute, but the cramping has begun, a hot belt tightening in my abdomen. Three hours later I am being dosed forty-eight drips per minute and the agony is real. Whose idea was it to have natural childbirth? Some version of me that had no idea what was in store.

"I want an epidural," I tell Tim. He and Yu-Yan look at me without expression, a wall of resistance. They are going with allegiance to my pre-labor wishes. I signed some form, even, that stated firmly how I wanted this to go. Well, now I want it to go differently, but no one is listening.

"Back labor, very painful," Yu-Yan says. She kneels on the bed by my knees and slides her hands up inside me as my body screams in pain from the Pitocin, from the baby attempting to makes its way scraping along the dry birth canal, from the assault of Yu-Yan's hands pushing against my body. The baby is turned, apparently, facing my back instead of facing my abdomen. This, added to the fact that my water broke days ago and that natural lubrication is no longer present, explains the excruciating pain the baby's progress is causing. Yu-Yan is up to her elbows now in a very small opening as here comes another contraction and the shrieking urge to push, push the baby, push Yu-Yan's arms and hands out of me, too.

"Can I have an epidural, please?"

"Epidural will slow down labor; baby will be in trouble," Yu-Yan says. She explains I've missed my window and now it's too late.

"Do you want some Demerol?" Tim asks. "It's okay for you to have Demerol."

"Yes," I say. I don't know what Demerol is.

Another contraction hits; the pain is the same, but as the Demerol kicks in, I feel dreamy, not as invested. In fact, as the stretches of relief grow shorter and the duration of each contraction grows longer, I'm traveling through an endless yellow desert. Each section of desert is hotter, the sun more excruciatingly intense than the one before. As I cross boundary after boundary, I understand that I have no choice but to proceed. I also understand that within the rules of this desert, if I continue on in this way, if the ramping of pain and boundaries doesn't stop, I will reach some final line, a demarcation that leaves sanity behind.

Tim will later tell the story of the night nurse, as broad shouldered as any army sergeant, coming in for her shift, just as a major contraction hits and the monitor shows the baby's heart rate slow.

"That nurse just walked over and looked at the situation," he will say. "Then she put her elbow on Chris's stomach and dropped. All her weight. Boom. And out popped Emily."

When Em is placed on my belly, warm, still sticky, part of the floating happiness, of the euphoria, is the cessation of pain. *I've just given birth to my father*, is my first thought when I see her: her long ears, the square shape of her head. I spend the night in the hospital. Tim goes home to find someone has thrown a rock through our bedroom window and our bed is covered in shattered glass. He puts on his sweats, pulls the hood up over his head, and crawls onto the bed, sleeps on top of the shards.

It's our first night home and Em isn't settling down, even as I nurse her hour after hour. Tim has rugby practice and, telling me he thinks this will be a good chance for me and the baby to bond, leaves us. At 8:00 P.M., after I have been nursing Em on and off since we got home from the hospital at 3:00 P.M., I am in a cold sweat. Nothing I'm doing is working. I'm so tired, it's so late, my nipples are sore and painful, and they need the break they won't be getting. I just want to sleep, and the vision of a life where I am able to roll over and close my eyes unencumbered seems suddenly like a long-lost utopia. At 10:00 P.M., Em releases my nipple and her eyes close. There is no way I'm going to risk waking her by putting her into the crib that was set up weeks ago with a matching rocking chair and curtains and bedding in a motif of bunnies and pink-and-blue clouds. It seems more natural to keep her here with me anyway, warm against my body, close, so if she wakes, so if something goes wrong—an unfamiliar fear runs through me: I feel so aware of her vulnerability—I will know it. I will soon read about *the family bed* and what feels right will have a name. For now, though I'm aching to stretch out fully, to lie prone, I stay as still as possible and lean my head back, close my eyes. For all of Em's babyhood, I will sleep when she sleeps. I attempt once to do what the books suggest, get cleaning done while she naps, but find myself exhausted and resentful the rest of the day when she is refreshed and I am not. She doesn't sleep steadily enough or deeply enough for me to use her nap times to catch up; she is restless and high-strung—was I right to see her similarities to my father?—and always in need of the soothing that nursing brings. My breasts ache and my nipples crack and bleed, but it also makes sense to me that nursing is nature's way of soothing and of bonding. I can feel Tim hovering on the outside of this new partnership, waiting for his chance to step in, for my craving for sleep to abate so I will relax, be less rigid about how things are done. I wonder when that will be.

"You need to get out of the house," Tim says at the end of Em's first week home.

I bring her to his rugby game and everything seems great until the sidelines erupt in a cheer and Em startles violently and then is racked with sobs. That night, she wakes up at 3:00 A.M. shrieking, drawing her legs up to her chest as if she is in agony. I try everything I can think of to soothe her; even nursing doesn't work, she spits out my nipple and screams harder, but I can find no source of this much discomfort. After another outing during the day and another night spent with Em screaming, I wonder if she is taking in the sights and sounds and activity of our outings but is unable to process them; if her nighttime screaming and writhing is a cleansing of sorts. After I attempt another rugby game and the screaming happens again at 3:00 A.M., we stop going anywhere. I hole up with her. Sure enough, when our days are quiet with very little outside stimulation, the screaming episodes don't happen.

"You're doing the right thing," my mother says. "It's important. Emily needs you."

Okay, but my mother gave up her music for us, gave up everything. It feels noble, and I'm up for this kind of sacrifice because there seems to be no alternative—being kept up in the wee hours of night with a screaming infant isn't going to make for any productivity—but I wonder if I'm going to be giving up on my dreams forever. I thought I would write while Em napped, but I'm napping while Em naps, to make up for being up a lot of every night because even on good nights, she wakes and needs soothing to go back to sleep. I have heard of leaving a baby and shutting the bedroom door at night, heard that it takes a week and the crying stops. *Because she stops trusting someone will care,* I tell Tim and myself. My mother agrees. Aren't I here to instill trust that she is loved and that her needs will be heard and met? If not that, then what? But the panic I used to feel at night in the Dakota when my mother was in bed has become a middle-of-the-day panic. I'm not getting anywhere with writing. Now that I'm no longer pregnant, eating is a struggle again. I don't know what to consider *healthy* other than blended salads, which leave me hungry. I go as long as I can not eating in the morning because as soon as I do, the guilt begins and builds to a feeling very close to depression. I consider the option of eating and making myself throw up to alleviate the guilt, as I did with my friend during our college days, but reject the idea. I'm a mother now. I need to set a good example.

"Em had an episode," Tim says. We are on the front stoop, and he and Em, eighteen months old, have returned from a walk. Em has just run past me up the front steps. I take immediate note that Tim, who doesn't like to make a big deal about anything, is telling me this before he even enters the house or puts down the extra jackets he is carrying. Cold fear, an icy hand closes around my heart.

"What kind of episode?"

"She seemed to pass out for a moment."

"What do you mean?" I turn and face him directly, look into his eyes, order him silently to change his story, to tell me something different this time.

"She was running on the sidewalk ahead of me and she tripped. I picked her up and she seemed to pass out for a few seconds as I was holding her." His eyes hold mine unwaveringly. There is no new story. He doesn't want this one as much as I don't want it. He's pale, shaken. Something happened that wasn't in his playbook for Em, for his child. The sudden chill in my solar plexus settles in deeper, makes itself at home. Em runs back to find me. She has taken off her shoes and holds her two matching dolls, Mae and Mollie, one in each arm. I pick her up.

"Did you have fun with Dad?"

"Yeah," she says, holding Mae and Mollie shoulder to shoulder, examining them. Whatever Tim saw must have been a fluke; she looks completely fine.

A few months later, Em and I are at the playground. I am holding her hand; she is walking along a low wall watching her little feet in the pink jellies she insists on wearing with everything, sporting her favorite checkered floppy hat, swinging her hips so her soft cotton Gymboree dress with stripes on the skirt twirls. Suddenly she jumps without any indication she is about to do so. I am unprepared and her hand slips—how did our hands become sweaty and slippery?—from mine and, instead of having what she trusted was there, my strength to keep her lifted in a slow-motion jump down, she falls through the thinnest of unsupported air, dropping four feet with nothing to stop her, and lands on the side of her head on the sidewalk. I know when I hear the sound—the hollow crack of an egg on a countertop—that this fall will have repercussions. Part of me wants to run now, as far away as I can, to not exist so I don't have to see the ruin of her, but instead I force myself to take the steps over to where she lies, her mouth open to cry but no sound emerging. *Oh God, I've killed her.*

I stoop and push my fingers under her, separating warm, soft flesh from hard pebbly cement. Her knees are drawing up into her stomach, her mouth opens but no sound comes out, she is slow-motion turning into an animal, a blue animal, her face drains of color, her neck arches back, her fingers curl into claws, her arms stiffen. Someone near me sprints into the house across the street and I'm still holding her, rocking her, when the fire trucks pull in, sirens screaming. A young paramedic puts an oxygen mask against her face. She is in a dreamy quiet now; the blue-clawed creature has uncurled and become human again, though she won't answer to her name and she looks around her at the sky, the tops of the trees, like nothing's really there.

"Ma'am, you're going to have to leave the room if you can't stop crying," the nurse says once we get to the hospital.

I am standing beside Em, who is lying in a hospital bed, as several nurses move around us. Am I crying? I didn't even notice. Another nurse approaches holding two large syringes in each hand. Em has had no drugs in her life thus far, no antibiotics, no aspirin. The Hahnemann Clinic in Berkeley is an office where homeopathic doctors practice. I like the comfort of its clinical feel, the lab coats, since every mother I know relies on her pediatrician's advice like it is gospel. But I also like the Elephant Pharm, which dispenses homeopathic remedies instead of *allopathic*, a word that exists now because alternative remedies are becoming fashionable.

"These are antibiotics," the nurse with the syringes says. Her dark brown hair is pulled too tightly back from her pink scalp. "If we inject them, they will go straight into her bloodstream and work faster."

Even in my daze, I feel a clear questioning that she should need antibiotics for hitting her head, but everyone is bustling about so efficiently, I want to believe they know what they're doing. Besides, I'm here for a miracle. Em is still looking around the room like she is in a dream, not focusing on anything or anyone.

The nurse positions herself and, raising each syringe, punches them, at the exact same time, one into each of Emily's thighs. Em shrieks, shrieks turn to sobs, other nurses hold her down as the syringe nurse too slowly empties the yellowy contents into Em's legs.

We are in a room, waiting for the doctor-ordered brain MRI. Em is hooked up to a gurney of octopus legs, thin tubes all feeding into her arms. We are alone; the door is closed. I have been told that if I can soothe her to sleep, we can lay her in the MRI machine with no medication. If I can't, they will sedate her for the process. I'm holding her body against mine with one hand so she can nurse, and pulling the IV pole with the other as I walk in slow circles around the room. I'm afraid of the sedation. She is already not waking up. I hear in my head, *Doctors don't understand the brain*, and it sounds like something my mother might have said to me once. I'm hearing it in her voice. The doctors want the MRI, that's their short-term goal, and sedation would work for that. But what if she never comes out of this creepy daze? Five minutes pass and she is still nursing and squirming in my arm, my skin and hers sweaty, damp, where we are touching. There is nothing here that is conducive to sleep: the glare of florescent lights, the bright black-and-white-checked linoleum floor. On the other side of the door, voices rise and fall, footsteps get loud then fade. She rolls against me, trying to get comfortable. I need to try a different tactic. I hum one of the many songs we listen to from her plastic cassette tape player with the primary-colored stop and start and rewind buttons, which I hook to the back of the baby jogger for walks and runs in the streets behind our house. *Inch by inch, row by row, gonna make this garden grow.* Our safe world of nursery songs, of Weemie, her stuffed lamb, of the baby jogger and our dogs and cats and our little cottage against the creek, seem like a fairy-tale dream, a lost world I have never appreciated enough. My knees go weak. *Inch by inch, row by row, someone bless these seeds I sow, someone warm them from below till the rain comes tumbling down.* Finally, I feel her weightless in my arm, the sign that she is surrendering to sleep, then heavy as she gives herself over to it, and I've done the impossible, though she has done her part, too, no doubt wanting to escape this bright, loud place with poking hands and cruel needles as much as I do. And then, suddenly, the door opens, letting in all the noise of the hospital bustle and a cold waft of air, and Em sits straight up, all my hard work undone.

"It's time," the nurse says.

————

Forty minutes later the doctor stands in front of Tim and me and tells us Em fell asleep in the MRI machine the moment she was laid on the table, so there was no need to administer a sedative, though I have never known her, in her entire young life, to fall asleep without the soothing of nursing. He says they can detect nothing abnormal on Em's brain in the MRI. We can take her home.

"So why did she have a seizure?" I ask Tim while we drive.

He shrugs. He doesn't know. Of course he doesn't know. No one knows. I should feel comforted that her scan was clear, but all that means to me is they didn't catch whatever was there. How is anyone supposed to bear this much love and helplessness?

Two hours later the three of us are lying in our bed, and Tim and Em are breathing deeply, eyes closed, faces smoothed in sleep. Tonight, Em fell asleep with no battle. Outside the quiet dark of the bedroom, the frogs are loud in the creek; their croaking reverberates against the sides of the hill and the sound thrums, magnifies. I'm afraid to give myself over to unconsciousness. What if she has another seizure while I'm not paying attention? The brain, so unknowable, is the perfect landscape for the fear of things that are undetectable, that lurk and hover, that will get us when we are least aware. If no one can tell me why this happened, then it could happen again and there's nothing I can do to prevent it. This fear feels familiar to me, it feels like a legacy, though it hasn't been handed to me overtly and with ceremony but rather insidiously, passed down without words. It's the fear my mother was responding to when she enforced the Program so dogmatically, when she made it her talisman. She must have believed that if we followed the tenants, we would be protected. It suddenly makes sense, her following of a charter that deviated so far from what everyone else was following. If we figured out the rules of the special canon and abided by them, we would be granted immunity from the woes the rest of humanity suffered. I look at Em, her face pale and perfect in sleep. What talisman do I have now? The Program isn't enough to stop brain damage or seizures. It's not enough to stop most things. The enormity of all that could hurt her presses down like the darkness around me. Then I notice a light shimmering in the corner. A beam from a streetlight? No, it's smoke. If I move, I'll wake Em, Tim, the dogs. I wait for it to dissipate, as smoke would, but this doesn't. It's still swirling in the far corner of the bedroom. The smoky swirl of light, I suddenly realize, has intention; I hear, without words, its message. It's saying, *Everything's all right.* I don't know how this could be, a light in the corner of my bedroom that has no obvious source, but I suddenly feel bathed in peace. This light *is* peace; it's love and comfort. I close my eyes, sleep for the first time this night. When I wake up the next morning, the light is gone but its message still feels clear, if only I can get past the worry to hear it.

Em and I are walking the dogs in the Walnut Creek Open Space. Kate, our Lab, runs by, dragging her leash as Em is taking a step. What are the odds, her foot comes down and makes contact with the gravel path at the exact same time the leash is underfoot, so that instead of finding solid ground, she steps onto a canvas leash moving at twenty-plus miles per hour. Her legs shoot out from under her and her head hits the only stone within ten feet of us.

I am holding her, running to the house outside the gate.

"Please call 911."

Em has a high fever; she has the flu. We are lying on the couch. Six months after the last seizure. My arms are around her and now she's titling her head back, looking at something on the ceiling over our heads.

"What are you looking at, Em?"

She doesn't answer. I sit up to examine her.

Her eyes are rolling back, her body is going stiff.

Now I am running with her in my arms to the fire station at the end of the block. It will take too much time to call 911. I reach it, knock. The firemen open the door, take her from me, give her oxygen. "We can take her to the hospital or you can take her," one says. "Or you can wait. Febrile seizures. She might be prone if she's had a seizure before. They usually grow out of them by five."

By five? She's not even three yet.

"Did you have too many blankets on her?"

She said she was cold. I had her piled high with blankets.

"You'll want to keep her fever down whenever she gets sick," he tells me. "I give my daughter a sponge bath in cool water, turn on a fan. Give her a fever reducer."

I remember the two syringes, the MRI, the thousands of dollars, Em's terror and mine in those corridors, and we head back home. Em is sitting up, coming out of it now.

You'll want to keep the fever down whenever she gets sick. For now I have been given a road map in the wilderness that is Em's brain. But I am alone with this; the doctors can't help. I am the first line of defense.

Em has a fever and I have moved her to my bed again so I can keep the fan on her and sponge her down with cool water when I think she's getting too hot. This is the protocol and I follow it unerringly.

"Nooooo, Maaaaam. Nooooo," she moans in her half sleep. She is so cold, her skin hurts, she wants to bundle up, but instead I force her into this nakedness and assault of cold air and water. I run the sponge down her arm, across her chest, her tummy, her thighs, angle the fan so it hits her. After a few moments I feel her skin and it's cool. I lie down next to her, close my eyes, and sleep for a few moments until I will wake up and sponge again.

———

My water breaks with Luke two days before his due date. This time I don't wait for the Pitocin; I drink a bottle of castor oil, which I have been told is a home remedy to induce labor, and it works. Like Em, Luke is turned so I am in the midst of another painful back labor. At one point, late in the night, in the midst of my contractions, I am screaming so loudly, Tim nods off to sleep on the chair in the corner of the hospital room and dreams that someone is wrapping piano wire around my fingers and pulling them off at their tips, one by one. This time Yu-Yan is stuck in traffic and is thirty minutes from reaching the hospital.

"I want an epidural," I tell the nurse.

"Your midwife will be here very soon," the nurse says.

"Give it to me before she gets here," I say.

I get my epidural and as the pain abates, tears run down my cheeks.

"Don't feel bad; you didn't fail." Tim leans in to reassure me.

"I'm not crying because I'm sad. I'm crying because the pain is gone. I'm. So. Happy."

With the epidural, my entire body relaxes and instead of slowing progress, as Yu-Yan had feared with Em, Luke slips out, effortlessly.

"My stomach hurts," Em says. I am holding her in my lap.

Luke is one week old and asleep in the rocking crib. I have given Em an antibiotic for strep throat, though she has had no drugs since the double injection of antibiotics in her thighs three years ago, and the fear of them is still screaming in me, my mother's programming alive and well, battling with the dilemma of having no choice in this situation, since strep leads to rheumatic fever and a weakened heart, not to mention the bacteria will cause a high fever that the doctor says I won't be able to contain. The pill is red, red like a stop sign, like a new wound, a color I couldn't imagine swallowing. The side effects listed on the bottle include stomach distress, so though she is in some pain, I want to believe that a stomachache falls within the parameters of normal. Suddenly she is arching back again, her body shaking and convulsing, and I am screaming to Tim to call the ambulance. I know already this one is too big to handle at home. This time I don't cry at her bedside; I don't want to be asked to leave. But, out in the waiting room, I do say to Tim, who is holding Luke, "Maybe she won't come out of it this time." Her blank looking around and seeing nothing has lasted almost ten hours. But she does come out of it, and the fireman was right. She is five and, though this seizure clocks the longest duration, it's her last. By now, someone has mentioned epilepsy and the fact that febrile seizures can be a precursor, but I won't know until she hits puberty that these childhood seizures will not translate into adult ones.

While Em is at school from 9:00 A.M. until noon and Luke naps, I try to write. In the afternoons I sit on the porch steps and watch them play. The answer to whatever I need to figure out with writing seems to be buried so deeply inside me, I need more time than the day affords. Still, I have a vague sense that everything I'm struggling with is connected. The middle, the longest, the least-structured part of the day is related to the middle, the longest, the least-structured part of a story is related maybe, somehow, to the middle of me, to the parts of myself that I haven't examined too closely or labeled and that I don't like very much. I decide this is about willpower. I face Act Two like it's a wave towering toward me. I take it bravely, try to swim up and over, muscle my way through, but the wave slams me flat on my back in the sand. I continue to attempt screenplay after screenplay. In screenwriting I get to stay on the surface of a story. A screenplay is a story told visually. From the outside. Going too deep to examine the story, myself, or the day, feels like I will drown.

Em and I visit Illinois and my mother's house in Queens. The first thing I notice is Illinois's house is wall-to-wall shag. We weren't allowed one rug and now she lives in carpets times a million.

I don't ask.

The musicians are arriving for rehearsal. My mother is in the kitchen with Em, stirring the *kitchari* simmering on the stove to feed them when they're through. I climb down the long flight of creaking wood steps into the basement to get something from my suitcase. Illinois has a drumstick in his hand, tapping in time as a young trumpet player plays a page of music. His back is to me; the young musician doesn't take his eyes off of Illinois's stick. I watch Illinois and the trumpet player for a moment, soak in the unspoken connection of shared passion and talent, then head back up the stairs without disturbing them.

My mother comes for two-week visits and sits crossed-legged on the floor to play with Em and Luke. The rest of the time, she cooks, never leaving the kitchen, so that it's impossible to eat anything without her eyes on us. She has switched completely now from following the tenants of the Program to following the science of Ayurveda, an ancient system of medicine, she explains, that was transcribed, according to legend, from the gods to human sages. According to Ayurvedic principles, she is *vata*. She says I am most likely *pitta*, which means all the foods I like most, like hot peppers, inflame my already inflamed *dosha*. She now drinks ginger tea with cumin, coriander, fenugreek, turmeric, and cinnamon, the specific herbs for her *dosha*, prescribed by Dr. Joshi. She spends hours peeling the ginger with a little knife, and eats the *kitchari* and drinks the tea, nothing else, three times a day. The smell of freshly peeled ginger, ghee, turmeric, and cumin fills our small house as she extols the virtues of this thousands-of-years-old *dosha*-pacifying food. I like *kitchari*; it's warm and soothing and it makes sense that there is real value in eating an ancient food that has been used for millennia to heal, but after a few days of eating only that, my body is screaming for more. By now, after years of their own struggles with food, my brothers have openly become omnivores. I feel, even more, the pressure of being the eldest, the only daughter, the only remaining legacy of her life's mission and purpose.

My mother is sure that Em is *pitta,* too, and after explaining the behavior that seems a carryover from the days of her being up at night screaming, her temper, to Dr. Joshi, he mails me a jar of little round balls made up of herbs to help cool her colon. If her colon is cooled, he tells my mother and my mother tells me, her temper will cool as well. If it's allowed to stay as it is, too hot, Dr. Joshi says permanent damage could result. It's possible, he says, that even her tendency toward seizures can be related to her inflamed colon. Swallowing one little ball a quarter of the size of an M&M can keep seizures at bay and soothe her intensity? This seems like the talisman I was hoping for. The problem is the herb balls are so pungent, they smell up the kitchen and Em won't touch them. My mother goes to the health food store with me. We buy ice cream, we buy peanut butter. I give her the ball in a spoon with each. She spits out the ice cream but swallows the peanut butter if I promise an ice cream chaser. In this way I am able to get the ball down her once a day. We do this for a year, at which point Em, who will grow up to forever hate peanut butter because of its association with the taste of the dark pungent balls, begs to be allowed to stop taking them. Despite my fear (what will protect her?), I acquiesce.

At mealtimes, my mother is satisfied to see me feeding Em and Luke kale and quinoa and tofu. Tim doesn't cook meat while she's visiting, so they don't have the opportunity to ask for it at night. Tim, though free like my brothers to veer from her dogma, says he doesn't want to be disrespectful, so while my mother visits, he stashes In-N-Out Burgers in the laundry hamper, taking bites whenever he goes in and out of the house. I can't betray her even in secret while she's with us, so I go back to feeling hungry all day.

"Do we have to have meat every night?" I ask Tim after my mother's visit. I forget how good it feels to be light. Despite the gnawing hunger I experience when she visits and I have to limit so much of what I would normally eat, I love the ease in my body that results.

It also suits me so much better, morally, not to eat animals.

"You can eat whatever you want," Tim says.

But I can't, because when his food is around at the end of a long day, sizzling in a pan or in the broiler, fat crisping and browning, juices running and pooling, and I can smell it from every room, I want it. If I don't eat it, I think about what I missed all the next day, the power of suggestion, and it lodges in my psyche and boomerangs around to hit me twice as hard the next night. Each night I go without, I am scraping something of me away, too, meat from bone, until it feels like there will be nothing left; all the good stuff, the best me, is best fueled with meat.

"Why can't we be vegetarian?"

"I'd never be vegetarian."

"That's so predictable. Do you like being a predictable male?"

"I like meat." He fake-growls at me and comes at me to tickle me, but I push his hands away. Why is he so bullheaded?

When Tim is with me visiting my dad in LA, Marge says she so appreciates a man's man. None of this pretending to be something you're not. He's masculine; it's just who he is. It's refreshing, she says.

My mother has invited me, Emily, and Luke on the SS *Norway* for the Jazz Cruise where Illinois is a featured musician. I love that my kids and I get to hang out "backstage" in my mother and Illinois's cabin as the Caribbean sunlight pours through the window and the ocean rolls by. Illinois's silk jacket and dark lavender shirt, his slacks and patent leather shoes are laid out on the bed, though he is still in his underwear, a white sleeveless undershirt and boxer shorts. My mother's outfit is laid out, too, her purple silk jacket still wrapped in dry cleaner's plastic. She makes Illinois freshly squeezed orange juice; she has carried the oranges and the squeezer on board, along with bags of dal and spices for *kitchari* and the seitan she stir-fries so it tastes like chicken. Now she is busy combing his hair the special way he likes it for performing, no exceptions, for the stage. Then she scurries over with his juice, hands him the glass. He sits back in his chair, undershirt on; it's almost time to dress but not yet. He accepts her ministrations; they are their rituals.

I'm back from the SS *Norway* trip. Tim and I find a house for sale one mile from our old house in Walnut Creek, in a new pasture. This one has floor-to-ceiling windows that back up against the hills and look out over the mountain. All wild grass and sunlight and leafy branches and sky. This house has the elegance of the Dakota; it sits high and majestic above the town, with the Shell Ridge line and Mount Diablo rising out of the foothills, filling our vista.

A Whole Foods goes up in Walnut Creek. Shopping feels like going to Disneyland, too good to be true. Healthy food that tastes good? That's marketed to appeal? No more sawdust floors and shapeless, brick-hard cookies. Lighting, skylights, a half-a-football-field-size section of thriving, beautiful produce, and deli counters filled with salads, slaws, sliced meats, dishes for every craving. My mother visits and I take her. I can't buy all the things I really want when she's here, so the store becomes a temptress for the two weeks we eat *kitchari* and drink only ginger tea. But as soon as she leaves, I guiltily go back, in baby steps, to buying the things I want.

"You have broken the chain," my brother Greg tells me when he visits. He watches me offer both Em and Luke quinoa and tofu, notices the fact that I tend to Luke, who seems to need chicken or steak at dinnertime to feel full, and Em, who is fine having only legumes all day. He means I am listening to them, not imposing my will and therefore will not be passing down the rigidity of dogma our mother passed down to us. Each of my brothers has had their own struggle with diet. Braddy tells me he can't eat one of anything. He devours an entire baked Safeway chicken in minutes, then looks around for the next thing to consume. Greg and Jay both feel as I do, guilt and self-recrimination when we eat certain foods, the backlash of self-flagellation. I am an adult, living with my own husband and children. I am free to eat what I want. But it's difficult for me to watch my children eat meat and I can't eat it myself during the day when I'm alone. Only with Tim and only when I'm distracted from what I'm actually doing. Otherwise, the guilt is blinding. So I eat too much cheese, too many sweets. My mother said sugar was poison, but it's still not that point of no return of meat. Yes, I have broken the chain of control and rigidity and guilt for my own children. The chain I haven't broken is the one still binding me.

Chapter 14

My father is eating a lunch salad with a business associate at Chasen's on Doheny Drive. He stands to go to the bathroom, puts his napkin on his seat, and the world dissolves out from under him. He is lying on the tile floor of the restaurant, watching people moving in slow motion above him, speaking down to him, their voices slowed to incomprehensible syllables.

I get the phone call from Marge. "Your father had a massive stroke." I will find out later that on the meds cocktail his doctor prescribed, green salad and blood thinners don't mix. In the hospital I find him in intensive care, his body shrunken to the size of an eleven-year-old boy's under his sheet. This can't be him, but it is. He is paralyzed on his left side. His speech is slurred beyond comprehension. His brain has changed, the area that controls short-term memory and inhibitions damaged. He will regain partial use of his left arm, his speech will become less slurred, he will laugh at his memory loss, but his crackling intelligence is dulled, the father we knew gone forever.

My father has ordered each of us to take a corner of his bedsheet.

His caregiver, Lynette; my father's skinny-necked assistant, Paul, who hopes to produce movies one day, which is the only reason he is here now, in this cat-urine-soaked condominium, because he is still hoping, despite all evidence that my father is dying; my brother Greg; and me.

My father's world has shrunk to the four walls of the condominium bedroom, where Marge deposited him after the stroke before she filed for divorce and disappeared. He orders Lynette around as if she were an entire movie crew. She never sleeps more than ten minutes day or night, but she talks to him about converting from Judaism to Catholicism so he is assured a place in heaven, which he does a few days before he dies.

"Lower me to the floor." Despite everything, his voice still commands. There is no question of disobeying. We man our posts.

In my father's mind, the air is too thin in the four-foot-altitude of his bed. Desperate to fill his lungs, suffocating with emphysema, he has probably been planning this move for days, telling no one. Biding his time, perhaps waiting for the right combination of visitors.

"Lower me to the floor!"

We look at one another. Are we really doing this?

"Lower me!" he says, desperate now.

We heave.

Maybe he has even been waiting for me, the oldest, the only girl, specifically, because he knows I won't refuse him.

"Lift!"

I pull the sheet taut. All of us, acting in unspoken unison, exert equal amounts of pull. Even so, he rolls onto his left, the paralyzed, side.

Greg and I step back; Lynette and Paul step forward. We lift him away from the bed. And slowly, with controlled strength, lower him to the in-need-of-a-shampoo beige carpet.

My father has come a long way from our apartment in the Dakota building to these three stained, mildewed, claustrophobic rooms.

He lies at our feet, trying, and failing, to breathe like every fish I ever watched die in the hold of his Boston Whaler.

"Lift me!" he roars again between gasps.

We bend our knees, grip, stand, pull the sheet with the rise of our bodies, raise his bulk, fat from the medications he's taking, somehow from the floor, up, up, slowly now, steady, onto the bed.

Lynette re-tucks the sheet around the mattress as my father lies, eyes wide, staring at the ceiling. Though his mouth is open and we can see him panting, his chest barely rises. No breath brings in enough air.

This time he doesn't ask us to move him. There is no place left to go.

"Where is Christine?" he asks from his bed. This is the last time I will see him alive.

"I'm right here, Dad," I say.

He looks past me to the door, still waiting.

Six days after my father dies, the crematorium calls. There had been a rush of deaths that week, but they are finally getting to him.

"Drink lots of water," the man in the shiny, ill-fitting suit tells me. "There's nothing like crying to dehydrate a person." He has a huge head and an unidentifiable accent. He stoops, his shoulders stiff, awkward, as if the orange-wallpapered rooms in this crematorium don't fit him any better than his jacket and trousers. He hands me a bottled water, holds out a box of Kleenex. I pull two tissues as he opens the door.

In life, my father filled a room. In death, at first I don't see him lying in the corner of this refrigerated crematorium display room.

When the doctor told my father he was going to die, five days before he actually did, my father ordered him to *get out of the f-ing hospital room*. He glared at us, daring us to live longer than him. Daring us to even try feeling smug that we were young and strong and upright, standing beside his prone, flattened form.

One of my brothers has turned on the air-conditioning in my father's Los Angeles condominium. I cross the carpet, step over the stains. In the living room, a miniature city of cardboard boxes forms an unintentional grid of blocks and streets and avenues across the dingy carpet. My brothers, Godzilla-size, move among them. I pull out folders with stacks of papers inside. Some of these papers are typed, but here is one with my father's scrawling handwriting, the first twenty pages, all he wrote, of his autobiography.

As a boy, I knew the Long Island Railroad as if it were a companion.

The words are heavy with emotion and self-importance, the tale of his boyhood town, Long Beach, New York, and his place within it. But the story trails off as if the railroad itself has taken an unexpected fork and my father can't follow it. I recognize the hesitancy and uncertainty of my own attempts at writing. I see my father, in these sentences, caught up in the magnitude of a story he wants to tell, trying to follow the threads of his ideas as they veer into new directions, multiply, and double back on him. He hesitates, confused, mistakes the confusion for restlessness, puts the yellow notepad in a drawer, telling himself he will come back to it. Sometimes, on a Sunday afternoon, he'd turn down the football game, pull these pages out of the drawer to read them to me. He liked the ring of his words. What he didn't like, clearly, was the sense he must have had that this story, so strong within him, the story of his own life, seemed to dissolve the harder he looked at it.

I pull out another, very worn notebook. *A Day in My Life*, in childish cursive, faded pencil, his thirteen-year-old self grinning in two-by-two, black-and-white and toothy, from the cover. *My Town, My Family*, a neat cursive paragraph page for each. I imagine the teacher's approval. I stop at the last page and really see it: *The Best Day of My Life*.

"Look," I say. I read out loud as he describes Long Beach's small movie theater, where he sat alone in the dark on sunny afternoons to see every movie that came through. *Clara Bow kissed me today. Douglas Fairbanks was here. I got their autographs.* But my brothers are looking through other piles; they don't notice, yet, how much rests on this, the day two movie stars came to my father's small town; one kissed him on the cheek and he fell in love.

My brothers have moved to my father's bedroom. I follow. His armoire smells of mothballs. They find a box in the closet that holds what is left of his valuables, gold cuff links, a gold money clip. An old Rolex watch.

In *A Christmas Carol*, Scrooge sees himself lying dead in his room, while a few neighbors haggle over the curtains that drape the four posters of his deathbed. I look over my shoulder. He never liked us going through his things.

In the armoire, his cashmere sweaters are stacked, neatly folded. The bottom drawer is filled with socks. This is the last time I will see these rooms, the books on his bookshelf, our macaw's wrought-iron birdcage sitting on the moisture-warped deck outside his bedroom door, his neatly folded socks and Hanes undershirts. The smell of him—faint sweat, shaving cream, hand lotion—that still lingers here will be aired out in the next few days, replaced by someone else's smell.

I take two pairs of cashmere socks from the drawer, one brown, one navy. The socks will keep me warm and remind me of his feet; he never liked them to be cold. From the armoire, an oversize dark gray—my favorite color—cashmere sweater. From the bookshelf: *Tuesdays with Morrie*. As I'm leaving I double back.

His reading glasses are still lying in the tray by his bed. They saw what he saw. I take them, too.

In our kitchen Tim shows me the letter Jesse, his new captain, whom Tim calls *the freak* because he is so good, has written to his fellow players on the Holy Mary College rugby team Tim has been coaching for four years. It begins, *I have been captain of every team I've ever been on. We need to work together not apart.* The season has just begun, one week, and already this rookie, whose Jewish father raised him after his mother left when he was two, has evaluated his teammates and is calling on them to step up, expecting excellence. I peek at Tim's face. He looks out the window as I read. He scratches the side of his mouth, waiting for me to see what he sees about this young man I have yet to meet.

"He reminds me of you," I tell him.

What I don't say is how much Tim reminds me of my father these days. He is often gruff, he keeps his methods to himself, and his players treat him as a godfather of sorts, an enigma.

They come to me with their observations of him. Tim is slowly transforming the rugby team he inherited at Holy Mary College into a national powerhouse.

"He likes to keep us off-balance. He never says what he's thinking."

"He's not human. Who else gets to work every day at five o'clock, works for eight hours, volunteer coaches in the afternoon, and still exercises four hours a day?"

"He never eats. He has no needs."

These players feel what I feel. I imagine a shared camaraderie.

Holy Mary's women's basketball game is a blur of ponytails, screeching rubber soles, layups, and three-point shots. In what Tim calls a gesture of goodwill from one Holy Mary's sport's team to another, Tim brings his team and me to watch. It's still early in the season, and I have yet to meet Jesse.

Tim calls, "Hey!" on our way out of the gym. Three men stand in an eddy by the door out of the current of the streaming crowd of exiting students. The tallest of the three has a pale beard, pale skin, pale eyes. He lifts his Gilly Callaghan–like chin when he sees Tim and gives a little laugh, as if it's a private joke that we're all here. He's still grinning when we reach them and I decide, based on his cocky tip of the chin, the confident glow in his eye, that this is he.

That spring Tim invites me to join the team on their rugby tour to Ireland. Luke, also on Easter break, is with us; Em is home with a babysitter so she doesn't miss school.

In the Dublin clubhouse after the game, Jesse is watching me. Around us, twenty-two-year-old man-boys scoop up the last forkfuls of rice-and-chicken dinner from their paper plates. Those not eating sidle up to the bar to pour foamy glassfuls of Irish beer. I wait for him to join them. Instead, in the shadows, amid empty wooden tables and upside-down chairs, the sweaty smell of chlorine and the black slick of just-mopped linoleum, I see him, tall and broad, jutting chin, horse-size thighs, place his foot behind him on the wall and lean. Like he has all the time in the world to do just what he is doing.

I am failing at eating strictly enough to maintain the euphoria of a fast. Being watched and noticed, I am suddenly lifted above all sadness. As much as Tim feels like home, it's nice to be this high again. It feels like something I can't do without.

I have never been this lost before. I don't even know the name of our hotel. We arrived in Cork, and I never looked. Now, around the skyline of brick towers and spiderweb bridges the sky darkens, glowing an unfamiliar steely blue, cadmium orange. Why is the river behaving like this? Taking me into a part of the city where I know I haven't been, though I'm tracing it backward, back the way I came. I have never lost my bearings in a city. But here the streets curve and swirl, sometimes running alongside each other, then suddenly crossing and crisscrossing like an optical illusion. I look behind me at the intersection I have just crossed. I passed a yellow planter box by an iron bench, but there is no planter box or bench now. Instead an unfamiliar bicycle sits propped against a green lamppost. It's as if Cork has a current and I am drifting farther and farther into unfamiliar waters regardless of how hard I paddle. For a moment I feel the urge to give up. Let go. Drift for real. Who would I be? Stripped of whatever it is I think of as *me*.

I see a guard in a blue cap with a gold brim standing in front of a shop. It feels like the second or third time I've passed him, though nothing about the white brick of this shop with the red shutters looks familiar.

"Can you help me?"

He is tall. He peers down.

"I followed the river down from my hotel." I remember a detail. "It used to be an orphanage. I can't find my way back."

He is broad shouldered with a long face, his mustache as thick as a cigar. He smiles and his face cracks open. The dazed feeling I have, as if I have already let go, as if I am already less myself than I was when I left the hotel, cracks a little with it.

"There are two rivers," he says in a thick brogue. I can barely understand him. "They run parallel through town, then branch off in different directions."

Did he say two rivers? He points and I see, on the other side of a small park, another lip of a blond-gray stone wall, the running water dark silver in the dusk. Yes, two, a stone's throw from each other. I had picked the wrong one when I came from the shop without knowing not to.

"Follow that and you'll come to a hill soon enough." He tips his hat.

I follow the river and, faster than I could have imagined, I leave the winding maze of shops behind. Soon the dark green hill and the hotel, redbrick and upright, come into sight. As I follow the long slope of the street toward them, I feel myself congealing. Like a genie returning to a bottle, I am returning to Luke, Tim, and the team in the hotel, and in one week, Em, my house and dog, my routine in California. It feels awkward, like birth, backward. As if I am fitting a slightly altered version of me back into its original frame.

But at least I am found. For now.

I answer the phone; it's my mother, trying to croak out words.

"Illinois died tonight."

She tells me Illinois had closed their annual gig at the Midsummer Night Swing concert at Lincoln Center for a sold-out crowd just a few days ago. Last month he had been awarded an honorary doctorate from the Julliard School in New York City.

"He was so proud," my mother had told me at the time. "He said receiving the honorary doctorate was the happiest moment of his life."

Now she sobs, "He wanted a chicken sandwich from White Castle. He asked for one. I made him some seitan instead." I hear her ragged intake of breath. "I should have gotten him the chicken sandwich. Maybe he would have been okay if he had had the chicken sandwich."

I am along with the team on tour in Argentina. Unlike Ireland, Tim didn't want me on this trip. *No women.* But Fay, the girlfriend of the assistant coach, Al, wanted to go, and Al needed her to have someone to pal around with.

Buenos Aires is muggy and hot. I am perpetually covered in sweat. I shower to find my clothes heavy and wet again in minutes. My hair sticks to the back of my neck; my underarms are soaked. The front door of our hotel opens onto a narrow thruway, more alley than street. Buses overhang the stained, uneven edges of sidewalk; taxis honk angrily. The heat rises in oily waves off the pockmarked, blackened concrete; the sour-sweet ammonia of urine; the muddy, vinegary liver of drying excrement; the alcohol of bus and taxi exhaust. Amid the honking and revving of motors, men and women hurry by, many with limps, limbs twisted and bent, half hidden under skirts. This is a place where arms and shoulders and stomachs and thighs are perpetually beaded, where cleavage is damp and glistening. Here, people bear their bodies, whole and misshapen. Despite the thread of familiarity in buses and taxis and dirty city streets, I remember we are not home.

The team is walking from the hotel to the waterfront for dinner. Like pebbles in a stream, Jesse, who has been on the team for three years now, stays just ahead of me, sometimes just behind. Now we approach a girl and a boy, sitting on a redbrick planter box, kissing urgently. The boy is dark-skinned, with a shiny mop of hair, the girl darker, her hair lighter, longer, sleeker. In his lap she turns to press against his skinny teenaged chest, and their tongues twist in and out of each other's mouths like snakes. They are not coming up for air. We approach, but it is clear that, for them, nothing exists except each other's hands and buttocks pressed on thighs, faces, mouths, and eyes. The sun is setting. The river is silver. The warm air smells of blossoms, the sour stink of open garbage cans, car exhaust, and mown grass as we pass these lovers pressed together in this sensual, hot, sultry night.

It's Sunday, and we're home from Argentina. The next morning, I turn over in bed and feel a piece of paper folded on my pillow.

Tim has already left for work. Half asleep, I reach for it, open it. In the semidarkness, I recognize my own handwriting, the blue pen, black now, from a copy machine.

We kissed.

I go cold, sit up. Really look. A page from the journal I had with me in Buenos Aires. Written the second to last night, after I had gone out to celebrate the birthday of one of the players and drank only a few sips of some mysterious homemade Argentine whiskey that made the warm night and the lights of the bar swirl for hours. Tim had stayed home. At four in the morning, standing outside the pub while waiting for a taxi, still swirling from the whiskey, Jesse and I had kissed.

"Do you want to do this?" Jesse had asked.

"Do you?" I said.

The next morning I find another page of my journal taped to the toilet seat.

"You're just going to torture me like this?" I call Tim at work.

"How is this torture? Put yourself in my position. Then you'll know what torture is."

Tim feigns affection in front of Em and Luke but turns his back to me as soon as we're alone. Rugby is over; Em and Luke have summer camps. I drive them around, grocery shop, clean the house, fold the laundry, feeling like a trauma victim. Eating feels like trying to swallow cement. I can see in the mirror how thin my face has become. All my jeans and T-shirts hang. The only thing I can get down are Starbucks mochas. I start early, tipping my tongue into white foam and sugary chocolate, breathing in the sweet steam, sipping. Heat is a carrier. This isn't a drink; it's a sugar transfusion. The high lasts all morning. I know there is some balance I am seeking. If I found it, I wouldn't want this exhilaration in a cup. But I don't want to not want it. I want my pores to open; I want to feel my cells breathing. I want to live on air; I want to float back up to where I was.

I begin eating dark chocolate to replace the mochas, which

are making me fat. But one square a day leads to two bars. I switch to coffee to replace the chocolate; soon one cup of coffee in the morning leads to drinking coffee all day. I try diets: no carb, no fat, all fat, no oil, no gluten, no nightshades, low-glycemic, proper food combining, only alkaline foods, all raw, no sugar. I've gone through every artificial sweetener I can get my hands on: stevia, aspartame, sucralose, saccharin. I swing in the opposite direction and live on sugar, then eliminate sugar and add caffeine back in, then subtract caffeine and go back to eating sugar. I want the feeling of aspiring and striving and wanting and needing.

A friend invites me—"I don't know what this is, but it looks interesting"—to a screening of *The Secret* at a small New Age-y book store in Walnut Creek. As we sit in the room amid the gathering of fold-out chairs, I feel wary. On the screen, people talk about how they pull things—houses, money, success—just by thinking about them. So hokey. So I'm surprised when I start to sob. What I'm hearing mostly, behind what these people on the screen are saying, is the comfort I remember coming from the swirling smoke-like light the night of Emily's first seizure. *Everything's all right.* I'm also hearing this: the high I've been looking for has been attainable all along. Like my mother said, it doesn't depend on anyone else, it exists inside of me. I just need to know where to look. On our way out, I buy *The Secret* from a stack of copies that have been set out on a table by the door, and the book beside it, *The Law of Attraction.* A few days later, I try to explain the law of attraction to my mother.

"That's nice, if it's something you like." She sniffs, disdain in her voice. It's not thousands of years old or validated by a guru who has been initiated into a divine lineage. It's coming from a middle-aged woman from Utah who says she is receiving blocks of thought from the nonphysical. But it's visualization thoroughly described, using desire as a road map. When we were on the

Program, it didn't take long to learn that just wanting something was the indication it wasn't good for me. Every religion I can think of counsels against desire. The idea that I can have what I want feels completely new. If I can have anything, what *do* I want?

Chapter 15

The clouds are impossibly dark. Like animated movie clouds, they are too black, moving too fast.

"They're angry," I say.

Tim snorts. "Clouds. Angry." He doesn't look at me. A year after the kiss, his anger still feels like a storm just beneath the surface.

The red kayak is packed with camp gear. Em, thirteen, and Luke, eight, sit inside, life jackets zipped, paddles at the ready. Yesterday, when Tim and I had hiked with our heavy packs to this beach, the kids chose to kayak, as they always do—paddling takes one-third of the time it takes to hike—the wind behind them. Hugging the shore to their second favorite camp spot on Pine Lake, a lake Tim had discovered when they were little, which he used to bring them to when I needed quiet time. Though the thumbnail of granite beach where we spent the night was tucked back from the lake and missed the full force of the wind, the clouds gnashed above us all night as Tim set up camp, boiled Top Ramen, joked with Em and Luke. The three of them tied a tarp between three trees in case the clouds opened, as they were threatening to do. Then Em and Luke strung worms on hooks and cast lines into the water, poles propped between rocks, settling down on a flat boulder, shoulders touching, to watch for the dip in the tip that meant they'd caught a pink stipple trout. Their muscle memory for setting up lines to hang the towels to dry, for finding which ziplock bag the seasoning is in, the Buck knife at the bottom of the ice chest to cut the salami, wrapping sandy wedges of cheese in a dirt-smudged quesadilla, squirts of mustard, meant they didn't need me here. This is the place where they had gone motherless on summer weekends and found they could thrive.

Now Em shifts herself in the kayak seat. The lake almost spills in around its sides. After only one night, we still have too many drinks and too much food left over.

"It's too full," I say.

Tim's lips tighten. "It's fine," he says. He pulls the bungee cord tight. Then, to Em and Luke: "Ready?"

I know we need to redistribute the gear. Tim and I need to take more in our packs and lighten the kayak. He is expecting too much of them. I am the outsider here, I tell myself. I have no authority; this is their world, not mine. But the truth is, I've been battling Tim's anger for a year now, and I'm tired.

Tim gives the kayak a shove. Using his momentum, Em and Luke row smoothly out of the cove, chattering with each other, Tim and I forgotten for now.

The plan is the reverse of the day before. Tim and I are to hike out to the truck while Em and Luke paddle along the shoreline to the dam three miles away. There we will pull the kayak out of the lake and load the pickup for home. But as Tim and I climb onto a boulder to watch the kids' progress, we see instantly that the seven-mile-long lake outside our protected cove has, without our knowing it during the night, become a black maelstrom. This is the day hundreds of lightning strikes start hundreds of fires across California. But we don't know that yet. Nor will I find out, not until I make it to the ranger station and the boat launch an hour from now, that there are craft advisories on Pine Lake. That no ranger has a boat big enough to safely take it out and look for our children.

The waves crash against the kayak that has already been picked up and taken by the wind. Though they've only gone twenty yards, neither Em nor Luke can hear me screaming for them to come back. Tim and I watch as, rowing hard, they are blown in the opposite direction, away from the dam side of the lake, across the black churning water, a vast angry sea now, toward the rougher, beachless shoreline miles away. Even in the distance, I can see how low they are in the water. So low that it looks, from my vantage point, like the lake is higher than the sides of the kayak. In moments they are a speck amid the vast sea-lake of black stormy whitecaps. And then they simply vanish, blown out of the range of my straining vision.

"Oh my God!" I scream. We still have an hour hike to get to the car. An hour. What will they be going through in that hour? Are they already in the lake? In the thin, sixty-degree, ocean-deep black lake water? I calculate in my head: even after we reach the truck, the boat launch and ranger station is another fifteen-minute drive. We push through the pine trees, running shoes sinking into the mossy bog, mosquitoes swarming in clouds above the soggy footing. Yesterday it had taken us two hours to hike to the cove. Now we're covering the return in more than double our previous speed. But it isn't fast enough. I feel like I'm in quicksand.

The forest opens onto a long, rocky dirt path that leads to the foot of a great slab of stone, mountain-size, bare and white like the moon. My running shoes grip the rock; my thighs and lungs and calves burn. Over boulders, through a long tangle of swamp, as fast as we can. But careful, too. Nothing can happen to us. We are the only people on the planet who know our kids are in a kayak in the middle of Pine Lake.

I climb onto another bald upward slope of granite and push forward. The heavy pack I'm wearing pulls me backward. I need to stop and breathe, my back aches, I am soaked with sweat, my lungs burn, desperate for oxygen in the altitude. Now comes the worst part: we have to leave the lake, lose sight of it completely in this stretch. I push on, feel Tim following, my breathing a rhythm I match my steps to. The white of the moonlike granite, the silence except for the sounds of my body. Finally the truck comes into view, parked up another long slope, three stories of granite still to go. *Don't think about how long this is taking.* But I feel hope, too. Miniature fireworks explode in my chest.

"I'll hike to the point," Tim says as he turns his back for me to dig in the pocket of his pack for the keys. "I can look for them there. Pick me up at the point," he adds.

I drive ninety miles an hour along the narrow mountain road. Does anything look familiar? That boulder, that big pine tree. Did I miss the turn? I don't know my way here. I haven't spent all those weekends they have, learning boulders and trees, landmarks to know which turns to take. Tim should be in the car with me. I should have forced him. What good is hiking to the point if Em and Luke aren't there? Now it's all come down to me.

I keep driving faster than is safe on the narrow, endless road. Boulders and trees come at me and speed past in a blur like the cartoon backgrounds of my childhood. If I make a wrong turn and end up in the labyrinthine roads of the Sierra Wilderness, I will never find my way out. I could find myself driving in these wilderness back roads for days, weeks. The old panic, my father leaning over me, his rage boiling, the type on the page unreadable to me, the letters meaningless. If Em had x amount of pine trees and boulders and Luke wanted y, how many pine trees and boulders would they both need? Panic that felt like shame. My brain shutting down. The belief that I couldn't do it in the clutch. The reason I had always relied on my mother and then Tim to be my compass.

A fork in the road ahead. Everything literally looks the same; there is nothing to distinguish going right from going left. The turn is coming fast now, but I want speed. Speed means the difference between living or dying in an icy lake. Panic is screaming in my head, but I'm not listening. Instead I can feel a lukewarm pit, like a solid calm seed sitting in the middle of my sternum. When I focus on that pit, I notice, I feel calm, too. I take a left and step on the gas, holding on to the steering wheel with both hands. Another fork. Another left. Is it left, left, right, or left, right, left? Another fork, I turn left again. The road veers around the largest boulder I have passed yet and then ahead, through the trees, I see it. The parking lot and, beyond that, the trailer that serves as the ranger station up here in the middle of nowhere. I turn in, come to a stop. Climb out of the truck, knock on the door of the RV. No answer. Everything is going much too slowly again. Where is the ranger? An older woman, coat pulled to her ears, comes around from the other side of the RV. She looks at me expectantly.

"My kids are in a kayak in the lake. They were blown to the other side. We don't know where they are."

The woman pulls a crackling radio out of the pocket of her coat. She talks into it: "Two kids are lost on the lake."

Minutes later the ranger pulls up in a golf cart. He radios the headquarters. The ranger on the radio says in a crackling voice that there is no boat big enough to take out safely to look for Em and Luke. The boat is being used in Sacramento.

"No boat?" I look at her blankly.

At the dock, at that moment, a fisherman is pulling his boat in with his son, to get out of the storm. The ranger drives the golf cart over. I see the fisherman look over at me. The ranger drives back.

"He'll take you."

I lock the truck. Walk over, climb onto the boat.

"I've seen a lot in my years on this lake," the fisherman tells me. "I have seen kayaks sink."

We speed across the lake, the fisherman and his son, a year or so younger than Luke. Jumping the waves, soaked with spray, we reach the spot where I last saw them over an hour ago now. There is nothing. Only empty black water. We head over to the opposite shore, where it had looked like they were blown. Waves crash against trees growing out of the water along the unforgiving shoreline.

We see a few people in tents and call to them, "Have you seen a red kayak? Two children?"

No. Sorry.

We move on. Up and down the lake. I see a red kayak on the beach of another island. Of course, there they are. Safe and sound. But a bald man and a woman with a baseball cap sit beside the kayak, waiting for the storm to abate. We ask more campers along the shore. No one has seen them. We pick Tim up from the point. He looks eagerly into the boat as we approach. I can tell by his smile that he thinks I have found them. Then he realizes. Poker-faced, he climbs in beside me, shakes hands with the fisherman, as if we do this every day, lose our children, climb into boats with strangers who have offered to find them. He looks at me, then says so only I can hear:

"I'm supposed to be the person protecting them."

My mother grew up with the threat of the mighty Mississippi over her shoulder. She came out of her childhood needing to believe she could control the uncontrollable. At times Tim seemed to encompass both my mother's need for control and a low burn of anger, reminiscent of my father. But what if anger and control were always and only an attempt to avoid what couldn't be faced? Our own helplessness?

We head to the most remote fjord on the lake. We will start there, work our way back. We follow the shoreline, looking into the woods for a kayak, for Em and Luke sitting beside it in the dirt. But at point after point there is nothing but pine trees, granite boulders. Rocks and pinecones strewn in the empty dirt. The fisherman has stopped chatting with us. We are all silent now as we motor along the shoreline. The fisherman is hugging close, following the fingers of inlets. I realize by how slow he is driving, the way he is scanning between the washed-up logs, that he is looking for debris now, for what would be floating if a kayak had sunk.

We have doubled back twice. We are running out of wilderness.

I can no longer call out, "Have you seen my children?" to people as we pass. The words choke in my throat, mix with sobs.

The fisherman calls for me: "Have you seen two children in a red kayak?"

No. Sorry. No. We'll keep our eyes open, though.

Finally there is no place else to look that makes sense. It has been two hours in this boat. Three since we last saw them. Wouldn't the kayak have washed up to a shore? All that was in it. Umbrellas. Ice chest. Chairs. Towels. (Frisbees.) Why hasn't anything floated up? I think of the kayak filling with water, sinking into the cold black depths of this lake. Em and Luke, exhausted from fighting the waves, sinking down with it.

We are heading back. I don't know how to face arriving at that boat launch without them. How to turn away from this lake and toward a future without my children.

Then Tim says, "We've driven by, but can we check it one more time?"

The dam.

It's impossible that they have made it without anyone seeing them. Without somehow crossing our path. But the fisherman and Tim seem glad for one more stop before the finality of the boat launch.

We turn toward the dam.

From a distance, my heart leaps—something red! As we get closer, I realize it is a bumper, one of four, strung along the dam to protect boats. We continue numbly. No one talking.

And then I see it. A slightly longer, thinner red pill–shaped object.

Could it be? We get closer. It's definitely something.

I start to sob. No sound, just sobbing soundlessly. The dam is in full sight and yes, the pill-shaped object is a kayak now. Two children stand beside it. Closer still and we can see Em's long honey-colored hair, Luke's bowl cut, his yellow life jacket. We pull up and the fisherman kills the engine. He leaps from the boat. In his eagerness, he catches his foot on a tie just off the bow and falls hard onto his hands and knees in the cold lake. He stands. His pants and shirt are dark, soaked with lake water. He strides over, knee-deep in the lake, and pulls Luke, though they have never met, hard against his chest.

Tim steps forward and unbuckles first Em's life vest, then Luke's.

"How did you get across the lake?" Tim's voice is tight with held-in emotion, his lips white and trembling.

"We rowed," Em says. "At first we were blown, but then we pointed into the wind. Just like you always say to do."

They found their way. Left to their own devices, they knew what to do and did it.

I say nothing; I just sit on my cushion on my seat in this fisherman's boat. Head bowed, my face in my hands.

Chapter 16

I need a regimen, something with parameters to follow, like the Program. Parameters make things so clear. It's easier to know when I'm succeeding or failing and therefore how to feel about myself. I decide to see how long I can go being vegan. No animal protein, period. At first I feel light. Hunger is muted. I observe my hunger; like the Ashram teaches, I am *the witness*. The lightness, the hunger, the high, feel like being in love without the love object. But after six months my hunger is a living thing with tentacles and teeth. I'm craving bloodred steak with the ferocity of my years on the Program. My legs ache and Tim says I cry at night in my sleep about the pain. I'm still going for extremes: the high and the feeling of living on the edge. Riding the razor's blade to feel alive. I thought my cravings would disappear, but they haven't. What am I trying to prove? No one is looking over my shoulder. Am I becoming my mother, trying to control the one thing I truly can control? I learn that a few of Tim's players are following a new diet called *Paleo*, where an adherent is allowed only meat and vegetables. A diet where meat is considered good for you? I try to let that sink in.

In Whole Foods I am given a sample of a vegan meal replacement powder. In the hours after I have a scoop, I feel balanced and light yet my hunger is satiated. After a few weeks of having the powder and feeling good, I notice something even more amazing.

If I eat something that weighs me down, a combination that doesn't sit right, I have a scoop in the midst of the discomfort and the heaviness lifts. Even eating steak suddenly seems like a nonevent. I read the ingredient label: probiotics, chlorella, maca, berry antioxidants, vitamins, vegan proteins, digestive enzymes. I have used digestive enzymes before and while they have helped, there is something in the combination of this specific powder that lifts the weight while also allowing for the euphoria I used to feel during a fast. The label on the container also reads, *high-density nutrition*. Dr. Cursio's Program was supposed to stimulate the cleansing of a fast while feeding us at the same time, but I never felt euphoria or lightness eating blended salads three times a day. Salads, even blended, were hard to digest and weighed me down. But this powder actually seems to achieve what Dr. Cursio was going for. And easily. I'm not in the kitchen all day; I'm not chained to juicers and blenders and crates' worth of vegetables I need to wash. All I need to do is add a scoop of powder to a glass of water and I feel good. And best of all, I feel free to eat whatever I want. No regimen needed; instead its opposite. Find my way by feeling for it. What feels right to me is unique to me and unique in each moment. No one else knows better than I do.

I've been accepted into a writing program. One hand grips the rock on the side of the crevasse, school, class—the lip that I cling to—so I can dip down into these darker realms I need to write from. I remember my struggles with the middle of the day, how tired I felt after I ate. I see now that that was partly why the middle of the day and the middle of any story felt like quicksand. To avoid animal protein, I ate too much cheese, too much bread, too much sugar. As soon as I ate, I'd need to take a nap. By the time I woke up, Em or Luke needed me or the most productive part of the morning had passed. I was going backward, without understanding why.

We hear about Jesse in increments. He makes the USA Sevens

team, plays in the Las Vegas tournament before thousands of people.

"You never said you were sorry, do you know that?" Tim and I are driving down to the South Bay to visit his mother for dinner. We cross the new Bay Bridge. The sunset is deep and hard, reds and purples and blues. The city glitters and I can see every light. It's been three years since I kissed Jesse. "In all this time. It's the one thing you haven't said."

Last week Luke was looking for a VHS tape to play in an old player he had found in the house he is living in near UC Berkeley, where he is a freshman. He came across, tucked in a drawer, Tim's and my wedding video, which I had not watched, because we hadn't had the correct machine, or when we had the right machine I couldn't find the tape, since a month after our wedding. Luke dusted off our old machine and turned it on.

In the video, my younger self kneels at the altar in front of the priest who is marrying us. Tim kneels beside me. Tim has tousled dark auburn hair and a chiseled face. His cheek dimples when he grins at me; he is gorgeous. He looks at me when the priest announces us man and wife, a quick glance, then ducks his head shyly and swallows. It's a private moment; he isn't sharing his feelings with me or with anyone. He's simply absorbing. Then, ready to let me in, he lifts his chin and our eyes meet. He's beaming. I have never seen this moment. I didn't register it then, I was so worried about how I looked and about all the details of the day, and I didn't register it when I watched the video after the wedding. Now, separated by decades, I can take in what I couldn't then: how lucky I was and how lucky I am, despite my impulses toward sabotage and despite having learned so completely to want what I couldn't have, to have Tim's steadfast adoration.

"I'm sorry," I say.

Chapter 17

My brother Jay helps my mother, eighty-two, move back to Los Angeles. He puts her in the same apartment as his nanny, Lolo, where there is an extra bedroom. It's near his house. She can walk to the ashram and to Erewhon, the old health food store where she used to buy all our vegetables when we first moved to California. She still follows the tenants of Ayurveda and eats *kitchari* with a small cut salad and bok choy or asparagus cooked in ghee, nothing else, three times a day.

It's Thanksgiving. We have gathered at Jay's. We are all in his kitchen, admiring the food my sister-in-law Macie has laid out, though we have all had a hand in cooking and prepping. Luke brined the turkey and we carried it down in the back of our car from Walnut Creek. Em's boyfriend, Eric, has made the corn bread. Jay has prepared his favorite sweet potato marshmallow dish. We are laughing and chatting now, gathering our plates, serving ourselves. My mother hasn't seen me eat meat since we started the Program. I have never admitted to her that I do. The last few times she was with us for Thanksgiving, I didn't have turkey, but this morning Em and Eric; Luke and his girlfriend, Amanda; and Tim and I woke up at 4:00 A.M. and made the six-hour drive to Los Angeles, Luke's brining turkey in the back of the car and on my mind. I've been looking forward to it all day. My brothers have continued to make it clear over the years that they want to be able to eat what they want to eat, but I haven't. Over the phone and through email she and I continue to share diet tips; she is in support of the vegan powder I use, but I have never brought up the subject of my eating meat. There never came a time when her happiness didn't feel tied to what I was eating. As we line up with our plates and forks, I consider forgoing the turkey. I feel all the old straitjackets descend, the old responsibility of being the only girl, her cohort. My mother is not eating anything. She had her *kitchari* earlier, though she is hovering in the kitchen, around the platters of sweet potatoes, string beans, salad, corn bread, turkey, watching what we each are choosing to put on our plates. It would be so much easier if I just didn't have any turkey. But now she is laughing at something Macie has said and I spear a slice of breast and tuck it under my salad. She laughs again with Macie and I spear two more slices.

I approach the table set for twelve; the only seat not taken is beside my mother. I check that the turkey is still hidden under my salad as I take my seat. If I don't pick it up or draw attention to it in any way, maybe she won't notice it's there. But I've chosen a slice with crispy skin, my favorite thing. It's more than the skin, of course. Eating this meat, now, is a validation of me. A validation of all I've come to understand about myself, a validation of the journey and also of the arrival. Eating this turkey doesn't mean I believe turkey is better for me than almonds or filberts or blended salad, but it does mean that I've created a life where there is room for less-than-perfect eating and where there is balance. Balance is its own kind of health, the kind I want most.

Beside me, my mother is holding a conversation with Braddy, seated on her other side. I eat some sweet potato, then a forkful of string beans, a spoonful of stuffing. A little bit of this, a little bit of that. After a few moments, I'm tired of stalling. Around me, everyone else is eating the turkey and it looks delicious. My heart is beating hard as I move the spring mix aside with my fork and stab the slice of turkey. Though she is still talking to my brother and isn't looking at me, I can feel her awareness. Alarm bells of adrenaline go off inside me, and the periphery of my vision blurs as I raise the piece to my lips and take a bite. My heart is pounding so hard, I can't taste anything. I chew anyway, swallow. She continues to talk to Braddy. I take another bite. She is still talking and responding to my brother as I swallow this bite, too. Had I expected her to shatter? Expected this to annihilate her? Jay calls to her from across the table and she answers, then she says something to Braddy's son, Otto, seated beside Jay. Otto responds. I feel the anticlimax of this moment, the waste. All these years I carried around the guilt and the burden and this was all I had to do? I take another bite, and my heart is still pounding but not as hard now. I chew. I'm not comfortable. I still can't taste the meat, though to her it must appear as though I'm eating this turkey easily. I look around the table at her children and grandchildren laughing with her and one another, enjoying this meal, their plates filled with beautiful food. What must she think of the fact that none of her offspring has followed in the extreme path she continues to take with diet and prescribed to us in our formative years? I wonder if it does indeed look like a careless, blithe decision to become the carefree eaters that my brothers and I must seem to her to be. Our easiness, now, belies all we have suffered, our struggles for normalcy over decades around eating. This is our gift to her: the sparing of any recrimination, the sparing of the personal battle we have each waged to get to who we are now.

Chapter 18

"I'm on a coconut water fast," my mother says over the phone from LA.

A hot prickle of worry. "You are?" I ask.

"I'm five days in, but I feel good. I've even been able to continue practicing."

She is tackling George Gershwin's *Rhapsody in Blue* for next Thanksgiving. She has a year, in which she plans to memorize all twenty-six pages. Last Thanksgiving she played Scott Joplin and handed out flyers she had made about the history of ragtime and jazz.

"I'm lucky my hands are so big," she says. "Gershwin was working with octaves in this piece. It's really meant for a man's hands."

This will be her third concert. Since she moved to Los Angeles from New York two years ago, she has been playing the piano and bassoon for her children and grandchildren at Jay's house when we gather for Thanksgiving.

"Are you sure you should be fasting for a week?" I say.

Her words are clipped when she answers, "I feel fine, Christine." I can hear the scold. She knows better than I do about these things. "I have energy. I slept all night last night, and my toe didn't bother me at all."

Her pinky toe has been keeping her up most nights. She is fasting, she tells me, because she believes the pain is due to the fact that the meridian attached to her gallbladder is blocked. The fast will clear the blockage. As proof that she needs to cleanse, she reports that the KinoTox pads she applies to her feet at night, which look like small Kotex pads and start off white and pink, are black and oily in the mornings as they work to draw out toxins, their purpose.

I make a note to myself to check in with her more frequently. I call her again at the end of the week.

"I break my fast tomorrow. I asked Lolo to buy egg yolks. I will eat *kitchari* and raw egg yolks for two days then introduce salads and cooked egg yolks. It's remarkable how much energy I feel from the coconut water."

Except she looks too skinny the next time I visit. I'm in LA to meet Francesca, whom I have only seen once since I moved to California. We had met by the campus at Berkeley, two years after I graduated from college. We were twenty-four, though at the time it had seemed like a lifetime had passed since our summers together.

I pick Francesca up from her hotel downtown and call my mom. She wants us to come to the apartment for lunch. "I've made kitchari," she tells me over the phone. I had given her a heads-up that we could come for lunch and she's ready. Francesca can't wait. As we drive through Los Angeles, she tells me, "I always loved the way your kitchen smelled in Point Lookout. Did I ever tell you that? Like vegetables, like tomatoes and cucumbers and lemon."

My mother lets us in to the small apartment. I have warned Francesca that there won't be a surface that isn't crowded with spices, dried roots, her preparations for three meals a day, hundreds of jars and tiny bowls filled with herbs, her fridge filled with juices she makes on Sunday now to last the week. Ron Portante, a psychic my mother started seeing when we moved to Beverly Hills, reported a vision of my mother in an earlier lifetime, standing off a crowded bazaar, witch-like, beckoning with a crooked finger, opening a cloak filled with fifty pockets, each with a different herbal remedy.

As expected, when Francesca and I enter, my mother's small kitchen and living room feel claustrophobic. Boxes are piled high in every corner, all the counter space is filled, the small coffee table and bookshelves are stacked high. It took my mother a year to go through all the boxes and files and belongings in Illinois's house, to send things to institutes, to foundations, to libraries. She has pared down her belongings, but I am reminded of why I like to travel so light in my life. I get the instant feeling of being weighed down, no escape, something I must have grown up feeling. She shows me how to use her new Coco Jack, a five-part system to open a coconut. It looks like a giant vice and requires several attempts and only partially works on the coconut she demonstrates with on her linoleum. She carries our bowls of yellow soupy *kitchari* and cut-up salad drenched in smeared avocado and lemon juice to a fabric ottoman that she has cleared off for our meal. She has steamed asparagus and dribbled it with olive oil. It seems like a feast, no longer weird because everyone has olive oil on vegetables and salad now. Even the *kitchari* seems like real food.

"This is delicious, Carol," Francesca says. I wolf it down, appreciating it, as I notice I do when her food is only a treat and no longer a three-meals-a-day, every-meal-the-same regimen. "I'm so happy I came."

The metallic hum of the juicer, my mother clinking jars together, shuffling around in her kitchen. Francesca here. I'm feeling flashbacks. I try to soak it in. Will the three of us ever be together again?

"I hope to see you again," Francesca says to my mother, reading my thoughts, when it's time to take her back to the hotel. "Let's not make it another thirty years."

I hug my mother, notice the sharp angles of her bony shoulders. Before I go, she wants me to make some ionized water; she has a brand-new ionization system installed under her small bathroom sink to remove tap water's impurities.

"Press the red button; when the light turns green, hold the glass under the spigot. Keep it there until the third beep, the light will turn yellow, flip the lever off."

I am suddenly twelve again. This is a lot of information to take in, but I want to prove I can manage her new system. I take the glass jar—my mother has no plastic in her kitchen—head down the narrow, stained carpeted hallway, crouch under the tiny sink. The ionization system is intimidating, it turns out. It looks like a science fair experiment: there are thin white spider-leg hoses going every which way, all attached to a large gleaming metal box. There is nothing remotely familiar about any of it. I push the red button, but it doesn't turn green. I push it again. No water comes out. Or maybe the water is dispensing from some other opening I haven't noticed yet.

"Mom, is the water supposed to come out after I push the button?"

It takes her a moment to get down the hall.

"No, no, no, Christine." Real annoyance as she comes up behind me. "Red, green, yellow. Let me do it."

I watch as water comes out of the first spigot. I would have liked to get it right, but there was no way to know.

"Some things never change." I'm back in the kitchen with Francesca. "She didn't think I could figure it out on my own. Maybe that's why it's taken me so long to believe I can."

"Mothers . . ." Francesca says.

I'm glad Francesca's there as witness. Glad I can name this now, even if it took several decades.

A month goes by, and I hear from Jay that my mother is doing another coconut water fast. Once she is done with the week, she implements, as a follow-up, a water fast every Sunday.

"Do you really need to fast once a week, Mom?" I ask her over the phone. "Do you think that's a good idea?"

"My toe is so much better," she says. "Can I put the phone down and play *Rhapsody in Blue*?" She has memorized twelve pages. She says she can feel George Gershwin in the room with her while she practices. She sees her neighbors when she goes down to the laundry room and they stop her and tell her how much they look forward to hearing her play.

Her playing sounds strong, her fingers on the keys forceful, the music beautiful, even through the phone. I trust her that she knows what's she's doing, that she's feeling better. That she doesn't want to bear the pain in her toe anymore and the fasts are the very thing that will solve the problem. So I expect and don't expect the call from Jay a few weeks later.

"I got a call from Marta," Jay tells me. Marta is my mother's new Ayurvedic practitioner in Los Angeles. "She said Mom called her and her words were garbled. When I got to the apartment, she was fine in every way, except that when she tried to speak, nothing came out."

I'm with the rugby team not far from Los Angeles.

"I'm getting on a plane."

"Wait and let's see what happens tonight," Jay says firmly. "She doesn't want to make a big deal out of this. She got mad at me when I suggested the hospital."

"Can you get her to go?"

"She's refusing."

"Can you force her? Pick her up and carry her into the car." To our mother, a hospital is a place where you go in healthy and don't come out.

"Forcing her in this condition might do more damage than good," Jay says.

The next day she agrees to go to Jay's acupuncturist, who tells her he can't work on her unless she has a medical okay. So, to my brothers' and my utter shock, Jay sends a photo to all of us of

my smiling mother sitting on a hospital bed, hooked up to elec-
trodes as they test her responses. She is cleared for acupuncture
and begins a whirlwind schedule of holistic practitioners.
Ayurvedic, acupuncture, body work. Later we will find out there's
a drug that, if administered within a few hours of a stroke, reverses
some of the brain damage. Her words return. Even so, she won't
let me visit: "Wait until I have the piece perfected. I want to play
it for you; I'm not ready yet." She is insistent. She doesn't want
me to see her when she can't find her words, I realize. She doesn't
want me to see her damaged. Impure.

"There's nothing for you to do, Christine. Come later, not now."

Her emails slowly evolve from missing a word or two out of
every sentence to back to her old sophisticated, erudite expres-
sions. She has returned to her old self, even fasting on Sundays
again, visiting her acupuncturist on Mondays, Marta on Tuesdays,
her kinesiologist on Thursdays, going for electrolysis on Fridays.
When I speak to her on the phone a week and a half after the
stroke, she is slightly halting, but if I hadn't known, I wouldn't
notice anything amiss. A few weeks more and she tells me she
has all of *Rhapsody in Blue* memorized, including the challeng-
ing second six pages she had been avoiding. Now she feels the
piece is ready and she wants me to come for a visit so she can
play it for me. We make plans for me to travel in two weeks, as
soon as the semester is over.

On Mother's Day she confides that after Jay dropped her back
at the apartment, after her visit at the house, she felt a deep longing for him. "I missed him. I don't know why. How long can you
stay?" There's a hunger in her voice that is unfamiliar—usually
she is so self-sufficient—but I sever the tendon in my leg a week
before I'm supposed to go to LA, and need emergency surgery.
On the other end of the phone, when I tell her, my mother is
silent. Surgery is her very last wish for herself or for me.

I talk to her for the last time on Friday, three days before the
scheduled operation. She says she is looking forward to seeing

me when I'm able to come. Two days later, on Sunday night, I get another call from Jay,

"I just want to let you know: Lolo just called. Mom isn't responding when Lolo shakes her. Apparently, Mom went into her room to meditate and didn't come out all day. When Lolo went in to check on her, she was lying on the bed. I'm heading over there now. I'll let you know."

Jay calls half an hour later. "Chris, Mom died."

She was sitting on the side of her bed and had then lain back, her arm across her forehead like she needed to rest for a moment, but she never got up. Her heart gave out or she had another stroke. We will never know, because my brothers and I agree that she wouldn't want to be carved up by doctors to find out. That seems like too much of a betrayal.

Chapter 19

Jay, Tim, Macie, and I enter my mother's bedroom. We have a few hours to clean out what took a lifetime to accumulate before Tim and I need to drive back to the Bay Area. Tim parks the truck under the first-floor stucco balcony. We decide to drop everything we are going to donate in the bed of the truck. Willie, the building manager, who acts in television commercials, has given us the go-ahead to use the empty Dumpster, also just off the balcony, for whatever we will be throwing away.

Jay opens the top drawer of the dresser that towers against the wall only inches from the foot of her bed. For now, she is all around us, in the heavy air, her smell, in these most treasured remnants from her life, for the last time.

"Forks," Jay says. He holds them out. Our Batman forks from Point Lookout. Woody Woodpecker and Robin. I haven't seen them since we were little. "Toss them?"

"No," I say. I take them from him.

There are more of our forks in the drawer, made for child-size hands, from our meals around the Point Lookout table. Meals and feeding, her offering sustenance to us. Later what she fed us represented her control, yes, but also the passing down of enlightenment. A new understanding that she believed would change everything. Jay pulls out a worn pillowcase with a mouse in yellow pajamas surrounded by white clouds. Mine when I was five, maybe six. He unfolds a tiny pair of boy's shorts, holds up a stuffed frog. I consider how many moves she made since the Dakota, to Long Island, then Beverly Hills, and to Queens, and finally ending in this room in Los Angeles. Secretly carrying these remnants of her children with her, telling no one, our childhood tucked in this drawer. She never said, *Don't grow up*, though I know she was missing us in the weeks before she died. Instead she carried us across the country and back again, carried us across her lifetime. Now Jay is under the small hallway sink, where I have cleared away the old ointments and creams. He pulls out the sci-fi water ionizer box and rips all the thin white hoses from their attachments to the sink's water supply, dismantling this most recent prized possession of hers in seconds. We pull the boxes from underneath her bed, from behind the clothes in the hall closet, gather books off the shelves, sift through all the stacks and piles and heaps. Five hours later, both the back of the truck and the Dumpster are filled to overflowing. The inside cab of the truck holds what I will save, the things most important to her: photos, my grandmother's hair combs, the purple jacket my mother wore for Illinois's performances on the *SS Norway,* her photo album from her trip to Atlantic City for the Miss America pageant. I save the article in which the journalist wrote that if my mother had played the piano instead of the bassoon for her talent, she would have won the pageant. Also in the backseat cab of the truck is the sewing machine, still too heavy for me to lift, that she spent so many hours bent over when we were children in the Dakota. We found it tucked in the back of the closet.

I feel like I am killing her all over again, handing what we have decided to donate to the man accepting Goodwill donations who says he loves jazz. All these items, painstakingly gathered and stored for a lifetime, and it took less than half a day to clear the apartment and thirty minutes to transfer everything from the car into the Goodwill bins. But there is also a freedom in clearing out all the vitamins and herbs and supplements; the jars of Derma

K and gardenia water and KinoTox pads and vitamin-D oil and bags of bath clay, jars filled with ionized water, with mysterious liquids, goopy with grime, dusty labels peeling. Bobby pins, hair clips, gathered in little round jars, all the evidence of her routine, her private and personal bath, stopped in an instant, made irrelevant. As if I have waited all my life for this moment. Her burden of things kept was our burden, pressing down on us still, even as we went about living our lives.

Chapter 20

The night my mother dies, Macie is standing in the backyard, lighting a candle to commemorate my mother's passing. Macie went to a meditation a few days ago for Vesak, a time when it is believed that the souls of Christ and Buddha come to Earth. As she lights the candles, my sister-in-law thinks about how, for my mother, this is an auspicious time to pass to the other realm, and as she says a short prayer, one of the lanterns in the three-hundred-year-old tree, the centerpiece of my brother's yard, begins to flicker. The lantern flickers for several moments as Macie stands there, feeling my mother's presence. Macie shares this with me and I lie in bed, racked with sadness, and I wish for my own experience of a flickering light. Suddenly my beside lamp begins to flicker. It flickers over and over for several moments—*is the lamp suddenly broken?*—then it stops. As I lie there, leaving the lamp on in case it flickers again, Tim asleep beside me, I'm flooded with the feeling of my mother, her smell, the security I felt when she was caring for me when I was little. The next morning when I open my computer to share with Macie the story of my own flickering light experience, I see an email sent after I had fallen asleep. In it Macie tells me that after Jay got back from the coroner, while he was getting ready for bed, the bathroom light began flickering, something it's never done. It flickered for several moments then stopped.

I dial Braddy, who lives in Tennessee, to share what's going on. Immediately he shouts to his girlfriend, Teresa, who's in the other room, to come.

"Jay and Chris had flickering lights, too."

Braddy tells me that that morning, he and Theresa had been meditating at their *puja*, where they have set up lights. The plastic LOVE light molded with letters that spell out *L-O-V-E* started flickering. As the flickering continued, Theresa said, "I wonder if that's your mother."

A few weeks later, I am lying in my bed, where my mother slept the last time she visited our house. It's morning and just getting light. I'm awake, but I haven't opened my eyes. I'm thinking of the flickering lights, thinking of my mother, wondering if I will have another experience that feels like communication. I open my eyes. In the middle of the plum tree that fills the window in the summer with its bounty of leaves and fruit, front and center, is a leaf, shaped not like a leaf at all, but like a heart, the size of my hand. That afternoon, the heart is gone—it was a trick of the light, I decide—but the next morning it's there again. It stays, greeting me every morning for the next three months.

"If anyone could transcend the line between living and non-living, it would be your mother," Pam, Illinois's daughter, says when I tell her about the leaf. "She had such a strong will."

The first storm of September brings a gloomy sky that hints of the winter to come, and in the accompanying high winds, the heart leaf I had come to rely on is ripped from its branch. That afternoon, I take the dog for a run in the hills behind our house. I wonder yet again if there will be any more signs that feel like communication. I imagine my mother as she might be now, free from the constraints of her body and from the parameters her struggles with health had seemed to dictate she follow. Knowing her, understanding now more than ever her love for us, I decide, yes, there will be more. Then something makes me stop midstride and look down. I am surrounded by fallen leaves, fifty or so, all around me at my feet, all in the shape of hearts.

In my mother's writings, she documented how ill she felt through all the years I counted as my childhood. I knew she had ailments, but she never shared the extent of her suffering, which now strikes me as brave—everything came down to her, all of our needs, four intense children, and my father's Godzilla-size raging. I think of the payoff she expected, after all her courage and battles, that didn't seem evident at the Thanksgiving table or elsewhere. My mother had been at the forefront, decades ahead of the rest of the world, believing her story was important: Illinois farm girl turned broadcasting executive's wife turned dietary revolutionary.

A few days ago I purchased an eight-dollar glass of green vegetable drink at a nearby coffee shop. The handwritten label listed kale and ginger and spinach and apple in the ingredients. I was tempted to tell the young woman who handed me the drink my history with juices like this one and how, once, it would have been the very last thing I would have wanted. Instead I thanked her, paid the eight dollars, and took a sip, noticing how all the flavors combined and worked together. The drink was cool and refreshing, and I thought again about my mother's legacy. Luke, at twenty-one, has a gourmet's palate. He prepares kale, which he grew up eating and still adores, almost every night. He relies on chlorella tablets to keep colds at bay, and he is passionate about the benefits of intermittent fasting. He also feels a gnawing hunger unless he has some kind of animal protein at night and loves, as I do, a well-prepared steak. Em, on the other hand, now twenty-seven, and as staunch a revolutionary as my mother was, is in a graduate program at Columbia, focused on changing the curriculum in schools to teach social justice. She has been known to follow austere eating patterns and almost seems to enjoy doing so, exploring how the limiting of certain foods can help her with various minor ailments of skin and digestion. She can happily live on legumes and vegan fare indefinitely, able to do what my mother could and I can't, eat Spartanly for the sake of how her body responds. While my brothers and I had to withdraw from so many activities that would have allowed us to fit in, my children are functioning normally in the world while, at the same time, they are highly interested in nutrition, because the "normal" world is interested in nutrition now, too.

Tucked inside the Star Wars folder, hidden at first behind the pages of notes about wandering her farm as a child and the documentation of symptoms and supplements, I find, after I return home from clearing out her belongings, the thing I least expect to find in my mother's writings: the beginnings of a screenplay. The several scenes and few pages of summary clearly have been written for a class; there are scrawlings in pen, an instructor's feedback, her name in the top corner written as Carol Romann. This was something she shared with no one, not even a mention, not even with her screenwriting sons.

I read a scene where the main character, *Claire*, has a college-age daughter, *Kristin*, who leaves home for what would turn out to be the last time, to spend the summer with her boyfriend, *Tom*. *Claire's* emotional reaction to that, her sadness kept hidden in real life, is here for me to see now when it's too late to ask her about it. I read a scene between *Claire* and her youngest son, here named *Jason*, in the Beverly Hills house; a scene with Pierre, called *Jean-Claude*, in which the romantic tension is thick enough to cut with a knife.

What is this movie about? her teacher's pen scrawls across the top of the first page.

My mother wrote as a response, just under his notes:

My main character wants . . . to discover the secret of vibrant health and beauty and to teach these truths to her children so that their lives can be enhanced and their potentials reached.

The goal . . . is for the main character to achieve her goal of radiant health and to have the nonbelievers around her, namely her husband, acquiesce to the truths she discovered.

My story is of a woman struggling to live.